RANDY ALCORN

IT'S ALL ABOUT JESUS

HARVEST HOUSE PUBLISHERS
EUGENE, OREGON

Cover design by Studio Gearbox

For bulk, special sales, or ministry purchases, please call 1-800-547-8979. Email: Customerservice@hhpbooks.com

It's All About Jesus

Published by Harvest House Publishers
Eugene, Oregon 97408
www.harvesthousepublishers.com

ISBN 978-0-7369-7995-5 (pbk)

Library of Congress Cataloging-in-Publication Data is on file at the Library of Congress, Washington, DC

Printed in the United States of America

20 21 22 23 24 25 26 27 28 / VP-RD / 10 9 8 7 6 5 4 3

To my five wonderful grandchildren,
who your Grams and I love with all our hearts

Jake Stump, may you depend on Jesus always and live in a way that others want to know him.

Matt Franklin, may you touch others with the love of Jesus, giving them reasons to believe in him.

Ty Stump, may you boldly declare your love for Jesus and put him first in all you do.

Jack Franklin, may you use your God-given creative gifts and imagination to glorify King Jesus.

David Franklin, may you love Jesus always and be his shining light that points the way to him.

Guys, I look forward, by the grace of Jesus, to one day—after the resurrection—walking with each of you on God's New Earth! When Grams and I leave this world, it will not be the end of our relationship with you, just an interruption. A great reunion awaits us in a far better world! Meanwhile, may our lives and yours be ALL ABOUT JESUS!

Pops

Acknowledgments

I want to express my heartfelt gratitude to Stephanie Anderson, Doreen Button, Chelsea Dudley, Brenda Abelein, and Kathy Norquist for helping me collect great quotations about Jesus; and to Stephanie and Doreen for helping me edit.

Thanks also to Harvest House editor Steve Miller and editor Kris Bearss for their excellent work.

Contents

Introduction

Why a book of great thoughts and quotations about Jesus? Well, can you think of anyone in human history whose birth, life, teachings, relationships, death, and promises are more important than those of Jesus? Who would come second? No one else is remotely close!

Even atheists and agnostics recognize that no one has affected life on Earth like Jesus. Every time we write a date, we're reminded of his impact—history falls into two parts, BC (before Christ) and AD (*anno Domini*, year of our Lord).

Each month, millions of people type "Who is Jesus?" or "Who is Christ?" into Internet search engines. Here's the problem: When I searched those questions, the first one yielded nearly 1.2 billion results, and the second, 1.6 billion. And the answers offered are diverse, contradictory, and confusing.

Christianity, the religion that bases itself on Christ, is the largest religion on the planet. One out of every three people worldwide believes in a man named Jesus who lived two thousand years ago! Sadly, however, even many professing Christians don't know what to believe about Jesus, and often believe things about him that contradict Scripture.

True Christ-followers understand that though there are many competing opinions about him, the only authentic Jesus is the one revealed in God's Word. Hence, they believe that Jesus was both man and God, was born of a virgin, lived a perfect life, performed great miracles, died for their sins, rose from the dead, and ascended to the right hand of God. And that isn't all. They believe that Jesus has made a way for them to have eternal life, delivering them from eternal Hell and granting them eternal life in Heaven. They believe that Jesus, the God-man, is going to return to Earth to set up his eternal kingdom.

Many people regularly gather to celebrate the person and work of Jesus Christ and consider Jesus to be their God, Savior, Judge, Example, Counselor, Friend, and Source of joy, even when persecuted or everything seems stacked against them. Some Christians are like my wife, who grew up in a home where her parents believed in Jesus, taught her about him, and took her every week to a Bible-teaching, Christ-centered church. Others are like me: not raised in a Christian home and ignorant of the gospel until they were teenagers or adults.

The world is full of people who naively embrace incorrect beliefs about Jesus. False teachers say whatever people want to hear, while demons in the invisible realm whisper lies about Jesus into our ears. This is why I follow every heading in this book with scripture first. Only secondly do I share what ordinary people—including me—have to say about Jesus. I believe that first by reading the Bible verses and then reading others' words about Jesus that are in keeping with Scripture, you can actually come to know many great truths about him through this book. That's a remarkable claim, but I stand by it.

Some clarifications: I decided not to include endnotes because I was finding that many endnotes were nearly as long as the quotations themselves, making less room for what matters most! Anyone interested in learning more about a specific author or quote can do a simple online search. (If you do this, you'll sometimes find quotations attributed to more than one person. I chose the source that seemed best documented, but occasionally said, "Attributed to" when I wasn't confident in the source but believed the quotation was worthy.)

I've also taken a liberty that, in the great majority of cases, avoids the distracting use of brackets. Suppose an author says, "Jesus went to the cross for us. He proved his love for us in his sacrifice." If the selected quotation begins with the second sentence, common practice is to quote it as "[Jesus] proved his love..." I believe it's true to the author's intent and less cumbersome to change the pronoun "He" to the antecedent noun "Jesus." Therefore, I'd quote that second sentence as "Jesus proved his love..." (I do not take this liberty with Scripture, where I use brackets.)

Also, I'm aware that not every person cited in this book was or is a Jesus-follower.

I quote Napoleon, Albert Einstein, and others who weren't known as believers, but particular things they said about Jesus seemed worthy of inclusion—perhaps even more so because while apparently not knowing him as Savior, they still recognized his unparalleled impact. Furthermore, various famous people said good things about Jesus while living biblically inconsistent or even immoral lives, treating others unjustly, or holding to doctrinal heresies. Some owned slaves and were advocates for segregation. Some, including the reformer Martin Luther, made anti-Semitic statements.

While I'm familiar with church history, it's impossible for me or anyone to know all the flaws of those I cite. I eliminated many quotations from godly people and have no doubt included a number from those who are less godly. I deliberately sought insights from many spiritually mature people, but my main focus was on the quality of the words about Jesus, not those who said them.

Please don't think, *I'm not going to read any further because I've heard that person said or did bad things, or holds to different doctrines, or posted a questionable tweet.* Instead, focus on the statement itself and the one person this book is truly about: Jesus Christ, the God-man.

My final caveat is that when I've thought there's something important not covered by others under a particular heading, I sometimes insert one from my own books or articles. This isn't because I think my comments are more noteworthy, but because they supplement what I didn't find as I searched the great quotes of others. I've tried to not just assemble quotations but paint a fuller picture of Jesus.

I've divided the book into four parts.

Part 1 declares who Jesus is—his nature, attributes, and characteristics.

Part 2 speaks of his transforming life, death, resurrection, return, and reign.

Part 3 explores the many powerful names and titles of Jesus.

Part 4 centers on Jesus in his beautiful relationships with his people.

While inspirational words about Jesus fill this book, the only ones that are truly inspired—in the sense of coming from God and carrying his full authority—originate from the Bible. Even if you think you're familiar with it, please don't skip over

Scripture to get to what others say! Our words don't compare to his. They usually have a short shelf life, while God's Word is eternal. He promises us this:

> As the rain and the snow
>   come down from heaven,
> and do not return to it
>   without watering the earth
> and making it bud and flourish,
>   so that it yields seed for the sower and bread for the eater,
> so is my word that goes out from my mouth:
>   It will not return to me empty,
> but will accomplish what I desire
>   and achieve the purpose for which I sent it (Isaiah 55:10-11 NIV).

I am one of countless people whose life Jesus has radically changed. I don't mean simply that the teachings of Jesus have changed me; I mean that Jesus himself, the real and living Jesus, came into my life as a teenager and, fifty years later, continues to transform me. I love my wife and children and grandchildren and friends dearly. But I love Jesus even more. And I believe that makes me a better husband, father, grandfather, and friend.

That's why I have always loved to read and think and talk about Jesus. As a very young Christian I bought a book of quotations about every aspect of the Christian life, and I pored over it again and again. My favorite quotes were those about Jesus himself, and also about his work in the lives of his followers. Several years ago I decided I wanted to compile the best of the best quotations about Jesus I could locate—both in great books and online (triple-checking for accuracy, which is imperative when using the Internet).

There are words from and about Jesus in many quotation books, but how many books have you seen where it's truly *all* about Jesus? It's likely this is the first. Compiling these quotes with the much-appreciated assistance of our Eternal Perspective Ministries staff has been a joy. While there are a lot of quotations here, I had to cut out two-thirds of what we collected because there simply wasn't space. It reminded me of the apostle John's statement at the end of his Gospel: "Jesus did many other things as well. If every one of them were written down, I suppose that even the whole world would not have room for the books that would be written" (John 21:25 NIV).

This collection is a drop in the ocean of what has been said about Jesus, which itself is a miniscule portion of all that could be said about him (and *will* be said in the ages to come!). But I believe it's a unique and particularly high-quality collection. God has profoundly used these words in my life over the past two years as I faced very difficult times. I pray God will use these insights just as mightily with you, to encourage you to love and trust and follow Jesus more.

In Christo solo is Latin for "In Christ alone." It was one of the five central assertions of the Reformation, and it means that salvation is by faith *only in Christ,* not by our own efforts. What could possibly be more important than contemplating this Jesus upon whom our entire lives, both present and eternal, depend?

Grow in the grace and knowledge of our Lord and Savior Jesus Christ; to Him be the glory, both now and to the day of eternity. Amen.
2 Peter 3:18 NASB

PART 1

The Nature and Attributes of Jesus

This precious Book, God's Word, tells us of one who resigned the throne and crown of heaven, exchanged the radiant robe of the universal King for the garment of a servant, descended to death, condescended to human want and woe and wickedness, lay in a lowly cradle in a cattle stall at Bethlehem, and hung upon a cross of shame of Calvary, that even those who crucified Him might be forgiven. Can you span the chasm between the throne of a universe and that cross? A crown of stars and a crown of thorns? The worship of the host of heaven and the mockery of an insulting mob?...There is nothing like it in history, not even in fable.

How can we understand? A man with human infirmities, without human sin or sinfulness; poor, yet having at His disposal universal riches; weak and weary, yet having the exhaustless energy of God; unable to resist the violence and insults of His foes, yet able to summon legions of angels at a word or wish; suffering, yet incapable of anything but perfect bliss; dying, yet Himself having neither beginning of days or end of years?

A.T. Pierson

If you're told you're going to meet someone important whom your friends know, you naturally ask them, "Who is he? What's he like? Where did he come from? What does he do? Is he the real deal? Does he live up to expectations?"

Because no other historical figure is as widely known, multitudes live with the illusion that they really *know* Jesus, when in reality they simply have various impressions *about* him. Impressions are not knowledge. They are a random collection of data picked up from family, friends, books, movies, articles, social media, and in some cases, experiences with churches or professing Christians. Many of these sources are either completely wrong, mostly wrong, or mostly right but with significant errors.

As a result, it is hard to imagine any subject more fraught with confusion, misinformation, and deception than the subject of who Jesus really is. And what a quandary! *The most important person who has ever lived is also the most misunderstood.* People often quote him—"Judge not," or "Whatever you ask in my name, this I will do," for instance—without understanding the context of his words, thereby entirely "missing" his meaning.

Thoughts flow the moment we hear the name *Jesus Christ.* The question is, which thoughts are true, and which are false? Even more important than his teachings on life and ethics is who Jesus actually claimed to be. As Kevin DeYoung has said, "Just about everybody in America likes Jesus, but few like him for who he truly is."

The doctrines of the deity and humanity of Christ, with all their implications, are vitally important not only to sound doctrine but to loving our Savior and Lord by seeing him more accurately. We are all theologians. The only issue is whether we're good ones or bad ones. Wouldn't you rather be a *good* one—especially when it comes to believing what's true about Jesus?

Sadly, many religious professionals deny Christ's deity, miracles, atonement, and/or resurrection and view the Gospel accounts as myth and distortion. To them, "the historical Jesus" was merely a moral teacher and example that the church turned into a god, falsely claiming that he performed miracles and was superhuman. These skeptical scholars suppose the Gospel accounts and the New Testament letters to be a human invention and argue that the church elevated Jesus to a divine status he never claimed. (This raises the question of why all the apostles were tortured, and every one of them but John died for what they believed. No one endures that kind of suffering for what they know to be a lie.)

Scripture itself, however, presents Christ not as myth, but history. It emphasizes the role of eyewitnesses. Seeking the historical Jesus while denying the Bible is like seeking to know what happened at Gettysburg while denying the historical records from Gettysburg.

Our faith in Christ is only as good as the authentic reality of the Christ we believe in. It shouldn't surprise us, then, that Satan will attack us by promoting false and unworthy views of the person and work of Jesus.

Peter wrote sobering warnings about those who give false portrayals of Jesus (2 Peter 2:1-3). The worst and most dangerous heresies misrepresent Jesus Christ, denying the truths about him and making him out to be less than he really is.

The apostle John also warned about misrepresentations of the Jesus he knew so well:

> Dear friends, do not believe every spirit, but test the spirits to see whether they are from God, because many false prophets have gone out into the world. This is how you can recognize the Spirit of God: Every spirit that acknowledges that Jesus Christ has come in the flesh is from God, but every spirit that does not acknowledge Jesus is not from God (1 John 4:1-3 NIV).

Since nothing is more important than who Jesus is and what he has done, naturally there are no greater truths—and in turn, no more pernicious and destructive heresies—than those concerning Jesus. If Jesus did not live, if he was not God, if he was not the Creator but merely one of the created, or if Jesus was not really a man, the consequences would be devastating in the lives of literally billions of people who have believed the words he spoke and the Bible's teachings about him.

Biblical Christianity is not simply a religion *about* Christ but a relationship *with* Christ. If we get it right about Jesus, we can afford to get some minor things wrong. But if we get it wrong about Jesus, in the end it won't matter what else we get right.

This is why I am starting this section with the greatest question Jesus ever asked anyone: "Who do you say I am?" Because our answer to that question, whether silent or spoken, is the single most important answer we will ever give.

Who Do You Say I Am?

When Jesus came to the region of Caesarea Philippi, he asked his disciples, "Who do people say the Son of Man is?" They replied, "Some say John the Baptist; others say Elijah; and still others, Jeremiah or one of the prophets." "But what about you?" he asked. "Who do you say I am?" Simon Peter answered, "You are the Messiah, the Son of the living God." Jesus replied, "Blessed are you, Simon son of Jonah, for this was not revealed to you by flesh and blood, but by my Father in heaven." **Matthew 16:13-17 NIV**

If you find it hard to believe in God, I strongly advise you to begin your search not with philosophical questions...but with Jesus of Nazareth. **John Stott**

Who is Jesus Christ? You've never met him in person, and you don't know anyone who has. But there is a way to know who he is. How? Jesus Christ–the divine Person revealed in the Bible–has a unique excellence and a spiritual beauty that speaks directly to our souls and says, "Yes, this is truth." It's like seeing the sun and knowing that it is light, or tasting honey and knowing that it is sweet. **John Piper**

Among the Jews there suddenly turns up a man who goes about talking as if He was God...Among Pantheists anyone might say that he was a part of God, or one with God: there would be nothing very odd about it. But this man, since He was a Jew, could not mean that kind of god. God, in their language, meant the Being outside the world Who had made it and was infinitely different from anything else. And when you have grasped that, you will see that what this man said was, quite simply, the most shocking thing that has ever been uttered by human lips. **C.S. Lewis**

The claims of Jesus are so startling that they...challenge us to make up our minds about this most remarkable person. Was he just a great teacher or was he much more? **Michael Green**

Everyone who comes in contact with Jesus has rendered a judgment on him. Even ignoring him is a decision about his identity. **Kevin DeYoung**

Reared in a carpenter shop...this young man gathered disciples about Him, and proclaimed Himself the Messiah. He taught and performed miracles for a few brief months and then was crucified; His disciples were scattered and many of them put to death; His claims were disputed, His resurrection denied and His followers persecuted; and yet from this beginning His religion spread until hundreds of millions have taken His name with reverence upon their lips and millions have been willing to die rather than surrender the faith which He put into their hearts. How shall we account for Him? "What think ye of Christ?" It is easier to believe Him divine than to explain in any other way what He said and did and was. **William Jennings Bryan**

The real question is not what are we to make of Christ, but what is He to make of us? The picture of a fly sitting deciding what it is going to make of an elephant has comic elements about it. **C.S. Lewis**

It takes a fantastic will to unbelief to suppose that Jesus never really "happened," and more to suppose that he did not say the things recorded of him—so incapable of being "invented" by anyone in the world at that time...We must therefore either believe in Him and in what He said and take the consequences; or reject Him and take the consequences. **J.R.R. Tolkien**

The most important question in anyone's life is the question asked by poor Pilate in Matthew 27:22: "What shall I do, then, with Jesus who is called Christ?" No other question in the whole sweep of human experience is as important as this. It is the choice between life and death, between meaningless existence and life abundant. **Dale Evans Rogers**

After six years given to the impartial investigation of Christianity, as to its truth or falsity, I have come to the deliberate conclusion that Jesus Christ was the Messiah of the Jews, the Saviour of the world, and my personal Saviour. **Lew Wallace**

The battle for human souls pivots on the issue of Christ's identity. He's the watershed, the dividing line between Hell and Heaven. Who do you believe, in your mind and deep in your heart, that he really is? Every person must give an answer—and whether our answer is right could not be more consequential or eternally significant. **Randy Alcorn**

Christ's Dual Nature: Fully God and Fully Human

God promised this Good News long ago through his prophets...As a man, he was born from the family of David. But through the Spirit of holiness he was declared to be God's Son with great power by rising from the dead. **Romans 1:2-4 NCV**

In Christ lives all the fullness of God in a human body. **Colossians 2:9 NLT**

"I and the Father are one." **John 10:30 NIV**

In order that the body of Christ might be shown to be a real body, he was born of a woman; but in order that his Godhead might be made clear he was born of a virgin. **Thomas Aquinas**

He who is over all, the blessed God, has been born; and having been made man, he is still God forever. **Hippolytus of Rome**

God has landed on this enemy-occupied world in human form...The perfect surrender and humiliation was undergone by Christ: perfect because He was God, surrender and humiliation because He was man. **C.S. Lewis**

Jesus Christ: the condescension of divinity, and the exaltation of humanity. **Phillips Brooks**

Jesus became as like us as God can be. **Donald English**

Christ's humanity is the great hem of the garment, through which we can touch his Godhead. **Richard Glover**

> Jesus is God spelling himself out in language that men can understand. **S.D. Gordon**

Remember, Christ was not a deified man, neither was he a humanized God. He was perfectly God, and at the same time perfectly man. **Charles Spurgeon**

Here are two mysteries for the price of one—the plurality of persons within the unity of God, and the union of Godhead and manhood in the person of Jesus. On these two mysteries, all else hangs. **J.I. Packer**

Attribute true and proper divinity to Christ. Attribute true and proper humanity to Christ. Do not so mingle the human and divine that you end up with a being neither human nor divine. Do not dissect Christ so that there are two persons in one being. **Ed Goodrick**

The gospel isn't the gospel if Jesus wasn't God or wasn't man. **Randy Alcorn**

If Jesus Christ is not true God, how could he help us? If he is not true man, how could he help us? **Dietrich Bonhoeffer**

He was God and man in one person, that God and man might be happy together again. **George Whitefield**

We…confess one and the same Son, our Lord Jesus Christ; the same perfect in Manhood; truly God and truly Man, in all things like unto us without sin…existing in two natures without mixture, without change, without division, without separation; the diversity of the two natures not being at all destroyed by their union, but the peculiar properties of each nature being preserved…not parted or divided into two persons, but one Lord Jesus Christ. **The Council of Chalcedon**

As human voice and instrument blend in one harmony, as human soul and body blend in each act of feeling, thought, or speech, so, as far as we can know, divinity and humanity act together in the thought and heart and act of the one Christ. **Archibald Alexander Hodge**

I know He was hungry, and I know that with five loaves He fed five thousand. I know He was thirsty, and I know that He turned the water into wine. I know he was carried in a ship, and I know that He walked on the sea. I know that He died, and I know that He raised the dead. I know that He was set before Pilate, and I know that He sits with the Father on His throne. I know that He was worshipped by angels…And truly some of these I ascribe to the human, and others to the divine nature. For by reason of this He is said to have been both God and man. **John Chrysostom**

The Christ was twofold: man is what was seen, but God is what was not seen. As man, he truly ate as we do…As God, he fed the five thousand with five loaves. **Cyril of Jerusalem**

Christ's temptations were utter nonsense if he were only a man. What man would ever be challenged to change a rock into a loaf of bread? **Source Unknown**

The impression of Jesus which the gospels give...is not so much one of deity reduced as one of divine capacities restrained. **J.I. Packer**

He was man and he was God, in order that since as man he suffered for us, so as God he might have compassion on us, and forgive our sins. **Irenaeus**

He is not humanity deified. He is not Godhead humanized...He is all that God is, and all that man is as God created him. **Charles Spurgeon**

Jesus Christ: The meeting place of eternity and time, the blending of deity and humanity, the junction of heaven and earth. **Source Unknown**

Jesus didn't put on a body as if it were a coat. He wasn't made of two separable components, man and God, to be switched on and off at will. Rather, he was and is and always will be a man *and* God. When Christ died, he might have appeared to shed his humanity; but when he rose in an indestructible body, he declared his permanent identity as the God-man. This is a mystery so great it should leave us breathless. **Randy Alcorn**

When Jesus came to earth he did not cease to be God; when he returned to heaven he did not cease to be man. **John Blanchard**

Christ's Deity

The leaders wanted to kill Jesus for two reasons. First, he had broken the law of the Sabbath. But even worse, he had said that God was his father, which made him equal with God. **John 5:18 CEV**

The entire fullness of God's nature dwells bodily in Christ...the head over every ruler and authority. **Colossians 2:9-10 CSB**

We are filled with hope, as we wait for the glorious return of our great God and Savior Jesus Christ. **Titus 2:13 CEV**

Of the Son he says, "Your throne, O God, is forever and ever, the scepter of uprightness is the scepter of your kingdom." **Hebrews 1:8 ESV**

God...did not, as one might have imagined, send men any servant, angel, ruler, or any of those who influence earthly things...Instead, he sent the very Creator and Fashioner of all things, the One by whom he made the heavens. **Unknown Christian in a letter to Diogenes, AD 150**

The deity of Christ is the key doctrine of the scriptures. Reject it, and the Bible becomes a jumble of words without any unifying theme. Accept it, and the Bible becomes an intelligible and ordered revelation of God in the person of Jesus Christ. **J. Oswald Sanders**

Jesus can't speak of judgment day without putting himself at the center of our cosmic conclusion—he is the Judge. He can't set eyes on Jerusalem without lamenting the way they've treated him for the last millennia. He can't mention Abraham without saying how terrific it was when they met—2,000 years earlier...He owns divine titles; accepts divine worship; performs divine acts; pronounces divine verdicts; and makes divine oaths. In short, he walks around planet earth like he owns the place. **Glen Shrivener**

Even the very creation broke silence at His behest and...confessed with one voice before the cross.... that He Who suffered thereon in the body was not man only, but Son of God and Savior of all. The sun veiled his face, the earth quaked, the mountains were rent asunder, all men were stricken with awe. **Athanasius of Alexandria**

Buddha never claimed to be God. Moses never claimed to be Jehovah. Mohammed never claimed to be Allah. Yet Jesus Christ claimed to be the true and living God. Buddha simply said, "I am a teacher in search of the truth." Jesus said, "I am the Truth." Confucius said, "I never claimed to be holy." Jesus said, "Who convicts me of sin?" Mohammed said, "Unless God throws his cloak of mercy over me, I have no hope." Jesus said, "Unless you believe in me, you will die in your sins." **Source Unknown**

In the whole history of the world, there is only one person who not only claimed to be God himself but also got enormous numbers of people to believe it. Only Jesus combines claims of divinity with the most beautiful life of humanity. **Timothy Keller**

The divinity of Jesus is not a dispensable extra that has no significance for our salvation. On the contrary, our salvation depends on it. We can be saved only by God Himself. **Klaas Runia**

The most pressing question on the problem of faith is whether a man as a civilized being…can believe in the divinity of the Son of God, Jesus Christ, for therein rests the whole of our faith. **Fyodor Dostoevsky**

If Jesus is not God, then there is no Christianity, and we who worship Him are nothing more than idolaters. Conversely, if He is God, those who say He was merely a good man, or even the best of men, are blasphemers. More serious still, if He is not God, then He is a blasphemer in the fullest sense of the word. If He is not God, He is not even good. **J. Oswald Sanders**

We believe in one God, the Father, all sovereign, the Maker of things visible and invisible; and in one Lord Jesus Christ, the Word of God, God of God, Light of Light, Son only-begotten…of the Father before all ages, through whom also all things were made. **Eusebius**

The good news is that in the face of Jesus Christ we see the very face of God, the One who has decided to be with us and for us in spite of our sin. **Kevin Vanhoozer**

Christ's Multifaceted Character

In him are hidden all the treasures of wisdom and knowledge. **Colossians 2:3 CSB**

The Spirit of the LORD shall rest upon him, the Spirit of wisdom and understanding, the Spirit of counsel and might, the Spirit of knowledge and the fear of the LORD. **Isaiah 11:2 ESV**

Most men are notable for one conspicuous virtue or grace. Moses for meekness, Job for patience, John for love. But in Jesus you find everything. **J. Oswald Sanders**

Jesus Christ is tender without being weak, strong without being coarse, lowly without being servile. He has conviction without intolerance, enthusiasm without fanaticism, holiness without Pharisaism, passion without prejudice...His life was life at its Highest. **Thomas Watson**

There is in the Lord Jesus a perfect evenness of various perfections. All the elements of perfect character are in lovely balance. His gentleness is never weak. His courage is never harsh. **C.I. Scofield**

Jesus is the Lion of Judah (Rev. 5:5) and the Lamb of God (Rev. 5:6)—He was lionhearted and lamblike, strong and meek, tough and tender, aggressive and responsive, bold and brokenhearted. **John Piper**

He combined child-like innocence with manly strength, all-absorbing devotion to God with untiring interest in the welfare of man, tender love to the sinner and uncompromising severity against sin, commanding dignity with winning humility, fearless courage with wise caution, unyielding firmness with sweet gentleness. **Philip Schaff**

He never spoke when it would have been wiser to remain silent, never kept silence when He should have spoken. Mercy and judgment blended in all His actions and judgments, yet neither prevailed at the expense of the other. **Oswald Sanders**

When we speak about wisdom, we are speaking about Christ. When we speak about virtue, we are speaking about Christ. When we speak about justice, we are speaking about Christ. When we speak about peace, we are speaking about Christ. When we speak about truth and life and redemption, we are speaking about Christ. **Ambrose**

He is the fountain of all truth, but He is more—He is truth itself. He is the source and strength of all beauty, but He is more—He is beauty itself. He is the fountain of all wisdom, but He is more—He is wisdom itself. In Him are all the treasures of wisdom and knowledge hidden away!...He is the fountain of love, but again, He is far more than that—He is love! **A.W. Tozer**

We must look at the complete Jesus revealed in Scripture, lest we remake him in our image, with his only attribute love. By seeing him in his holiness and love, his truth and his grace, we'll learn to see the fullness of his beauty. **Randy Alcorn**

If you leave out Christ, you have left the sun out of the day and the moon out of the night. You have left the waters out of the sea and the floods out of the river...you have left joy out of heaven, you have robbed *all* of its all. There is no gospel worth thinking of, much less worth proclaiming, if Jesus be forgotten. **Charles Spurgeon**

Jesus of Nazareth, without money and arms, conquered more millions than Alexander the Great, Caesar, Mohammed, and Napoleon; without science and learning, he shed more light on things human and divine than all philosophers and scholars combined; without the eloquence of school, he spoke such words of life as were never spoken before or since, and produced effects which lie beyond the reach of orator or poet; without writing a single line, he set more pens in motion, and furnished themes for more sermons, orations, discussions, learned volumes, works of art, and songs of praise than the whole army of great men of ancient and modern times. **Philip Schaff**

If Jesus is the Bread of Life, loss of Jesus means starving. If Jesus is the Light of the World, loss of Jesus means darkness. If Jesus is the Good Shepherd, loss of Jesus means wandering alone and lost. If Jesus is the resurrection and the life, loss of Jesus is eternal death. And if Jesus is the Lamb of God, sacrificed for our sins, loss of Jesus means paying that price for ourselves. **Rebecca McLaughlin**

Only Christ is the whole of man's happiness; the sun to enlighten him, the physician to heal him, the wall of fire to defend him, the friend to comfort him, the pearl to enrich him, the ark to support him, the rock to sustain him under the heaviest pressures. **Isaac Ambrose**

What the sun is to the day, what the moon is to the night…such is Jesus Christ to us. What bread is to the hungry, clothes to the naked…such is Jesus Christ to us. What the husband is to his spouse, what the head is to the body, such is Jesus Christ to us. **Charles Spurgeon**

Jesus is the giver of our life and the rock of our hope. He is our safety and our future. He is our righteousness, our sanctification, our inheritance. You find that He is all of this in the instant that you move your heart toward Him in faith. **A.W. Tozer**

Christ's Humanity

When the fullness of time had come, God sent forth his Son, born of woman, born under the law. **Galatians 4:4 ESV**

He went down with them and came to Nazareth, and He continued in subjection to them...And Jesus kept increasing in wisdom and stature, and in favor with God and men. **Luke 2:51-52 ESV**

After fasting forty days and forty nights, he was hungry. **Matthew 4:2 NIV**

Jesus Christ ended the remoteness of God by coming to earth as a man himself...The austere God who spoke to the Old Testament heroes in thunder and lightning is now as real and touchable, as human, as flesh and blood can make him. **Calvin Miller**

He it is by whom all things were made, and who was made one of all things; who is the revealer of the Father, the creator of the Mother; the Son of God by the Father without a mother, the Son of man by the Mother without a father; the Word who is God before all time, the Word made flesh at a fitting time, the maker of the sun, made under the sun...unutterably wise, in His wisdom a babe without utterance; filling the world, lying in a manger. **Augustine**

God eternal became a child so that through his life, death and resurrection, we would become the children of God. **Paul David Tripp**

Jesus was so fully human that even those who lived and worked with him for 30 years, even those brothers who grew up in his own household, did not realize that he was anything more than another very good human being. They apparently had no idea that he was God come in the flesh. **Wayne Grudem**

Even Jesus, the one and only Son of God, as a young man "grew in wisdom and stature, and in favor with God and men" (Luke 2:52). Because our Lord himself had to go through developmental stages and gain wisdom through experience (although, unlike ourselves, his progression did not involve trial and error), we can be assured that he empathizes with our weaknesses and struggles (Hebrews 2:18; 4:15)...But because he is God, we can be equally confident that Jesus will help us to overcome those weaknesses and gain life-empowering insight through those struggles. ***The Knowing Jesus Study Bible***

When I look at Jesus' warm and intimate friendship, my heart fills with praise that Jesus was...a man. A man of flesh-and-blood reality. His heart felt the sting of sympathy. His eyes glowed with tenderness. His arms embraced. His lips smiled. His hands touched. Jesus as male! Jesus invites us to relate to him as the Son of Man. And because he is fully man, we can relate to Jesus with affection and love. **Joni Eareckson Tada**

We know Jesus was God. But He was also a man—He got tired; He got hungry; He knew what it was to have crowds pressing around Him all the time; He knew what it was to have His privacy invaded. But He kept right on letting the crowds into His life. He kept on teaching, healing, confronting the powers of hell. **Nancy DeMoss Wolgemuth**

When God entered time and became a man, he who was boundless became bound. Imprisoned in flesh. Restricted by weary-prone muscles and eyelids. For more than three decades, his once limitless reach would be limited to the stretch of an arm, his speed checked to the pace of human feet. I wonder, was he ever tempted to regain his boundlessness?...With one word, he could've transformed the hard earth into a soft bed, but he didn't...With an arch of his brow, he could've paralyzed the hand of the soldier as he braided the crown of thorns. But he didn't. **Max Lucado**

The mystery of the humanity of Christ, that he sunk himself into our flesh, is beyond all human understanding. **Martin Luther**

By His own descent to the earth He has prepared our ascent to heaven. Having received our mortality, He has bestowed on us His immortality. Having undertaken our weakness, He has made us strong in His strength. Having submitted to our poverty, He has transferred to us His riches. **John Calvin**

He became what we are that he might make us what he is.
Athanasius of Alexandria

Christ's Human Limits

Jacob's well was there, and Jesus, tired as he was from the journey, sat down by the well. **John 4:6 NIV**

After this, Jesus knew that everything had been done. So that the Scripture would come true, he said, "I am thirsty." **John 19:28 NCV**

On the Sabbath he began to teach in the synagogue, and many who heard him were astonished, saying, "Where did this man get these things? What is the wisdom given to him? How are such mighty works done by his hands? Is not this the carpenter, the son of Mary and brother of James and Joses and Judas and Simon? And are not his sisters here with us?" And they took offense at him. **Mark 6:2-3 ESV**

Although he was crucified in weakness, he now lives by the power of God. **2 Corinthians 13:4 NLT**

For the first 30 years of his life Jesus lived a human life that was so ordinary that the people of Nazareth who knew him best were amazed that he could teach with authority and work miracles. **Wayne Grudem**

Jesus didn't do it all. Jesus didn't meet every need. He left people waiting in line to be healed. He left one town to preach to another. He hid away to pray. He got tired. He never interacted with the vast majority of people on the planet. He spent thirty years in training and only three years in ministry. He did not try to do it all. And yet, he did everything God asked him to do. **Kevin DeYoung**

Jesus was morally perfect from conception, and an infinity before that, but Scripture tells us he grew in understanding through life experiences. Incredibly,

Jesus "learned obedience from what he suffered" (Hebrews 5:8). Growing and learning cannot be bad; the sinless Son of God experienced them. They're simply part of being human—his humanity was real, not imaginary. **Randy Alcorn**

To obey to the point of death requires the ability to die, and for this, Jesus had to be human. **Bruce Ware**

Jesus...is weak because he refuses to trust his own strength and instead submits to the Father's will and depends upon the Spirit. This is a godly weakness that models the self-denying path of faith and obedience. Ironically, the disciples' apparent strength is actually perilous weakness, but Jesus's apparent weakness is in fact the truest kind of strength, because humble dependence will empower him to walk the road the Father has set before him. **Trevor Laurence**

Jesus...was at times physically weak, for during his temptation in the wilderness he fasted for 40 days (the point at which a human being's physical strength is almost entirely gone, and beyond which irreparable physical harm will occur if the fast continues)...When Jesus was on his way to be crucified, the soldiers forced Simon of Cyrene to carry his cross (Luke 23:26), most likely because Jesus was so weak, following the beating he had received, that he did not have strength enough to carry it himself. The culmination of Jesus' limitations in terms of his human body is seen when he died on the cross (Luke 23:46). His human body ceased to have life in it and ceased to function, just as ours does when we die. **Wayne Grudem**

By a Carpenter mankind was created and made, and by a Carpenter mete it was that man should be repaired. **Desiderius Erasmus**

The only way to make sense, then, of the fact that Jesus came in the power of the Spirit is to understand that he lived his life fundamentally as a man, and as such, he relied on the Spirit to provide the power, grace, knowledge, wisdom, direction, and enablement he needed, moment by moment and day by day, to fulfill the mission the Father sent him to accomplish. **Bruce Ware**

Christ's Humility

Jesus knew that the Father had put all things under his power, and that he had come from God and was returning to God; so he got up from the meal, took off his outer clothing, and wrapped a towel around his waist. After that, he poured water into a basin and began to wash his disciples' feet, drying them with the towel that was wrapped around him. **John 13:2-5 NIV**

Your attitude should be the same as that of Christ Jesus: who, being in very nature God, did not consider equality with God something to be grasped, but made himself nothing, taking the very nature of a servant, and being found in appearance as a man, he humbled himself and became obedient to death—even death on a cross. **Philippians 2:5-8 NIV**

> The Ancient of Days became the infant of days throughout whose entire number he experienced humiliation...No one has ever descended so low because no one has ever come from so high. **Mark Jones**

If people ask, "Why did he not appear by means of other parts of creation, and use some nobler instrument, as the sun or moon or stars or fire or air, instead of man merely?" let them know that the Lord came not to make a display, but to teach and heal those who were suffering. **Athanasius of Alexandria**

Though the King of the Universe, He didn't have the honor of being born in the palace of a king. He wasn't born in Rome, the world's political capital, or Athens, the philosophical capital, or Alexandria, the intellectual capital, or even Jerusalem, the religious capital. He was born in tiny Bethlehem, which means simply "House of Bread." **Randy Alcorn**

When Jesus came in the form of a servant, he was not disguising who God is. He was revealing who God is. **John Ortberg**

Jesus Christ served others first; he spoke to those to whom no one spoke; he dined with the lowest members of society; he touched the untouchable. He had no throne, no crown, no bevy of servants or armored guards. A borrowed manger and a borrowed tomb framed his earthly life. **Charles Colson**

Jesus...made a career of rejecting marks of status or privilege: He touched lepers, washed the feet of his disciples, befriended little children, encouraged women to join his entourage, and finally, submitted to crucifixion by a foreign power. Everything about Jesus spoke of servitude. **Eugene H. Peterson**

The Lord ate from a common bowl, and asked the disciples to sit on the grass. He washed their feet, with a towel wrapped around His waist—He, who is the Lord of the universe! **Clement of Alexandria**

It is relatively easy to serve those above us—even the world expects this—but Jesus served downward. **Jerry Bridges**

Jesus Christ knew who He was. He knew where He had come from, and why he was here. And He knew where He was going. And when you are that liberated, then you can serve. **Howard Hendricks**

Jesus lost all his glory so that we could be clothed in it. He was shut out so we could get access. He was bound, nailed, so that we could be free. He was cast out so we could approach. **Timothy Keller**

Christ ceased not to be a King because He was like a servant, nor to be a lion because He was like a lamb, nor to be God because He was made man, nor to be a judge because He was judged. **Henry Smith**

Christ's Sinlessness in Temptation

Then Jesus was led by the Spirit into the wilderness to be tempted by the devil. **Matthew 4:1 NIV**

Judas had betrayed Jesus...He returned the thirty silver coins to the chief priests and leaders and said, "I have sinned by betraying a man who has never done anything wrong." **Matthew 27:3-4 CEV**

For our sake he made him to be sin who knew no sin, so that in him we might become the righteousness of God. **2 Corinthians 5:21 ESV**

We do not have a high priest who is unable to empathize with our weaknesses, but we have one who has been tempted in every way, just as we are—yet he did not sin. **Hebrews 4:15 NIV**

The first Adam was tested in the God-blessed garden and fell. The second Adam was tested in the God-cursed desert, and won. **Russell Moore**

Jesus was not tempted to see if He would fall. He was tempted to show that He could not fall. **J. Vernon McGee**

There is one fail-safe method available to each of us for resisting temptations...we have to fight back with God's truth. Each time Jesus was tempted his response began with the same phrase: *It is written.* ***The Knowing Jesus Study Bible***

The complete absence of sin in the life of Jesus is all the more remarkable because of the severe temptations he faced, not only in the wilderness, but throughout his life. **Wayne Grudem**

A catalog of virtues and graces, however complete, would merely give us a mechanical view. It's the spotless purity and the sinlessness of Jesus as acknowledged by friend and foe that raises His character high above the reach of all others...It's the absolute perfection of Christ's character that makes Him a moral miracle in History. It's futile to compare Him with saints and sages, ancient or modern. **Philip Schaff**

Some have objected that if Jesus did not sin, then he was not truly human, for all humans sin. But that objection simply fails to realize that human beings are now in an abnormal situation. God did not create us sinful, but holy and righteous. Adam and Eve in the Garden of Eden before they sinned were truly human, and we now, though human, do not match the pattern that God intends for us when our full, sinless humanity is restored. **Wayne Grudem**

No critic of Jesus has ever been taken seriously. His life was the epitome of virtue. **Richard Halverson**

His deity is demonstrated by his own claims supported by his divine attributes and miraculous activities. His humanity is demonstrated by the virgin birth and his human attributes, activities, relationships, trials, and temptations. One peculiarity of his humanity was sinlessness, but this did not make him something other than human. ***The Knowing Jesus Study Bible***

Jesus perfectly lived what he perfectly taught. **Herman H. Horne**

Christ's Emotions

When Jesus saw her weeping, and the Jews who had come with her also weeping, he was deeply moved in his spirit and greatly troubled. And he said, "Where have you laid him?" They said to him, "Lord, come and see." Jesus wept. **John 11:33-35 ESV**

As he approached Jerusalem and saw the city, he wept over it. **Luke 19:41 NIV**

Jesus took Peter, James and John along with him, and he began to be deeply distressed and troubled. "My soul is overwhelmed with sorrow to the point of death," he said to them. "Stay here and keep watch." **Mark 14:33-34 NIV**

At that time Jesus, full of joy through the Holy Spirit, said, "I praise you, Father, Lord of heaven and earth, because you have hidden these things from the wise and learned, and revealed them to little children." **Luke 10:21 NIV**

"I have told you this so that my joy may be in you and that your joy may be complete." **John 15:11 NIV**

As he saw the crowds, his heart was filled with pity for them, because they were worried and helpless, like sheep without a shepherd. **Matthew 9:36 GNT**

In the temple courts he found people selling cattle, sheep and doves, and others sitting at tables exchanging money. So he made a whip out of cords, and drove all from the temple courts, both sheep and cattle; he scattered the coins of the money changers and overturned their tables. To those who sold doves he said, "Get these out of here! Stop turning my Father's house into a market!" **John 2:14-16 NIV**

It is impossible to contemplate the character of Jesus, with serious and devout attention, and not be charmed with it. We see in him, all the human passions in the highest perfection. His joys were grave, his griefs were just. His gentleness and his severity, his holiness and his humanity were in perfect harmony with each other. **John Fawcett**

Unfortunately, most portrayals of Jesus show him as stoic and unemotional. But Scripture says otherwise. Jesus experienced compassion (Matthew 9:36; Luke 7:13), anger (John 2:15-17), and agony so intense that his capillaries burst (Luke 22:44). **Randy Alcorn**

Jesus had a full range of human emotions. He "marveled" at the faith of the centurion (Matt. 8:10). He wept with sorrow at the death of Lazarus (John 11:35). And he prayed with a heart full of emotion...(Heb. 5:7). **Wayne Grudem**

A Jesus who never wept could never wipe away my tears. **Charles Spurgeon**

Jesus wept. The Savior sobbed. Messiah moaned. God Almighty shed tears. What more proof of God's heart and emotions and care and understanding do we want? **Randy Alcorn**

Christ's Love

Now before the Feast of the Passover, when Jesus knew that his hour had come to depart out of this world to the Father, having loved his own who were in the world, he loved them to the end. **John 13:1 ESV**

When we were still helpless, Christ died for the wicked at the time that God chose. It is a difficult thing for someone to die for a righteous person. It may even be that someone might dare to die for a good person. But God has shown us how much he loves us—it was while we were still sinners that Christ died for us! **Romans 5:6-8 GNB**

By this we know love, that he laid down his life for us. **1 John 3:16 ESV**

Who shall separate us from the love of Christ?...Neither death nor life, neither angels nor demons, neither the present nor the future, nor any powers, neither height nor depth, nor anything else in all creation, will be able to separate us from the love of God that is in Christ Jesus our Lord. **Romans 8:35, 38-39 ESV**

We sinned for no reason but an incomprehensible lack of love, and He saved us for no reason but an incomprehensible excess of love. **Peter Kreeft**

Though our feelings come and go, God's love for us does not. **C.S. Lewis**

The love of God, as manifested in Jesus Christ, is what I would wish to be the abiding object of my contemplation; not merely to speculate upon it as a doctrine, but so to feel it, and my own interest in it, as to have my heart filled with its effects, and transformed into its resemblance. **John Newton**

Don't you need a fountain of love that won't run dry? You'll find one on a stone-cropped hill outside Jerusalem's walls where Jesus hangs, cross-nailed and thorn-crowned. When you feel unloved, ascend this mount. Meditate long and hard on heaven's love for you. **Max Lucado**

Jesus corrects my foggy conceptions of God. Jesus reveals a God who comes in search of us, a God who makes room for our freedom even when it costs the Son's life, a God who is vulnerable. Above all, Jesus reveals a God who is love. **Philip Yancey**

The outstretched arms of Jesus exclude no one, not the drunk in the doorway, the panhandler on the street, gays and lesbians in their isolation, the most selfish and ungrateful in their cocoons, the most unjust of employers and the most overweening of snobs. **Brennan Manning**

Jesus did not identify the person with his sin, but rather saw in this sin something alien, something that really did not belong to him, something that merely chained and mastered him and from which he would free him and bring him back to his real self. Jesus was able to love men because he loved them right through the layer of mud. **Helmut Thielicke**

Christianity does not involve the belief that all things were made for man. It does involve the belief that God loves man and for his sake became man and died. **C.S. Lewis**

Behold, what manner of love is this, that Christ should be arraigned and we adorned, that the curse should be laid on His head and the crown set on ours. **Thomas Watson**

When you realize that every breath is a gift from God. When you realize how small you are, but how much he loved you. That he, Jesus, would die, the son of God himself on earth, then you...you just weep. **Angela Bassett**

Christ's death for us isn't proof of our value as wonderful people. Rather, it shows his unfathomable love that he would die for rotten people, "wretches," like you and me. **Randy Alcorn**

Our vision is so limited we can hardly imagine a love that does not show itself in protection from suffering...The love of God did not protect His own Son...He will not necessarily protect us—not from anything it takes to make us like His Son. **Elisabeth Elliot**

Whenever you are tempted to doubt the love of God, Christian reader, go back to Calvary. **A.W. Pink**

Because he was thrown into *that* storm for you, you can be sure that there's love at the heart of *this* storm for you. **Timothy Keller**

God does not accept me just as I am; He loves me despite how I am. He loves me just as Jesus is; He loves me enough to devote my life to renewing me in the image of Jesus. **David Powlison**

In Christ, there is nothing I can do that would make You love me more, and nothing I have done that makes You love me less. **J.D. Greear**

We please Him most not by frantically trying to make ourselves good, but by throwing ourselves into His arms with all our imperfections, and believing that He understands everything and loves us still. **A.W. Tozer**

No skeletons will ever fall out of our closets. Jesus will never say, "Had I known you'd done that, I'd never have let you into Heaven." He knows all our sins and he died for every one of them. No exceptions. Jesus has seen us at our worst and still loves us. **Randy Alcorn**

Every day we may see some new thing in Christ. His love has neither brim nor bottom. **Samuel Rutherford**

Christ's Compassion and Gentleness

When [Jesus] saw the crowds, he had compassion on them, because they were harassed and helpless, like sheep without a shepherd. **Matthew 9:36 NIV**

When the Lord saw her, his heart was filled with pity for her, and he said to her, "Don't cry." **Luke 7:13 GNB**

Filled with compassion, Jesus reached out his hand and touched the man. "I am willing," he said. "Be clean!" **Mark 1:41 NIV**

With infinite love and compassion our Lord understood the human predicament. He had deep empathy with people; he saw their needs, their weaknesses, their desires, and their hurt. He understood and was concerned for people. Every word he spoke was uttered because he saw a need for that word in some human life. His concern was always to uplift and never to tear down, to heal and never hurt, to save and not condemn. **Charles L. Allen**

He did not want praise or adulation or to impress people with who or how many followed Him. He stopped over and over again for just one person, for just one life. **Heidi Baker**

True to His own counsel, He manifested the wisdom of the serpent and the simplicity of the dove. His tremendous inner strength never degenerated into mere self-will. He mastered the difficult art of displaying sympathy without surrendering principle. **J. Oswald Sanders**

Remember that even Jesus' most scathing denunciation—a blistering diatribe against the religious leaders of Jerusalem in Matthew 23—ends with Christ weeping over Jerusalem (v. 37). Compassion colored everything He did. **John MacArthur**

No matter how low down you are; no matter what your disposition has been; you may be low in your thoughts, words, and actions; you may be selfish; your heart may be overflowing with corruption and wickedness; yet Jesus will have compassion upon you. He will speak comforting words to you; not treat you coldly or spurn you, as perhaps those of earth would, but will speak tender words, and words of love and affection and kindness. Just come at once. **Dwight L. Moody**

If you know Jesus, then the hand holding yours bears the calluses of a carpenter who carried a cross for you. When he opens his hand, you see the gnarled flesh of his nail scarred wrists. When you might think he doesn't understand your pain, realize you don't understand the extent of his. **Randy Alcorn**

There never was his like among the choicest of princes...The heaviest end of the cross lies ever on his shoulders. If he bids us carry a burden, he carries it also. If there is anything that is gracious, generous, kind, and tender, yea lavish and superabundant in love, you always find it in him. **Charles Spurgeon**

When the church isn't for the suffering and broken, then the church isn't for Christ. Because Jesus, with His pierced side, is always on the side of the broken. **Ann Voskamp**

If we'd witnessed firsthand Gethsemane and the march to Golgotha and the horrific cross, we'd never question God's empathy or love. **Randy Alcorn**

The tears of Christ are the pity of God. The gentleness of Jesus is the long-suffering of God. The tenderness of Jesus is the love of God. **Alexander Maclaren**

The man who surrenders to Christ exchanges a cruel slave driver for a kind and gentle Master, whose yoke is easy and whose burden is light. **A.W. Tozer**

"The Lord your God is in your midst...he will rejoice over you with gladness; he will quiet you by his love; he will exult over you with loud singing" (Zephaniah 3:17). The Lord of the Cosmos—who was comforted in the arms of a Galilean peasant girl who no doubt sang to him—kneels down, picks us up, wipes the tears from our eyes, and rejoices over us with singing? Incredible. But absolutely true. **Randy Alcorn**

Christ's Happiness

"I have told you this to make you as completely happy as I am." **John 15:11 CEV**

At that very time the Son rejoiced greatly in the Holy Spirit, and said, "I praise You, O Father." **Luke 10:21 NASB**

...Looking to Jesus, the author and perfecter of our faith, who for the joy that was set before him endured the cross, despising the shame, and is seated at the right hand of the throne of God. **Hebrews 12:2 ESV**

"You [Jesus] have loved righteousness and hated wickedness; therefore God, your God, has anointed you with the oil of gladness beyond your companions." **Hebrews 1:9 ESV**

Before you ever had a happy moment, or your great-grandparents had a happy moment, or Adam and Eve had a happy moment—before the universe was even created—God the Father and God the Son and God the Spirit were enjoying a perfect and robust relational delight in one another. **Steve DeWitt**

The doctrine of the Trinity beautifully resolves the apparent problem of God's love preexisting any object of his love. The happiness of Father, Son and Holy Spirit infinitely predated creation...It means happiness didn't begin with the first human who experienced it. It also explains how God could be displeased with His creatures and their sin without disrupting his innate happiness. And it assures us that when we meet Jesus on the other side of death and He says, "Enter into your Master's happiness," we won't have to work up our own happiness, but will immerse ourselves in His. **Randy Alcorn**

Jesus Christ is the happiest being in the universe. His gladness is greater than all the angelic gladness of heaven. He mirrors perfectly the infinite, holy, indomitable mirth of his Father. **John Piper**

I have always been impressed by the fact that God is happy—and that this ineffable and continuous joy lived in the soul of Christ. **Olivier Messiaen**

The Common English Bible captures these words of one that many commentators believe is none other than God's all-wise Son: "I was having fun, *smiling* before him all the time, *frolicking* with his inhabited earth and delighting in the human race" (Proverbs 8:30-31, emphasis added)...Here he's seen as playfully interacting with his Father and his creation. What an amazing portrayal of the preincarnate happiness of Jesus! **Randy Alcorn**

The joy of the Lord is not something trifling. It's a playfulness that created and sustains the universe, a laughter that guides history to its glorious end. **Dylan Demarsico**

We are happy to think Christ is happy. I do not know whether you have ever drank that joy, Believer, but I have found it a very sweet joy to be joyful because Christ is joyful. **Charles Spurgeon**

Jesus, despite the sad world he inhabited, was the prime host and the prime guest of the party. Jesus let himself be doused with perfume. He attended to wedding wine and wedding garments. The Bible is full of merriment. The feast outruns the fast. It is crammed with...lambs and fatted calves, grapes, pomegranates, olives, dates, milk, and honey. **Tim Hansel**

Somehow or other, and with the best intentions, we have shown the world the typical Christian in the likeness of a crashing and rather ill-natured bore—and this in the Name of one who assuredly never bored a soul in those thirty-three years during which He passed through this world like a flame. **Dorothy Sayers**

Jesus has a gladness that exceeds that of all people (which makes sense, because he created us). If we were to ask a random group, "Who is the happiest human being who ever lived?" few people—including few believers—would give what Hebrews 1:9 tells us is the correct answer: *Jesus.* **Randy Alcorn**

The Gospel is the Gospel of happiness. It is called, "the glorious Gospel of the blessed God" (1 Timothy 1:11). A more correct translation would be, "the happy God." Well, then, adorn the Gospel by being happy! **Charles Spurgeon**

Christ's Humor

"How can you think of saying to your friend, 'Let me help you get rid of that speck in your eye,' when you can't see past the log in your own eye?" **Matthew 7:4 NLT**

"You blind guides, straining out a gnat and swallowing a camel!" **Matthew 23:24 ESV**

"It is easier for a camel to go through the eye of a needle than for someone who is rich to enter the kingdom of God." **Matthew 19:24 NIV**

It is a bit odd that within the Church the humor of Jesus is so roundly ignored...Since God created humor, it makes sense that Jesus would use humor to communicate with humanity. **Tim Shenk**

There are numerous passages...which are practically incomprehensible when regarded as sober prose, but which are luminous once we become liberated from the gratuitous assumption that Christ never joked...Once we realize that Christ was not always engaged in pious talk, we have made an enormous step on the road to understanding. **Elton Trueblood**

Jesus was a master of wordplay, irony and satire, often with an element of humor intermixed. **Leland Ryken**

The humor of Jesus is subtle...The Sermon on the Mount, for instance, doesn't begin with a joke to warm up the crowd. But throughout his ministry Jesus displays great wit, command of the language, a gift for irony and word plays, and impeccable timing—all hallmarks of great comedians. **Tim Shenk**

Rebuffed by the Samaritans, James and John addressed Jesus: "Lord, do you want us to call down fire from heaven to consume them?" (Luke 9:53-54). Although Jesus turned down this request and rebuked the requesters, nonetheless he nicknamed this duo "the sons of thunder" (*Boanerges*; see Mark 3:17). Given their futile desire to bring down lightning, and thunder, from heaven, this nickname, no matter how gently bequeathed, was bound to be the subject of much humor in numerous retellings of the story. **Leonard Greenspoon**

Scripture includes dozens of passages in which it's hard to imagine Jesus not smiling: holding children in his arms (Matthew 19:13-15), raising a child from the dead (Luke 7:11-17), making his outrageous statement about swallowing a camel (Matthew 23:24), and contemplating the love he and his Father have for each other and us (John 15:9). **Randy Alcorn**

Jesus was no serious, dour-faced, religious teacher who never smiled and looked down his nose at those who did. I believe one reason Jesus attracted the crowds He did is because of the sparkle in His eye, and the constant half-smile which hinted at a secret joke only He knew...The humor of Jesus is probably closer to what we would call wit, satire, and irony. When understood, the humor of Jesus rarely makes you laugh out loud, but you might smile, or even chuckle, when you see His point. **Jeremy Myers**

If there is a single person within the pages of the Bible that we can consider to be a humorist, it is without doubt Jesus. **Leland Ryken**

Jesus referred to the shrewd and ruthless political leader Herod as "that fox" (Luke 13:32)...It certainly wouldn't have been lost on the crowd that those pointy-eared varmints were nuisances, not terrors. Jesus was poking fun at a vicious, immoral, murderous tyrant by comparing him not to a lion or a bear but to a fox! Imagine people going home and telling their friends, "You won't believe what Jesus called Herod!" **Randy Alcorn**

Did Jesus have a sense of humor? Well, he created laughter. And think of the crowd he dined with. These rabble-rousers quickly earned Jesus a reputation as a drunkard and a glutton, and it wasn't because they served water and crackers. This was a wild group, and surely such a crowd got rolling in laughter from time to time, if only from the joy they were experiencing being with Jesus...Imagine his own happiness at having these very lost sheep back at his side. **John Eldredge**

Enemies often criticized Jesus for dining with the dregs of society—tax collectors and prostitutes, those written off as "sinners" by the religious elite. He pled "no contest" to that charge...These were surely people who knew how to party, and our Lord was in the thick of it. With his witty jokes and funny stories, Jesus would have become the life of these parties, in more ways than one. **Randy Petersen**

Jesus went to the wedding because he liked the people, he liked the food, and heaven forbid, he may have even wanted to swirl the bride around the dance floor a time or two. (After all, he's planning a big wedding himself.)...It's been awhile since I pegged Jesus as a party-lover. But he was. His foes accused him of eating too much, drinking too much, and hanging out with the wrong people!...Jesus took time for a party...shouldn't we? **Max Lucado**

It is more than reasonable to assume that the happiest person in the universe, after taking our flesh and our sorrows, untarnished by his own sin, often boiled over with the best of laughter. **Isaac Adams**

If Jesus was truly human, he laughed. Humor is a fundamental part of having human emotions. Can you imagine Jesus going to dinner parties and never laughing? Can you picture him changing water into wine to keep a wedding party rolling and never cracking a smile? Can you fathom a master story teller who never used humor? **Donald Sweeting**

We certainly wouldn't attribute to Jesus any sinful emotions or forms of behavior, and it would seem to me the only reason to think he didn't laugh would be if we first came to the conclusion that laughter is evil. **R.C. Sproul**

I think one of the reasons we never really hear much about the humor, hilarity, and joy of Jesus is because so many people (perhaps Christians most of all, God forgive us!) are genuinely and tragically convinced that God is far too serious to ever have a good time. **Trent Sheppard**

If you can't picture Jesus teasing and laughing with His followers, you need to reevaluate your theology of Creation and Incarnation. We need a biblical doctrine of humor that prepares us for an eternity of celebration, spontaneous laughter, and overflowing joy. **Randy Alcorn**

Christ's Glory

This was Jesus' first miracle, and he did it in the village of Cana in Galilee. There Jesus showed his glory, and his disciples put their faith in him. **John 2:11 CEV**

Father, I want those you have given me to be with me where I am, and to see my glory, the glory you have given me because you loved me before the creation of the world. **John 17:24 NIV**

He is the radiance of the glory of God and the exact imprint of his nature, and he upholds the universe by the word of his power. **Hebrews 1:3 ESV**

Jesus has been counted worthy of more glory than Moses—as much more glory as the builder of a house has more honor than the house itself. **Hebrews 3:3 ESV**

When you read the Gospels, you are seeing God's perfections...in all their breath-taking, real-life forms. You can know the glories of God from the Old Testament, but in Jesus Christ they come *near*. **Timothy Keller**

In Bethlehem, it happened again—God's glory came down to be with his people. This time there was only a small band of shepherds to witness its arrival...erasing the darkness with its brilliant effulgence as Jesus' birth was announced (Luke 2:8-14)...John 1:14 tells us that "the Word became flesh and made his dwelling among us. We have seen his glory, the glory of the One and Only, who came from the Father, full of grace and truth." ***The Knowing Jesus Study Bible***

I think He must have been just a plain-looking Jew, for Judas had to kiss Him to tell which one He was...But when He opened His mouth, glory came out, and men and women either rejected the glory or they followed the glory. **A.W. Tozer**

One short glimpse, one transitory vision of his glory, one brief glance at his marred, but now exalted and beaming countenance, would repay almost a world of trouble. **Charles Spurgeon**

Oh for a thousand tongues to sing my great Redeemer's praise,
the glories of my God and King, the triumphs of his grace!
My gracious Master and my God, assist me to proclaim,
to spread through all the earth abroad the honors of thy name.
Jesus! the name that charms our fears, that bids our sorrows cease;
'tis music in the sinner's ears, 'tis life, and health, and peace. **Charles Wesley**

Christ's desire for us to see his glory should touch us deeply. What an unexpected compliment that the Creator of the universe has gone to such great lengths, at such sacrifice, to prepare a place for us where we can behold and participate in his glory. **Randy Alcorn**

When the people of God reach heaven…we shall see, with our eyes, that very body which was born of Mary at Bethlehem, and crucified at Jerusalem between two thieves: the blessed head that was crowned with thorns; the face that was spit upon; the hands and feet that were nailed to the cross; all shining with inconceivable glory. **Thomas Boston**

Christ's Authority

Jesus came and said to them, "All authority in heaven and on earth has been given to me." **Matthew 28:18 NRSV**

When Jesus finished these sayings, the crowds were astonished at his teaching, for he was teaching them as one who had authority, and not as their scribes. **Matthew 7:28-29 ESV**

[The Father] raised Christ from the dead and seated him at his right hand in the heavenly realms, far above all rule and authority, power and dominion, and every name that is invoked, not only in the present age but also in the one to come. And God placed all things under his feet and appointed him to be head over everything for the church, which is his body, the fullness of him who fills everything in every way. **Ephesians 1:20-23 NIV**

I saw a mighty angel proclaiming in a loud voice, "Who is worthy to break the seals and open the scroll?"...I wept and wept because no one was found who was worthy to open the scroll or look inside. Then one of the elders said to me, "Do not weep! See, the Lion of the tribe of Judah, the Root of David, has triumphed. He is able to open the scroll and its seven seals." **Revelation 5:2-5 NIV**

Jesus has been exalted. Through his resurrection and ascension the King has been enthroned...The universe is his. His authority is absolute and exhaustive. You will never breathe air that doesn't belong to him and you will suffocate if you try. **Sam Allberry**

How can we so readily slight the Christ of God who has limitless authority throughout the universe? **A.W. Tozer**

Plenty of people...have made up a "Jesus" for themselves, and have found that this invented character makes few real demands on them. He makes them feel happy from time to time, but doesn't challenge them, doesn't suggest they get up and do something about the plight of the world. Which is, of course, what the real Jesus had an uncomfortable habit of doing. **N.T. Wright**

Madonna, Oprah, Dr. Phil, the Dalai Lama, and probably a lot of Christian leaders will tell us that the point of religion is to get us to love each other. "God loves you" doesn't stir the world's opposition. However, start talking about God's absolute authority, holiness...Christ's substitutionary atonement, justification apart from works, the necessity of new birth, repentance, baptism, Communion, and the future judgment, and the mood in the room changes considerably. **Michael Horton**

His authority on earth allows us to dare to go to all the nations. His authority in heaven gives us our only hope of success. And His presence with us leaves us with no other choice. **John Stott**

I must follow my Lord. No matter what...It is His voice I must listen to, not the voices of those around me, however strident, however persuasive. It is His Word that must govern my life, not the words of others. **Stu Weber**

Christ's Power

Through his power all things were made—things in heaven and on earth, things seen and unseen, all powers, authorities, lords, and rulers. All things were made through Christ and for Christ. **Colossians 1:16 NCV**

Jesus said, "Whatever you ask in my name, this I will do, that the Father may be glorified in the Son. If you ask me anything in my name, I will do it." **John 14:13-14 ESV**

Then all those in the synagogue, when they heard these things, were filled with wrath, and rose up and thrust him out of the city; and they led him to the brow of the hill on which their city was built, that they might throw him down over the cliff. Then passing through the midst of them, he went his way. **Luke 4:22-24, 28-30 NIV**

Christ is the radiance of the glory of God and the exact imprint of his nature, and he upholds the universe by the word of his power. **Hebrews 1:3 ESV**

In Hebrews 1:3, the Greek translated "upholds" is *phero,* "to carry," the same word used in Luke 5:18 when the paralyzed man was carried on his mat to Jesus. Jesus carries the entire universe as men carry a cot. **Randy Alcorn**

Jesus is the only one who can speak to a man in the grave and tell him to come forth. **Priscilla Shirer**

He that believes most the love and power of Jesus will obtain the most in prayer. **Robert Murray M'Cheyne**

Admit it: When your heart is being wrung out like a sponge, when you feel like Morton's salt is being poured into your wounded soul, you don't want a thin, pale, emotional Jesus who relates only to lambs and birds and babies. You want a warrior Jesus. You want a battlefield Jesus. You want his rigorous and robust gospel to command your sensibilities to stand at attention...When you're in a dark place, when lions surround you, when you need strong help to rescue you from impossibility, you don't want "sweet." You don't want faded pastels and honeyed softness. You want mighty. You want the strong arm and unshakable grip of God who will not let you go—no matter what. **Joni Eareckson Tada**

Power, no matter how well-intentioned, tends to cause suffering. Love, being vulnerable, absorbs it. In a point of convergence on a hill called Calvary, God renounced the one for the sake of the other...Jesus invoked a different kind of power: love, not coercion. **Philip Yancey**

He puts people in positions where they are desperate for his power, and then he shows his provision in ways that display his greatness. **David Platt**

Given his divine power, perhaps the greatest wonder is not that Jesus went to the cross but that he *stayed* on it. **Randy Alcorn**

Christ's Sovereignty

A furious squall came up, and the waves broke over the boat, so that it was nearly swamped. Jesus was in the stern, sleeping on a cushion. The disciples woke him and said to him, "Teacher, don't you care if we drown?" He got up, rebuked the wind and said to the waves, "Quiet! Be still!" Then the wind died down and it was completely calm. He said to his disciples, "Why are you so afraid? Do you still have no faith?" They were terrified and asked each other, "Who is this? Even the wind and the waves obey him!" **Mark 4:37-41 NIV**

In love he predestined us for adoption as sons through Jesus Christ, according to the purpose of his will. **Ephesians 1:4-5 ESV**

For we are God's masterpiece. He has created us anew in Christ Jesus, so we can do the good things he planned for us long ago. **Ephesians 2:10 NLT**

We know that for those who love God all things work together for good, for those who are called according to his purpose. **Romans 8:28 ESV**

The Father loves the Son and has given all things into his hand. **John 3:35 ESV**

Now Christ is the visible expression of the invisible God. He existed before creation began, for it was through him that everything was made, whether spiritual or material, seen or unseen. Through him, and for him, also, were created power and dominion, ownership and authority. In fact, every single thing was created through, and for him. He is both the first principle and the upholding principle of the whole scheme of creation. **Colossians 1:16-17 PHILLIPS**

There is not a square inch in the whole domain of our human existence over which Christ, who is Sovereign over all, does not cry: "Mine!" **Abraham Kuyper**

The brow once crowned with thorns now wears the diadem of universal sovereignty; and that arm, once nailed to the cross, now holds in it the scepter of unlimited dominion. He who lay in the tomb has ascended the throne of unbounded empire. **John Eadie**

The empty tomb of Jesus tells you that there is nothing that has the power to defeat God's plan of redeeming grace. **Paul David Tripp**

There's not a plant or flower below,
But makes Thy glories known;
And clouds arise, and tempests blow
By order from Thy throne. **Isaac Watts**

The Christian is joyful, not because he is blind to injustice and suffering, but because he is convinced that these, in the light of the divine sovereignty, are never ultimate. The Christian can be sad, and often is perplexed, but he is never really worried, because he knows that the purpose of God is to bring all things in heaven and on earth together under one head, even Christ. **Elton Trueblood**

He moves the ever-moving wheels of circumstances. No sparrow falls, no leaf decays, but in accordance with His ordering mind. He wills, and things occur. Chance is a figment of a dreaming pillow. It never was. It never can be. Thus to the child of God there is no trifle or unimportant event. **Henry Law**

No power in this world, however powerful, acts outside of the sovereign reign and plan of a God who died for us. **Marshall Segal**

My aim is that you would be filled with a well-grounded amazement at the absolute authority and sovereignty of Jesus Christ over this world and over his unstoppable mission to gather his sheep from all the unreached peoples of the world, *and* that many of you would hear the voice of God calling you irresistibly, joyfully, to leave your home and go to a place of greater need for the everlasting good of lost people and for the fame of Jesus Christ. **John Piper**

Christ's Infinity

Of the increase of his government and of peace there will be no end.
Isaiah 9:7 ESV

I pray that you, being rooted and established in love, may have power, together with all the Lord's holy people, to grasp how wide and long and high and deep is the love of Christ, and to know this love that surpasses knowledge—that you may be filled to the measure of all the fullness of God. **Ephesians 3:17-19 NIV**

"I am the Alpha and the Omega," says the Lord God, "who is and who was and who is to come, the Almighty." **Revelation 1:8 ESV**

There are two hundred and fifty-six names given in the Bible for the Lord Jesus Christ, and I suppose this was because He was infinitely beyond all that any one name could express. **Billy Sunday**

History is too fragile and indeterminate a structure to contain Jesus; like—using the imagery of one of His own parables—the old wineskins into which new wine cannot be put, or like the worn cloth which cannot be patched with new. How shabby, how patched and repatched, how thread-bare and faded this fabric of history is, compared with the ever-renewed, gleaming and glistening garment of truth! **Malcolm Muggeridge**

His life, his spirit, his personality is incomparably greater than anything he said, or did, or taught. **Rufus M. Jones**

Because Christ was God, did he pass unscorched through the fires of Gethsemane and Calvary? Rather let us say, because Christ was God he underwent a suffering that was absolutely infinite. **Augustus Strong**

He has already loved us with infinite love and there is no way that infinitude can be increased. **A.W. Tozer**

How can Christ be less than God, when he says, "Lo, I am with you always, unto the end of the world" (Matt. 28:20)? How could he be omnipresent if he were not God? How could he hear our prayers, the prayers of millions scattered through the leagues of earth, and attend to them all, and give acceptance to all, if he were not infinite in understanding and infinite in merit? **Charles Spurgeon**

Christ is the ocean, in which every drop is infinite compassion. He is the mountain towering above the mountains, in which every grain is God's own goodness. **Henry Law**

Jesus will not come back to tweak this problem and that. He will return with a massive correction of all systemic evil forever... "Of the increase... forever ascending, forever enlarging, forever accelerating, forever intensifying. There will never come one moment when we will say, "This is the limit. He can't think of anything new. We've seen it all." No. The finite will experience ever more wonderfully the infinite, and every new moment will be better than the last. **Ray Ortlund Jr.**

There will always be more to see when we look at Jesus, because his infinite character can never be exhausted. We could—and will—spend countless millennia exploring the depths of His being. **Randy Alcorn**

Christ's Righteousness

Behold, the days are coming, declares the LORD, when I will raise up for David a righteous Branch, and he shall reign as king and deal wisely, and shall execute justice and righteousness in the land. In his days Judah will be saved, and Israel will dwell securely. And this is the name by which he will be called: "The LORD is our righteousness." **Jeremiah 23:5-6 ESV**

The LORD is righteous; he loves righteous deeds; the upright shall behold his face. **Psalm 11:7 ESV**

Dear children, don't let anyone deceive you about this: When people do what is right, it shows that they are righteous, even as Christ is righteous. **1 John 3:7 ESV**

For you who fear my name, the sun of righteousness shall rise with healing in its wings. **Malachi 4:2 ESV**

The righteousness of Jesus Christ is one of those great mysteries, which the angels desire to look into, and seems to be one of the first lessons that God taught men after the fall. **George Whitefield**

Jesus, Sun of righteousness,
Brightest beam of love divine,
With the early morning rays
Do Thou on our darkness shine,
And dispel with purest light
All our long and gloomy night. **Freiherr Christian Knorr von Rosenroth**

Millions have stopped trying to establish their own righteousness, and have put their hope and trust in the King of kings whose name is "*Jehovah* is our righteousness." **John Piper**

Christ in his life was so righteous, that we may say of the life, taken as a vehicle, that it is righteousness itself...He lived out the law of God to the very full, and while you see God's precepts written in fire on Sinai's brow, you see them written in flesh in the person of Christ. **Charles Spurgeon**

The Lord Jesus Christ has done what we ought to have done—and suffered what we ought to have suffered. He has taken our place and become our substitute both in life and death, and all for the sake of miserable, corrupt, ungrateful beings like ourselves. Oh, is not His name then rightly called, "The Lord our Righteousness"? **J.C. Ryle**

The only sin Jesus had was mine, Luther's and yours—and the only righteousness we can ever have is His. **A.W. Tozer**

The only king who fulfilled all righteousness was Jesus Christ. He is the man of Psalm 1:1. It was Jesus who did not walk, did not stand, and did not sit in the seat of scoffers. It was Jesus who meditated on the law day and night, often withdrawing from the crowds and from his disciples to pray. It was Jesus' food to do the will of the One who sent him. *He* delighted in the law of God always. And Jesus, although perfectly righteous, was counted as one who was wicked, so that we would be counted as righteous if we receive him by faith alone. **Nicholas Davis**

> The only way sinners can get past the gates of heaven is by wearing the robes of somebody else's righteousness...the righteousness of Jesus Christ. **R.C. Sproul**

He is the Rock, the refuge, the ruler, the ransom, the refiner, the redeemer, the righteousness and the resurrection of all humble souls. **William Plumer**

In a sin-broken world, where all our lives are touched by the corruption, selfishness, and injustice of those who rule us, it is sweet comfort to know that the One who would establish his rule over us is righteous all the time and in every possible way. It is sweet to know that all corruption and injustice will end someday, and he will rule over us in perfect righteousness forever. **Paul David Tripp**

Our Lord Jesus Christ is coming as the Sun of Righteousness to dispel all the sin clouds of earth and to bring in the reign of everlasting righteousness. **H.A. Ironside**

Christ's Holiness

Set your hope on the grace to be brought to you when Jesus Christ is revealed at his coming...as he who called you is holy, so be holy in all you do, for it is written: "Be holy, because I am holy." **1 Peter 1:13, 15-16 NIV**

It was indeed fitting that we should have such a high priest, holy, innocent, unstained, separated from sinners, and exalted above the heavens. **Hebrews 7:26 ESV**

The four living creatures, each of them with six wings, are full of eyes all around and within, and day and night they never cease to say, "Holy, holy, holy, is the Lord God Almighty, who was and is and is to come!" **Revelation 4:8 ESV**

Jesus is holiness with a face. **Nancy DeMoss Wolgemuth**

The Transfiguration was the "Great Divide" in the life of our Lord. He stood there in the perfect, spotless holiness of his manhood; then he turned his back on the glory and came down from the Mount to be identified with sin. **Oswald Chambers**

Jesus sweated blood. He withstood the test. He ran the whole race. We cannot make such claims. We have not been tested that hard, or humiliated that comprehensively...We are in the ABCs of the kindergarten of the school of temptation. By not falling into temptation, Jesus ran the whole race, while I collapsed in the first mile. **Rosaria Butterfield**

We dare not choose God's love over his holiness. If God's love outstripped his holiness, then why send Jesus to the cross? If love trumps holiness, then why not dispense with the crucifixion altogether? God's holiness and love, combined at Calvary, constitute the only way to save sinners and still satisfy God's perfect nature. **Randy Alcorn**

Jesus Christ had to come to this world because we could never be holy enough to know God. We had to borrow our holiness from God's Son. **David Jeremiah**

Grant me never to lose sight of the exceeding sinfulness of sin, the exceeding righteousness of salvation, the exceeding glory of Christ, the exceeding beauty of holiness, the exceeding wonder of grace.
The Valley of Vision: A Collection of Puritan Prayers and Devotions

Christ's Faithfulness

"The Lord, the Lord, a God merciful and gracious, slow to anger, and abounding in steadfast love and faithfulness." **Exodus 34:6 ESV**

> The Lord will fulfill his purpose for me; your steadfast love, O Lord, endures forever. Do not forsake the work of your hands.
> **Psalm 138:8 ESV**

Let us hold fast the confession of our hope without wavering, for he who promised is faithful. **Hebrews 10:23 ESV**

There's not much in life that is perfectly reliable, but Jesus is and will always be. **Paul David Tripp**

Others may have proved faithless—all other help may have failed you—friendship help, promised help, expected help...but, has Christ ever failed you? **John MacDuff**

Be assured, if you walk with Him and look to Him, and expect help from Him, He will never fail you. **George Müller**

Jesus Christ is not a security from storms. He is the perfect security in storms. **Kathy Troccoli**

We are secure, not because we hold tightly to Jesus, but because he holds tightly to us. **R.C. Sproul**

My security as a Christian does not reside in the strength of my faith but in the indestructibility of my Savior. **Sinclair Ferguson**

Because of all that Jesus has done, I can look at him and say, "Yes, Lord, I will trust you. You've proven yourself." **Randy Alcorn**

When Jesus is in His rightful place, all insecurity will fade away and His lasting loveliness will become the mark of your life. **Leslie Ludy**

For 86 years I have served Jesus Christ and he has never abandoned me. How could I curse my blessed king and savior?
Polycarp (as he was being martyred)

Christ's charge and care of these that are given to Him, extends even to the very day of their resurrection, that He may not so much as lose their dust, but gather it together again, and raise it up in glory to be a proof of His fidelity; for, saith He, "I shall lose nothing, but raise it up again at the last day." **Thomas Brooks**

Only believe, don't fear. Our Master, Jesus, always watches over us, and no matter what the persecution, Jesus will surely overcome it. **Lottie Moon**

I can take the check of Christ's trustworthiness to the bank. I can cash that check again and again and it will never bounce. It is guaranteed by the eternal rock, the triune God. I can trust Christ's promises. I can trust his plan. I can trust his timing. I can trust his methods. I can trust his love for me. **Nanci Alcorn**

Christ's Grace

The wages of sin is death, but the free gift of God is eternal life in Christ Jesus our Lord. **Romans 6:23 ESV**

You know the grace of our Lord Jesus Christ, that though he was rich, yet for your sakes he became poor, so that you through his poverty might become rich. **2 Corinthians 8:9 NIV**

Grace is a person. And his name is Jesus. **Judah Smith**

To know Jesus is the shortest description of true grace; to know him better is the surest mark of growth in grace; to know him perfectly is eternal life. **John Newton**

He is the most magnanimous of captains. If there is anything gracious, generous, kind and tender, lavish, and superabundant in love, you always find it in him. **Charles Spurgeon**

There is the stormy North side to Christ. But be sure of this: there is more divine grace in one of Jesus' blizzards than in all the "sunshine" Satan ever tricked you into. **William Vander Hoven**

Passing in front of Moses, God identified himself as "abounding in love and faithfulness" (Exodus 34:6). The words translated *love* and *faithfulness* are the Hebrew equivalents of *grace* and *truth.* Christ's hearers had seen truth in the Law of Moses, but it was Christ who personified grace. The law could only reveal sin. Jesus alone could *remove* it. **Randy Alcorn**

God hath long contended with a stubborn world, and thrown down many a blessing upon them; and when all his other gifts could not prevail, he at last made a gift of himself. **Henry Scougal**

> Christ offers something for nothing: He even offers everything for nothing. **C.S. Lewis**

Jesus' standards were much higher than those of the Pharisees (Matthew 5:17-48). He never lowered the bar. He always raised it. But He also empowers those who know Him to, by His grace, jump higher than the law demanded. **Randy Alcorn**

Jesus comes...for the wobbly and the weak-kneed who know they don't have it all together, and who are not too proud to accept the handout of amazing grace. **Brennan Manning**

Jesus did not come to strike a balance between grace and truth. He brought the full measure of both. **Andy Stanley**

Most sinners loved being around Jesus. He drew them out of the night like a light draws moths. They enjoyed his company and invited him to their parties. People sensed Jesus loved them, even when speaking difficult words. He was full of grace *and* truth. **Randy Alcorn**

O Son of God, grace was in all thy tears; grace came bubbling out of thy side with thy blood; grace came forth with every word of thy sweet mouth; grace came out where the whip smote thee, where the thorns pricked thee, where the nails and spear pierced thee. O blessed Son of God, here is grace indeed!...Grace to make sinners happy, grace to astonish devils! **John Bunyan**

Don't wonder why God might despise us—the reasons are obvious. Wonder why He loves us. His grace to us in Christ Jesus, not his wrath, is what's so surprising. **Randy Alcorn**

The truth is, God doesn't grade on a curve; he grades on a cross. **Jefferson Bethke**

When you hear of a notorious sinner, instead of thinking you do well to be angry, beg of Jesus Christ to convert, and make him a monument of his free grace. **George Whitefield**

We were not merely misguided subjects; we were rebels and traitors against the King. Yet God adopts us as his children and happily gives us a seat at his table. If this seems less than amazing, then we really don't grasp the meaning of grace. **Randy Alcorn**

Grace is *costly* because it calls us to follow, and it is *grace* because it calls us to follow *Jesus Christ*. It is costly because it costs a man his life, and it is grace because it gives a man the only true life. **Dietrich Bonhoeffer**

The Savior pours out grace for you to finish the race. He pours out more grace when you stumble, grow weary, fall down, lose heart. He stands at the head of the course and, while all the saints who have gone before line the roadway and cheer riotously, He stretches out His arms wide in exuberant welcome, exultant congratulation. **Mark Buchanan**

Your genetic predispositions, your sinful tendencies, the moral failures of your past, the culture you live in, the path you have taken so far in your life—none of these are destined to have the last word in your life. God's grace toward you in Christ has the last, the lasting, and the determining word in your life. **Nancy Guthrie**

When you and I come to lie upon our death beds, the one thing that should comfort and help and strengthen us there is the thing that helped us in the beginning...The Christian life starts with grace, it must continue with grace, it ends with grace. **Martyn Lloyd-Jones**

Christ's Mercy

The Lord is merciful and gracious, slow to anger and abounding in steadfast love. **Psalm 103:8 ESV**

Because of his great love for us, God, who is rich in mercy, made us alive with Christ even when we were dead in transgressions—it is by grace you have been saved. **Ephesians 2:4-5 NIV**

We could never recognize the Father's grace and mercy except for our Lord Jesus Christ, who is a mirror of his Father's heart. **Martin Luther**

There is more mercy in Christ than sin in us. **Richard Sibbes**

I am fallen, flawed and imperfect. Yet drenched in the grace and mercy that is found in Jesus Christ, there is strength. **Adam Young**

Jesus doesn't avoid those who mess up. Jesus runs to those who mess up. **Matt Chandler**

Let your tears fall because of sin; but, at the same time, let the eye of faith steadily behold the Son of man lifted up...Our sinnership is that emptiness into which the Lord pours his mercy. **Charles Spurgeon**

I offer you salvation this day; the door of mercy is not yet shut, there does yet remain a sacrifice for sin, for all that will accept of the Lord Jesus Christ, He will embrace you in the arms of His love. **George Whitefield**

Christ has flung the door of mercy wide open and stands in the door calling and crying with a loud voice to poor sinners. **Jonathan Edwards**

The down-and-out, who flocked to Jesus when he lived on earth, no longer feel welcome. How did Jesus, the only perfect person in history, manage to attract the notoriously imperfect? And what keeps us from following in his steps today? **Philip Yancey**

Nobody ever got anything from God on the grounds that he deserved it. Having fallen, man deserves only punishment and death. So if God answers prayer it's because God is good. From His goodness, His lovingkindness, His good-natured benevolence, God does it! **A.W. Tozer**

What could the Lord Jesus Christ have done for you more than he has? Then do not abuse his mercy, but let your time be spent in thinking and talking of the love of Jesus. **George Whitefield**

Christ's Care for All Nations and Races

And they sang a new song: "You are worthy to take the scroll and to open its seals, because you were slain, and with your blood you purchased men for God from every tribe and language and people and nation." **Revelation 5:9 NIV**

Jesus Christ is the center of the human race. With Him there are no favored races...He is the Son of Man—not a Son of the Jewish race only. He is the Son of all races no matter what the color or tongue. **A.W. Tozer**

Jesus was not a white man; He was not a black man. He came from that part of the world that touches Africa and Asia and Europe. Christianity is not a white man's religion and don't let anybody ever tell you that it's white or black. Christ belongs to all people; He belongs to the whole world. **Billy Graham**

Christ was born in the first century, yet he belongs to all centuries. He was born a Jew, yet He belongs to all races. He was born in Bethlehem, yet He belongs to all countries. **George W. Truett**

The supreme character lives in this: that he combines within himself, as no other figure in human history has ever done, the qualities of every race. **C.F. Andrews**

The death and resurrection of the Son of God for sinners is the only sufficient power to bring the bloodlines of race into the single bloodline of the cross. **John Piper**

Every racial barrier is broken down in Christ. Because of His work on the cross, we're all part of the same family. We share the same Father, and the same brother Jesus, and that means we're family. **Randy Alcorn**

We see the fitness of His death and of those outstretched arms: it was that He might draw His ancient people with the one and the Gentiles with the other, and join both together in Himself. **Athanasius of Alexandria**

Jesus made no ethnic distinctions in who He died for, so why would His people make ethnic distinctions in who we fellowship with? **Shai Linne**

Christ's work on the cross put racism to death: "He himself is our peace, who has made the two groups one and has destroyed the barrier, the dividing wall of hostility" (Ephesians 2:14). On the New Earth, the work of reconciliation will be complete, and we'll celebrate our unified diversity by singing praise to Jesus that His blood has ransomed people for God from every tribe. God is the Creator and lover of human diversity. Christ is glorified not simply by the total number who worship him, but because this number represents every race, nation and language. **Randy Alcorn**

There is one race: the human race. In Christ, we are to be one people representing many beautiful ethnicities. **John M. Perkins**

The problem of race is deep and wide and requires seismic change...The problem of race is not "out there." It's "in here," in the human heart. And though there is no task in heaven or on earth more difficult than changing the human heart, I believe in the One who can do it. It requires a supernatural solution. **Benjamin Watson**

Like the current earthly Jerusalem, the New Jerusalem will be a melting pot of ethnic diversity. But unlike the current city, the groups in the New Jerusalem will be forever united by their common worship of King Jesus, Healer of all nations. **Randy Alcorn**

Christ's Care for All People

"There is forgiveness of sins for all who repent." **Luke 24:47 NLT**

"Let it be known to you that this salvation of God has been sent to the Gentiles; they will listen." **Acts 28:28 ESV**

In reading this, then, you will be able to understand my insight into the mystery of Christ...This mystery is that through the gospel the Gentiles are fellow heirs, fellow members of the body, and fellow partakers of the promise in Christ Jesus. **Ephesians 3:4-6 NIV**

Luke, as the only Gentile writer in the New Testament...made an implicit statement that all peoples—Jews and Gentiles alike—are invited into a relationship with God through Jesus. Luke's point was not that all of humanity will be saved but that salvation is equally offered to all of humanity (Luke 24:46-47). ***The Knowing Jesus Study Bible***

Jesus honored the dignity of people, whether he agreed with them or not. He would not found his kingdom on the basis of race or class or other such divisions. **Philip Yancey**

Part of the exquisite beauty of salvation is its simplicity. Any man, woman, or child can come to Christ with absolutely nothing to offer Him but simple faith—just as they are. **Beth Moore**

Jesus accepted material support from wealthy women, and gratefully accepted the extravagant anointing of his body with an expensive perfume. Christ's birth attracted poor shepherds and rich kings. His life on earth drew many—both poor and wealthy. And regardless of their means, Jesus was pleased to accept into his Kingdom *all* who would bow their knee before the Messiah. **Randy Alcorn**

So many people feel isolated, not good enough, defined by the labels they wear rather than the identity they have in Christ. The love of Christ tells us that we're accepted; that we belong. **Sheila Walsh**

God is near to lowliness; he loves the lost, the neglected, the unseemly, the excluded, the weak and broken. **Dietrich Bonhoeffer**

Jesus does not look for people who are perfect and have never failed or made mistakes to be in his family. Instead, he is drawn toward people who recognize their failures and see their need for him. **Nancy Guthrie**

The religion which has introduced civil liberty is the religion of Christ and His apostles…which acknowledges in every person a brother, or a sister, and a citizen with equal rights. **Noah Webster**

Jesus would go anywhere, talk to anyone. And wherever He went, He would stop for the one—the forgotten one, the one who was rejected, outcast, sick, even stone dead. Even a thief who was dying for his crimes on the cross next to Him. In the Kingdom of God's love there is no sinner who cannot come home. **Heidi Baker**

Peace on Earth will not be accomplished by the abolition of our differences but by a unifying loyalty to King Jesus, a loyalty that transcends our differences and is enriched by them. **Randy Alcorn**

Christ's Concern for Women

Soon afterward Jesus began a tour of the nearby towns and villages, preaching and announcing the Good News about the Kingdom of God. He took his twelve disciples with him, along with some women who had been cured of evil spirits and diseases. Among them were Mary Magdalene, from whom he had cast out seven demons. **Luke 8:1-2 NLT**

All these with one accord were devoting themselves to prayer, together with the women and Mary the mother of Jesus, and his brothers. **Acts 1:14 ESV**

The family tree of Christ startlingly notes not one woman but four. Four broken women—women who felt like outsiders, like has-beens, like never-beens...And Jesus claims exactly these who are wandering and wondering and wounded and worn out as His. He grafts you into His line and His story and His heart, and He gives you His name, His lineage, His righteousness. **Ann Voskamp**

Now consider this: the first person to hold the newborn Christ was Mary of Nazareth, and the first person to touch the newly risen Christ, however briefly, was Mary of Magdala. God placed himself in a woman's care when he came to earth, then entrusted a woman to announce his resurrection when he came back to life. **Liz Curtis Higgs**

Not only did Jesus notice women, He called them out of the shadows and into faith. It wasn't by accident that many of His recorded conversations were with women or that many of His miracles placed women in starring roles. Jesus deliberately chose it to be this way. What's more, women were among His best students and most dynamic and daring disciples. No wonder women loved His instruction! **Chuck Swindoll**

Perhaps it is no wonder that the women were first at the Cradle and last at the Cross. They had never known a man like this Man—there never has been such another. A prophet and teacher who never nagged at them, never flattered or coaxed or patronised; who never made arch jokes about them, never treated them either as "The women, God help us!" or "The ladies, God bless them!"; who rebuked without querulousness and praised without condescension...who had no uneasy male dignity to defend; who took them as he found them and was completely unself-conscious. There is no act, no sermon, no parable in the whole Gospel that borrows its pungency from female perversity; nobody could possibly guess from the words and deeds of Jesus that there was anything "funny" about woman's nature. **Dorothy L. Sayers**

Christ's Immutability

Jesus Christ is the same yesterday and today and forever.
Hebrews 13:8 NIV

He also says [about the Son], "In the beginning, Lord, you laid the foundations of the earth, and the heavens are the work of your hands. They will perish, but you remain; they will all wear out like a garment. You will roll them up like a robe; like a garment they will be changed. But you remain the same, and your years will never end." **Hebrews 1:10-12 NIV**

In a world that prizes the new, the progressive, and the evolved, we need to be reminded that...since he remains the same, so does his truth. **Kevin DeYoung**

Jesus Christ is your righteousness and he is never going to change...When you wake tomorrow, he will still be your righteousness, before you have done anything to enjoy God's favour...Your spirit needs to bask in the brilliant sunlight of this reality. **Terry Virgo**

Jesus is always the same to the meek, the mourner, the brokenhearted, the penitent sinner. His attitude is always the same toward those who love Him, the honest-hearted person...He never turns them away. He is ready with forgiveness. He is ready with comfort. He is ready with blessing. **A.W. Tozer**

In our fluctuations of feeling, it is well to remember that Jesus admits no change in his affections; your heart is not the compass Jesus saileth by. **Samuel Rutherford**

For those who feel their lives are a grave disappointment to God, it requires enormous trust and reckless, raging confidence to accept that the love of Jesus Christ knows no shadow of alteration or change. **Brennan Manning**

If the Lord be with us, we have no cause of fear. His eye is upon us, His arm over us, His ear open to our prayer—His grace sufficient, His promise unchangeable. **John Newton**

Nothing about our Lord Jesus Christ has changed down to this very hour. His love has not…cooled off, and it needs no increase because He has already loved us with infinite love and there is no way that infinitude can be increased…It is hard for us to accept the majestic simplicity of this constant, wonder-working Jesus. We are used to getting things changed so that they are always bigger and better! **A.W. Tozer**

Set NOT your hearts on the flowers of this world. They shall fade and die. Prize the Rose of Sharon and the Lily of the Valley. He changes not! Live nearer to Christ than to any person on this earth; so that when they are taken, you may have Him to love and lean upon. **Robert Murray M'Cheyne**

Christ's Uniqueness and Incomparability

No one has ever seen God. The one and only Son, who is himself God and is at the Father's side—he has revealed him. **John 1:18 CSB**

Jesus did many other things as well. If every one of them were written down, I suppose that even the whole world would not have room for the books that would be written. **John 21:25 NIV**

Salvation is found in no one else, for there is no other name under heaven given to mankind by which we must be saved. **Acts 4:12 NIV**

"I am the Alpha and the Omega, the First and the Last, the Beginning and the End." **Revelation 22:13 NLT**

Of the religions of the world, Christianity is unique because it stems from the uniqueness of Jesus Christ, the greatest man who ever lived. In Jesus, we have One who has virtually changed every aspect of human life. **John Hampton Keathley III**

His beauty is eternal, and His reign shall never end. Jesus is in every respect unique, and nothing can be compared with Him. **Joseph Ernest Renan**

The sages and heroes of history are receding from us, and history contracts the record of their deeds into a narrower and narrower page. But time has no power over the name and deeds and words of Jesus Christ. **William Ellery Channing**

All heroes are shadows of Christ. **John Piper**

Caesar hoped to reform men by changing institutions and laws; Christ wished to remake institutions and lessen laws by changing men. **Will Durant**

Jesus and Alexander died at thirty-three,
One lived and died for self; one died for you and me. **Charles Ross Weede**

Jesus was a teacher, but somehow not just a teacher. He was claiming to have announced something or discovered something or inaugurated something in a way teachers never did. **John Ortberg**

I have read in Plato and Cicero sayings that are very wise and very beautiful; but I never read in either of them: "Come unto me all ye that labor and are heavy laden." **Augustine**

Socrates taught for 40 years, Plato 50, and Aristotle 40—a total of 130 years. But their contributions to our chief problems are next to nil. Then came Jesus of Nazareth, who taught for just over three years, and he gave the solution to the problems of evil and death—himself! **Desmond Ford**

Jesus didn't just bring us good news. He himself is the good news. **Randy Alcorn**

Alexander, Caesar, Charlemagne, and I have founded empires. But on what did we rest the creations of our genius? Upon force. Jesus Christ founded his empire upon love; and at this hour millions of men would die for him. **Napoleon Bonaparte**

A cannonball travels only two thousand miles an hour; light travels two hundred thousand miles a second. Such is the superiority of Jesus Christ over Napoleon. **Victor Hugo**

The major difference between Shakespeare and Christ, is that if Shakespeare came into this room we would all stand in honor and respect. But if Jesus were here, we would all humbly bow and worship Him. **Charles Lamb**

I am a Jew, but I am enthralled by the luminous figure of the Nazarene. Jesus is too colossal for the pen of phrase-mongers, however artful…No man can read the gospels without feeling the actual presence of Jesus. His personality pulsates in every word. No myth is filled with such life. **Albert Einstein**

Jesus Christ stands alone, unique and supreme, self-validating, and the Holy Ghost declares Him to be God's eternal Son. **A.W. Tozer**

Jesus's coming is apocalyptic not only in that it is revelatory but in that it is an upheaval, a liberating invasion of the cosmos…Jesus enters not merely the history of the first century but the history of the cosmos. His crucifixion is the crucifixion of the cosmos; sin and death are now defeated. New creation invades the present evil age…Jesus is inaugurating the new heavens and the new social order in the midst of a world of darkness. **Patrick Schreiner**

Everything that Jesus Christ touched, he utterly transformed. **D. James Kennedy**

It is Jesus Christ, and Jesus Christ alone, who makes sense out of everything in this world. **A.W. Tozer**

Jesus Christ is the center of all, and the goal to which all tends. **Blaise Pascal**

Christ's Continuity (from Heaven to Earth to Heaven)

"Look at my hands. Look at my feet. You can see that it's really me. Touch me and make sure that I am not a ghost, because ghosts don't have bodies, as you see that I do." **Luke 24:39 NLT**

"Men of Galilee," they said, "why do you stand here looking into the sky? This same Jesus, who has been taken from you into heaven, will come back in the same way you have seen him go into heaven." **Acts 1:11 NIV**

Jesus Christ was the same person from the point of his conception, to his birth, his childhood, his ministry, and his death, resurrection and ascension. He will be the same Jesus who returns to Earth to set up his eternal kingdom. **Randy Alcorn**

Make no mistake: if he rose at all it was as His body; if the cells' dissolution did not reverse, the molecules reknit, the amino acids rekindle, the Church will fail. Let us not mock God with metaphor, analogy, sidestepping transcendence; making of the event a parable, a sign painted in the faded credulity of earlier ages; let us walk through the door. **John Updike**

If resurrection meant the creation of a new body, Christ's original body would have remained in the tomb. Jesus said to his disciples after his resurrection, "It is I myself," emphasizing he was the same person—in spirit and body—who was crucified. **Randy Alcorn**

It was in the flesh that Christ was raised from the dead. Because the very same body that fell in death, and which lay in the tomb, also rose again. If, therefore, we are to rise again after the example of Christ—who rose in the flesh—we will certainly not rise according to that example unless we ourselves will also rise again in the flesh. **Tertullian**

The way in which Jesus ascended up to heaven was calculated to demonstrate the continuity between his existence in a physical body here on earth and his continuing existence in that body in heaven. **Wayne Grudem**

The incarnation isn't temporary; it's permanent. Christ rose in the glorified human body he will have forever. It's not that Jesus became a baby, and 33 years later after the resurrection and ascension suddenly stopped being a man. No, the second member of the triune God will be a human being for all eternity, reigning on the New Earth. **Randy Alcorn**

Christ's Presence and Nearness

Now in Christ Jesus you who once were far away have been brought near by the blood of Christ. **Ephesians 2:13 NIV**

Let your gentleness be evident to all. The Lord is near. **Philippians 4:5 NIV**

"Never will I leave you; never will I forsake you." **Hebrews 13:5 NIV**

You can know the glories of God from the Old Testament, so overwhelming and daunting, but in Jesus Christ they come *near*. He becomes graspable, palpable. **Timothy Keller**

Nowhere is God so near to man as in Jesus Christ. **Richard Baxter**

God is everywhere. His truth and his love pervade all things as the light and the heat of the sun pervade our atmosphere. But...God does not touch our souls with the fire of supernatural knowledge and experience without Christ. **Thomas Merton**

Eden's greatest attraction was God's presence. Sin's greatest tragedy was that God no longer dwelt with his people. But this all changed with Christ's incarnation (John 1:1, 14). God walking with Adam and Eve in the garden was a wonderful preview of the God-man Jesus coming down from Heaven to live forever with people on Earth. **Randy Alcorn**

It is quite clear that the whole teaching of Jesus Christ about God, expressed alike in His words and in the whole fashion and mould of His character, implies that God is always nearer, mightier, more loving, and more free to help every one of us than any one of us ever realizes. **D.S. Cairns**

Jesus is happy to come with us, as truth is happy to be spoken, as life to be lived. **Francis of Assisi**

Jesus departed from our sight that he might return to our hearts. He departed, and behold, he is here. **Augustine**

If you think God is far away and indifferent, here is the surprising revelation. From the foundation of the world, God knew your sufferings and declared he himself would take human form and participate in them (which means that we, too, could share in his). This is not a distant, indifferent God. **Edward Welch**

We can go through anything because Jesus goes before us. **Max De Pree**

Our loving Lord is not just present, but nearer than the thought can imagine—so near that a whisper can reach Him. **Amy Carmichael**

Loneliness is an opportunity for Jesus to make Himself known. **F.B. Meyer**

Be of good comfort; the hardest that can come shall be a means to mortify this body of corruption, which is a thousand times more dangerous to us than any outward tribulation, and to bring us into nearer communion with our Lord Jesus Christ, and more assurance of His kingdom. **John Winthrop**

As there is the most heat nearest to the sun, so there is the most happiness nearest to Christ. **Charles Spurgeon**

Prayer for God's presence to be seen and enjoyed is quite startling to a world that prefers for God to be an absentee Father that just sends a big child-support check each month. Because we're sinful, we would prefer God to give us our demands while demanding nothing in return. We love to set the agenda. But Jesus teaches us here that God's presence precedes his provision. His agenda is far better than ours. **John Onwuchekwa**

Abide in Me, says Jesus. Cling to Me. Stick fast to Me. Live the life of close and intimate communion with Me. Get nearer to Me. **J.C. Ryle**

We are never nearer Christ than when we find ourselves lost in a holy amazement at his unspeakable love. **John Owen**

A Christian has a union with Jesus Christ more noble, more intimate and more perfect than the members of a human body have with their head. **John Eudes**

Where is Christ? At the right hand of God (Hebrews 12:2). In terms of his human body, Christ is in one location, and only one. But despite his fixed location at God's right hand, Jesus is here now, living within us (Galatians 2:20). If he indwells those who are saints and yet sinners now, how much more will he be able to indwell us in the world to come when there will be no sin to separate us from him? **Randy Alcorn**

Christ's Influence

If anyone is in Christ, he is a new creation. The old has passed away; behold, the new has come. **2 Corinthians 5:17 ESV**

We all, with unveiled face, beholding the glory of the Lord, are being transformed into the same image from one degree of glory to another. For this comes from the Lord who is the Spirit. **2 Corinthians 3:18 ESV**

Jesus produced mainly three effects: hatred, terror, adoration. There was no trace of people expressing mild approval. **C.S. Lewis**

Those who meet Jesus always experience either joy or its opposites, either foretastes of Heaven or foretastes of Hell. Not everyone who meets Jesus is pleased, and not everyone is happy, but everyone is shocked. **Peter Kreeft**

Few people felt comfortable around Jesus; those who did were the type no one else felt comfortable around. The Jesus I met in the Gospels was anything but tame. **Philip Yancey**

Jesus Christ is to me the outstanding personality of all time, all history, both as Son of God and as Son of Man. Everything he ever said or did has value for us today and that is something you can say of no other man, dead or alive. There is no easy middle ground to stroll upon. You either accept Jesus or reject him. **Sholem Asch**

The world crucified Jesus because they couldn't stand Him! There was something in Him that rebuked them and they hated Him for it and finally crucified Him. **A.W. Tozer**

Men may love him or hate him, but they do it intensely. **T.R. Glover**

One of Jesus' specialties is to make somebodies out of nobodies.
Henrietta C. Mears

God became man to turn creatures into sons; not simply to produce better men of the old kind but to produce a new kind of man. **C.S. Lewis**

He is the greatest influence in the world today. There is...a fifth Gospel being written—the work of Jesus Christ in the hearts and lives of men and nations.
William Griffith Thomas

No one who meets Jesus ever stays the same. **Philip Yancey**

Jesus Christ turns life right side up, and Heaven outside in. **Carl F.H. Henry**

The first person to write about him—who would become known as Paul—said that Jesus appeared to him unbidden and unwanted. And he had a strange way of continuing to show up where he was not always sought or even welcome.
John Ortberg

Rodney Stark, sociologist at the University of Washington, points out that when a major plague hit the ancient Roman Empire, Christians had surprisingly high survival rates. Why? Most Roman citizens would banish any plague-stricken person from their household. But because Christians had no fear of death, they nursed their sick instead of throwing them out on the streets. **Kenneth L. Woodward**

Jesus inhabited the slave role. Paul calls himself a slave of Christ, loves a runaway slave as his very heart, and insists that slave and free are equal in Christ. With no room for superiority, exploitation, or coercion, but rather brotherhood and shared identity, the New Testament created a tectonic tension that would ultimately erupt in the abolition of slavery. **Rebecca McLaughlin**

No one's words have been read more, studied more, quoted more, debated more, pondered more, written and lectured about more, translated into more languages, fueled more literacy efforts around the world, and shaped more diverse cultures than the words of Jesus. **Jon Bloom**

A secular British curmudgeon named Malcolm Muggeridge was brought up short while visiting an Indian leprosarium run by the Missionaries of Charity. As he saw Mother Teresa in action, he realized with the force of sudden insight that humanists do not run leprosariums. **John Ortberg**

PART 2

The Birth, Life, Death, Resurrection, Return, and Reign of Jesus

He was born in an obscure village, the child of a peasant woman. He worked in a carpentry shop until he was thirty, and then for three years he was an itinerant preacher.

When the tide of popular opinion turned against him, his friends ran away. He was turned over to his enemies. He was tried and convicted. He was nailed upon a cross between two thieves. When he was dead, he was laid in a borrowed grave.

He never wrote a book. He never held an office. He never owned a home. He never went to college. He never traveled more than two hundred miles from the place where he was born. He never did one of those things that usually accompanies greatness.

Yet all the armies that ever marched, and all the governments that ever sat, and all the kings that ever reigned, have not affected life upon this earth as powerfully as has that One Solitary Life.

James Allan Francis

When we look at the life of Jesus, we see something unparalleled in all human history. As a carpenter's son, and especially as the eldest son, he was an integral part of the family business. He worked hard, long hours. As did other Jewish children of his place and time, he studied and knew much of the Old Testament Scriptures by heart. He was like the other children with one major difference—he never sinned. That would have made him popular with some people, and very unpopular with others.

But let's go back further. As God the Father directly oversees every child's conception and formation, so he did with Jesus, again with a startling difference. In this case, the child conceived was the Son who had always, from eternity past, lived with his Father and the Holy Spirit. God was overseeing the human conception of his eternal Son under the power of the Spirit; Jesus experienced what his forefather David did: "[God] knit me together in my mother's womb" (Psalm 139:13 NIV).

Most likely, given the angel's appearance to Mary before Christ's conception and the travel time from Mary's home to Elizabeth's, Messiah had been conceived no more than ten days before the preborn John jumped for joy at the presence of the unborn Jesus (Luke 1:44 NIV). Later the shepherds, the angels, Simeon, and Anna were overcome with happiness at Christ's birth. This same Jesus who stepped out of eternity and into time is the source of our eternal happiness. The Jesus who dwells within every believer, who came down from Heaven and returned there, will one day actually bring Heaven down to the New Earth—forever (Revelation 21:1-4 NIV).

We live our lives between the first coming of Christ and the second. We look back to that first Christmas and the life of Jesus on Earth. At the same time we look forward to the return of the resurrected Christ when we, his resurrected people, will live with him forever on the New Earth.

There are those who say that doctrine doesn't matter and that we should just love Jesus. But who *is* this Jesus we are to love? What did Jesus really teach? What was the gospel message he preached? What example did he set for us? What was his mission, how did he pray, what miracles did he perform?

Why did he go to the cross for us when he didn't have to? How could he remain on the cross when all he had to do was to utter the words "Take me down" to be relieved of unthinkable suffering? Why was it necessary for him to shed his blood? What really happened at his death, and what was the meaning of his resurrection? What happened at the ascension and why does it matter? How and when will Christ return? How will he reign over his eternal kingdom on the New Earth, and in what sense will we—his people—reign with him?

These and many other questions will be answered in this section. Are you ready to learn and grow and think greater, wider, and deeper thoughts about Jesus than you ever have? May He expand your mind and touch your heart through what you're about to read!

Christ's Incarnation and Virgin Birth

By this you know the Spirit of God: every spirit that confesses that Jesus Christ has come in the flesh is from God. **1 John 4:2 NRSV**

Here is the great mystery of our religion: Christ came as a human. The Spirit proved that he pleased God, and he was seen by angels. Christ was preached to the nations. People in this world put their faith in him, and he was taken up to glory. **1 Timothy 3:16 CEV**

In the sixth month of Elizabeth's pregnancy, God sent the angel Gabriel to Nazareth, a town in Galilee, to a virgin pledged to be married to a man named Joseph, a descendant of David. The virgin's name was Mary...The angel went to her and said, "Do not be afraid, Mary; you have found favor with God. You will conceive and give birth to a son, and you are to call him Jesus. He will be great and will be called the Son of the Most High...his kingdom will never end."

"How will this be," Mary asked the angel, "since I am a virgin?"

The angel answered, "The Holy Spirit will come on you, and the power of the Most High will overshadow you. So the holy one to be born will be called the Son of God. Even Elizabeth your relative is going to have a child in her old age, and she who was said to be unable to conceive is in her sixth month. For no word from God will ever fail."

"I am the Lord's servant," Mary answered. "May your word to me be fulfilled." **Luke 1:26-27, 30-38 NIV**

The Incarnation is the most stupendous event which ever can take place on earth, and after it henceforth, I do not see how we can scruple at any miracle on the mere ground of it being unlikely to happen. **John Henry Newman**

Christ took our flesh upon him that he might take our sins upon him. **Thomas Watson**

The greatness of God was not cast off, but the slightness of human nature was put on. **Thomas Aquinas**

The miracle of the cross was made possible by the miracle of the incarnation. The angels must have been stunned to see the second member of the triune God become a human being. **Randy Alcorn**

Because of our physical hunger we know there is bread; because of our spiritual hunger we know there is Christ. **Malcolm Muggeridge**

It is fitting that a supernatural person should enter and leave the earth in a supernatural way...His birth was natural, but His conception was supernatural. His death was natural, but His resurrection was supernatural. **John Stott**

Jesus Christ did not remain at base headquarters in heaven, receiving reports of the world's suffering from below and shouting a few encouraging words to us from a safe distance. No, he left the headquarters and came down to us in the front-line trenches, right down to where we live **Helmut Thielicke**

It has never been quite enough to say that God is in his heaven and all is right with the world; since the rumor is that God had left his heavens to set it right. **G.K. Chesterton**

Christians believe in the virgin birth of Jesus. Materialists believe in the virgin birth of the cosmos. Choose your miracle. **Glen Scrivener**

For me it is the virgin birth, the Incarnation, the resurrection which are the true laws of the flesh and the physical. Death, decay, destruction are the suspension of these laws. **Flannery O'Connor**

If Jesus Christ were not virgin born, then...He inherited the nature of that father; as that father had a nature of sin, then Jesus Himself was a lost sinner and He Himself needed a Savior from sin. Deny the virgin birth of Jesus Christ and you paralyze the whole scheme of redemption by Jesus Christ. **I.M. Haldeman**

Though He was God, He became a man. He was the Ancient of Days, yet He was born at a point in time. He created worlds and companied with celestial beings, yet He came to live in a family setting on earth. **Henry Gariepy**

At Bethlehem God became man to enable men to become the sons of God. **C.S. Lewis**

He was created by a mother whom he created. He cried in the manger in wordless infancy, he the Word, without whom all human eloquence is mute. **Augustine**

No priest, no theologian stood at the cradle of Bethlehem. And yet, all Christian theology finds its beginnings in the miracle of miracles, that God became human. **Dietrich Bonhoeffer**

Christ's Birth

For to us a child is born, to us a son is given; and the government shall be upon his shoulder, and his name shall be called Wonderful Counselor, Mighty God, Everlasting Father, Prince of Peace. **Isaiah 9:6 ESV**

Now the birth of Jesus Christ took place in this way. When his mother Mary had been betrothed to Joseph, before they came together she was found to be with child...Behold, an angel of the Lord appeared to him in a dream, saying, "Joseph, son of David, do not fear to take Mary as your wife, for that which is conceived in her is from the Holy Spirit." **Matthew 1:18-20 ESV**

[Mary] gave birth to her firstborn son and wrapped him in bands of cloth, and laid him in a manger, because there was no place for them in the inn. **Luke 2:7 NRSV**

[Mary] looks into the face of the baby. Her son. Her Lord. His Majesty. At this point in history, the human being who best understands who God is and what he is doing is a teenage girl in a smelly stable. She can't take her eyes off him. Somehow Mary knows she is holding God. *So this is he.* She remembers the words of the angel. "His kingdom will never end."

He looks like anything but a king. His face is prunish and red. His cry, though strong and healthy, is still the helpless and piercing cry of a baby. And he is absolutely dependent upon Mary for his well-being.

Majesty in the midst of the mundane. Holiness in the filth of sheep manure and sweat. Divinity entering the world on the floor of a stable, through the womb of a teenager and in the presence of a carpenter. **Max Lucado**

They all were looking for a king to slay their foes and lift them high.
Thou cam'st, a little baby thing that made a woman cry.
George MacDonald

Where you would have expected angels, there were only flies. Where you would have expected heads of state there were only donkeys, a few haltered cows, a nervous ball of sheep, a tethered camel, and a furtive scurry of curious barn mice.

Except for Joseph, there was no one to share Mary's pain. Or her joy. Yes, there were angels announcing the Savior's arrival—but only to a band of blue-collar shepherds. And yes, a magnificent star shone in the sky to mark his birthplace—but only three foreigners bothered to look up and follow it. Thus, in the little town of Bethlehem...that one silent night...the royal birth of God's Son tiptoed quietly by...as the world slept. **Ken Gire**

Late on a sleepy, star-spangled night, those angels peeled back the sky just like you would tear open a sparkling Christmas present. Then, with light and joy pouring out of Heaven like water through a broken dam, they began to shout and sing the message that baby Jesus had been born. The world had a Savior! The angel called it "Good News," and it was. **Larry Libby**

Joyful, all ye nations, rise.
Join the triumph of the skies.
With angelic host proclaim,
"Christ is born in Bethlehem!" **Charles Wesley**

The birth of Jesus is the sunrise of the Bible. Towards this point the aspirations of the prophets and the poems of the psalmists were directed as the heads of flowers are turned toward the dawn. **Henry Van Dyke**

The most outstanding record that is graven on the scroll of time is the date of the birth of Jesus Christ. No issued document is legal, no signed check is valid, and no business receipt is of value unless it bears the statistical reference to this great historic event. **Homer G. Rhea Jr.**

For millions of people who have lived since, the birth of Jesus made possible not just a new way of understanding life but a new way of living it. **Frederick Buechner**

The coming of Christ by way of Bethlehem manger seems strange and stunning. But when we take him out of the manger and invite him into our hearts, then the meaning unfolds and the strangeness vanishes. **Neil Strait**

If Jesus were born one thousand times in Bethlehem and not in me, then I would still be lost. **Corrie ten Boom**

So God throws open the door of this world—and enters as a baby. As the most vulnerable imaginable. Because He wants unimaginable intimacy with you. What religion ever had a god that wanted such intimacy with us that He came with such vulnerability to us?...So vulnerable that His bare, beating heart could be hurt? Only the One who loves you to death. **Ann Voskamp**

A God who was *only* holy...would have simply demanded that we pull ourselves together, that we be moral and holy enough to merit a relationship with him. A deity that was an "all-accepting God of love...this God of the modern imagination would have just overlooked sin and evil and embraced us. Neither the God of moralism nor the God of relativism would have bothered with Christmas. **Timothy Keller**

The baby of Bethlehem was Creator of the universe, pitching his tent on the humble camping ground of our little planet. God's glory now dwelt in Christ. He was the Holy of holies. People had only to look at Jesus to see God. **Randy Alcorn**

Long before silver bells jingled, Christmas lights twinkled, and horse-drawn sleighs went dashing through the snow, God reached down from heaven with the best gift of all. Love, wrapped in swaddling clothes. Hope, nestled in a manger. **Liz Curtis Higgs**

In our world too, a Stable once had something inside it that was bigger than our whole world. **C.S. Lewis**

Come to earth to taste our sadness,
he whose glories knew no end;
by his life he brings us gladness,
our Redeemer, Shepherd, Friend.
Leaving riches without number,
born within a cattle stall;
this the everlasting wonder,
Christ was born the Lord of all. **Charles Wesley**

Human logic says the King of kings should have been born in a palace, surrounded by luxury. Instead, the only door open to the humble Savior was a dirty stable. Amazingly, and revealingly, this was all by God's design. Why is this good news for us? Because the Savior offered himself on our behalf, we won't find "No Vacancy" signs in Heaven. If we've made our reservations by receiving God's gift in Christ, then Heaven is wide open with plenty of room for all of us. **Randy Alcorn**

No other God have I but Thee; born in a manger, died on a tree.
Martin Luther

Christ's Teaching

A crowd built up to such a great size that he had to get into an offshore boat, using the boat as a pulpit as the people pushed to the water's edge. He taught by using stories, many stories. **Mark 4:1-2 MSG**

"Blessed are those who are persecuted because of righteousness, for theirs is the kingdom of heaven." **Matthew 5:10 NIV**

"Blessed are you when people insult you, persecute you and falsely say all kinds of evil against you because of me. Rejoice and be glad, because great is your reward in heaven, for in the same way, they persecuted the prophets who were before you." **Matthew 5:11-12 NIV**

"If anyone slaps you on the right cheek, turn to them the other cheek also." **Matthew 5:39 NIV**

"Love your enemies! Pray for those who persecute you! In that way, you will be acting as true children of your Father in heaven. For he gives his sunlight to both the evil and the good, and he sends rain on the just and the unjust alike." **Matthew 5:44-47 NLT**

"Seek ye first the kingdom of God, and his righteousness; and all these things shall be added unto you." **Matthew 6:33 KJV**

"Do not worry about tomorrow, for tomorrow will worry about itself. Each day has enough trouble of its own." **Matthew 6:34 NIV**

"In everything, therefore, treat people the same way you want them to treat you, for this is the Law and the Prophets." **Matthew 7:12 NASB**

"Whoever does the will of my Father in heaven is my brother and sister and mother." **Matthew 12:50 NIV**

"'You must love the Lord your God with all your heart, all your soul, and all your mind.' This is the first and greatest commandment. A second is equally important: 'Love your neighbor as yourself.' The entire law and all the demands of the prophets are based on these two commandments." **Matthew 22:36-40 NLT**

"Whoever wants to be a leader among you must be your servant, and whoever wants to be first among you must be the slave of everyone else." **Mark 10:43-45 NLT**

"Whatever you ask for in prayer, believe that you have received it, and it will be yours. And when you stand praying, if you hold anything against anyone, forgive them, so that your Father in heaven may forgive you your sins." **Mark 11:24-25 NIV**

"No servant can serve two masters, for either he will hate the one and love the other, or he will be devoted to the one and despise the other. You cannot serve God and money." **Luke 16:13 ESV**

Jesus answered, "What I teach is not my own teaching, but it comes from God, who sent me." **John 7:16 GNB**

"Now I am giving you a new commandment: Love each other. Just as I have loved you, you should love each other." **John 13:34 NLT**

"In my Father's house are many rooms...I am going there to prepare a place for you. And if I go and prepare a place for you, I will come back and take you to be with me that you also may be where I am." **John 14:2-3 NIV**

"Don't you know me, Philip, even after I have been among you such a long time? Anyone who has seen me has seen the Father. How can you say 'Show us the Father'? Don't you believe that I am in the Father, and that the Father is in me?" **John 14:9-10 NIV**

His storytelling fulfilled the prophecy: "I will open my mouth and tell stories; I will bring out into the open things hidden since the world's first day." **Matthew 13:35 MSG**

Who was Jesus?...He was the world's greatest storyteller. Ask him a question; he'd answer with a story. Give him a crowd of people listening intently; he told them stories. Give him an argument; he'd give you a story. Give him a real tricky, catchy question; he'd give you a real tricky, catchy story. Have you ever watched a seven-year-old listening—inhaling—a story? Eyes wide, mouth slung open, mind churning, he lives, accepts, and believes…Jesus knew what he was doing. **Lois A. Cheney**

Jesus made everything so simple and we have made it so complicated. He spoke to the people in…everyday words, illustrating His messages with never-to-be forgotten stories. **Billy Graham**

If Jesus Christ is only a teacher, then all he can do is to tantalize us, to erect a standard we cannot attain to; but when we are born again of the Spirit of God, we know that he did not come only to teach us, he came to make us what he teaches we should be. **Oswald Chambers**

The message of Christ is not Christianity. The message of Christ is Christ. **Gary Amirault**

The most striking feature of the teaching of Jesus is that he was constantly talking about himself. It is true that he spoke much about the fatherhood of God and the kingdom of God. But then he added that he was the Father's "Son," and that he had come to inaugurate the kingdom. Entry into the kingdom depended on men's response to him. He even did not hesitate to call the kingdom of God "my kingdom." This self-centeredness of the teaching of Jesus immediately sets him apart from the other great religious teachers of the world. **John Stott**

It is impossible to be a follower of Christ while denying, disregarding, discrediting, and disbelieving the words of Christ. **David Platt**

When Jesus Christ utters a word, He opens His mouth so wide that it embraces all Heaven and earth, even though that word be but in a whisper. **Martin Luther**

You never get to the end of Christ's words. There is something in them always behind. They pass into proverbs; they pass into laws; they pass into doctrines; they pass into consolations; but they never pass away, and after all the use that is made of them they are still not exhausted. **Arthur Penrhyn Stanley**

Christ's Good News

He came to Nazareth, where he had been brought up. And as was his custom, he went to the synagogue on the Sabbath day, and he stood up to read. And the scroll of the prophet Isaiah was given to him. He unrolled the scroll and found the place where it was written, "The Spirit of the Lord is upon me, because he has anointed me to proclaim good news to the poor. He has sent me to proclaim liberty to the captives and recovering of sight to the blind, to set at liberty those who are oppressed, to proclaim the year of the Lord's favor." And he rolled up the scroll...And the eyes of all in the synagogue were fixed on him. And he began to say to them, "Today this Scripture has been fulfilled in your hearing." **Luke 4:16-19 ESV**

He said to them, "Let us go somewhere else to the towns nearby, so that I may preach there also; for that is what I came for." **Mark 1:38 NIV**

The gospel is not good advice to men, but good news about Christ; not an invitation to us to do anything, but a declaration of what God has done; not a demand, but an offer. **John Stott**

The gospel is so simple that small children can understand it, and it is so profound that studies by the wisest theologians will never exhaust its riches. **Charles Hodge**

Jesus Christ did not say "Go into the world and tell the world that it is quite right." The Gospel is something completely different. In fact, it is directly opposed to the world. **C.S. Lewis**

If you get rid of Christ from your creed, you have at the same time destroyed all its good news. **Charles Spurgeon**

Jesus came to wreck our lives, so that he could join us to his. We cannot build Christian churches on a sub-Christian gospel. People who don't want Christianity don't want almost-Christianity. **Russell Moore**

It is Christ who lived the life that we couldn't. It is Christ who died that death that we deserve. It is Christ who appeased God's wrath. It is Christ that rose from the dead…It is Christ who we are commanded to place our faith in. It is Christ who saves us and it is Christ that gives us eternal life. **Jackie Hill Perry**

Religion is a human activity dedicated to the job of reconciling God to humanity and humanity to itself. The Gospel, however—the Good News of our Lord and Savior, Jesus Christ—is the astonishing announcement that God has done the whole work of reconciliation without a scrap of human assistance. **Robert Farrar Capon**

Christ did not die to forgive sinners who go on treasuring anything above seeing and savoring God. And people who would be happy in heaven if Christ were not there, will not be there. The gospel is not a way to get people to heaven; it is a way to get people to God. **John Piper**

Christ's Example

Once Jesus was in a certain place praying. As he finished, one of his disciples came to him and said, "Lord, teach us to pray, just as John taught his disciples." Jesus said, "This is how you should pray: 'Father, may your name be kept holy. May your Kingdom come soon. Give us each day the food we need, and forgive us our sins, as we forgive those who sin against us. And don't let us yield to temptation.'" **Luke 11:1-4 NLT**

Jesus, knowing that the Father had given all things into his hands, and that he had come from God and was going back to God…knelt down and washed the apostles' feet. **John 13:3 ESV**

Follow my example, as I follow the example of Christ. **1 Corinthians 11:1 NIV**

Imitate God, therefore, in everything you do, because you are his dear children. **Ephesians 5:1 NLT**

Our Lord lived his life…to give the normal standard for our lives.
Oswald Chambers

Even those who have renounced Christianity and attack it, in their inmost being still follow the Christian ideal, for hitherto neither their subtlety nor the ardour of their hearts has been able to create a higher ideal of man and of virtue than the ideal given by Christ of old. **Fyodor Dostoevsky**

Jesus was not a whisperer. No one ever saw Him close to His neighbor's ear, looking stealthily around lest some one should overhear what He was going to say. He stood upright, looked men squarely and kindly in the eye, and spoke what He had to say right out, boldly, frankly, that the whole world might hear; and when He did speak privately to His disciples, He told them to shout it from the housetops. **Samuel Logan Brengle**

Sometimes I wonder how Jesus would have fared in this day of mass media and high-tech ministry. I can't picture him worrying about the details of running a large organization. I can't see him letting some make-up artist improve his looks before a TV appearance. And I have a hard time imagining the fund-raising letters Jesus might write. **Philip Yancey**

Jesus…did not attain a state of perfection by carrying around in his pocket a list of rules and regulations, or by seeking to conform to the cultural mores of his time. He was perfect because he never made a move without his Father. **Thomas Skinner**

Hang that question up in your houses, "What would Jesus do?" and then think of another, "How would Jesus do it?" for what he would do, and how he would do it, may always stand as the best guide to us. **Charles Spurgeon**

To become Christlike is the only thing in the whole world worth caring for. **Henry Drummond**

Have a great aim—have a high standard—make Jesus your ideal...Make him an ideal not merely to be admired but also to be followed. **Eric Liddell**

Stop tinkering with your soul and look away to the perfect One. **A.W. Tozer**

Whatever you fix your eyes on is what you will encourage; fix your eyes on Jesus. **Mark Parker**

In the Christian life our primary teacher in the way of happiness is Christ. He is our mentor; we are his disciples. And it is by observing him, listening to him, learning from him, following his teachings, and imitating his example that we grow in happiness. **Paul J. Wadell**

We must imitate Christ's life and his ways if we are to be truly enlightened and set free from the darkness of our own hearts. Let it be the most important thing we do, then, to reflect on the life of Jesus Christ. **Thomas à Kempis**

The character of Jesus is immensely attractive. It embodies all that we ourselves would, in our best moments, like to be. **Michael Green**

As God's only Son, Jesus came to Earth and gave His life so that we may live. His actions and His words remind us that service to others is central to our lives and that sacrifice and unconditional love must guide us and inspire us to lead lives of compassion, mercy, and justice. **George W. Bush**

It would be well if there were as great a similarity between the life of Christ and the life of Christians, as there is between a just copy and the original. What He was by nature, we should be by grace. **William Secker**

If Jesus Christ the Lord of glory was willing to be obedient unto death, how much more should sinners saved by grace who owe everything to God give back to the God who saved them the life which He has redeemed. **John F. Walvoord**

Christ's Obedience

"He who sent me is with me. The Father has not left me alone, for I always do those things that please him." **John 8:29 ESV**

He went a little beyond them, and fell on His face and prayed, saying, "My Father, if it is possible, let this cup pass from Me; yet not as I will, but as You will." **Matthew 26:39 NASB**

Through the obedience of the one man the many will be made righteous. **Romans 5:19 NIV**

He humbled Himself by becoming obedient to the point of death, even death on a cross. **Philippians 2:8 NASB**

Jesus's greatest work on earth was accomplished by submitting and not by "doing." **Vaneetha Rendall Risner**

Jesus never had any distraction or deviation. His Father's will was always before Him, and it was to this one thing that He was devoted. **A.W. Tozer**

In everything, He stayed true, heartbeat to heartbeat, with the Father's desires. Jesus lived for God alone; God was enough for Him. Thus, even in its simplicity and moment-to-moment faithfulness, Christ's life was an unending fragrance, a perfect offering of incomparable love to God. **Francis Frangipane**

Jesus did not always live up to others' expectations. But He knew how to separate the grain of God's will from the chaff of man's will. **Randy Alcorn**

Doing the will of God was delightful and refreshing to the soul of Christ: he took as much pleasure in it, as a hungry man does in eating and drinking. **John Gill**

The Lord Jesus died for the ungodly. He was obedient at all costs: He bore everything, and went down into the dust of death, man's hatred, God's desertion, and Satan's power; we find Him there at the cost of everything. **John Nelson Darby**

For this reason, Christ had to live a life of perfect obedience to God in order to earn righteousness for us. He had to obey the law for his whole life on our behalf so that the positive merits of his perfect obedience would be counted for us. **Wayne Grudem**

The very resources Jesus used to live his obedient life are resources given also to all of us who trust and follow him. **Bruce Ware**

Christ's Mission

The Spirit of the Lord God is upon me, because the Lord has anointed me to bring good news to the poor; he has sent me to bind up the brokenhearted, to proclaim liberty to the captives, and the opening of the prison to those who are bound; to proclaim the year of the LORD's favor, and the day of vengeance of our God; to comfort all who mourn; to grant to those who mourn in Zion—to give them a beautiful headdress instead of ashes, the oil of gladness instead of mourning, the garment of praise instead of a faint spirit; that they may be called oaks of righteousness, the planting of the LORD, that he may be glorified. **Isaiah 61:1-3 ESV (see Luke 4:18-19, where Jesus applies this to himself)**

"...I in them and you in me, that they may become perfectly one, so that the world may know that you sent me and loved them even as you loved me." **John 17:23 ESV**

He who was seated on the throne said, "Behold, I am making all things new... Write this down, for these words are trustworthy and true." **Revelation 21:5 ESV**

From Jesus' youth, indeed even from his birth, the cross cast its shadow ahead of him. His death was central to his mission. **John Stott**

Jesus understood his mission. He was not driven by the needs of others, though he often stopped to help hurting people. He was not driven by the approval of others, though he cared deeply for the lost and the broken. Ultimately, Jesus was driven by the Spirit. He was driven by his God-given mission. He knew his priorities and did not let the many temptations of a busy life deter him from his task. **Kevin DeYoung**

The mission God gave Jonah meant possible death and suffering...Jonah, however, refused to go, thinking only of himself. The mission God gave Jesus, however, meant *certain* death and infinite suffering, and yet he went, thinking not of himself but of us. **Timothy Keller**

The only One who was able to recognize and follow His purpose from the beginning was Jesus. He alone was able to obey consistently and please God completely. And His divine mission was to make a way for each of us to do the same. **Charles R. Swindoll**

God had only one Son, and He was a missionary and a physician. **David Livingstone**

Jesus is passionate about justice and compassionate toward the needy, especially those who have no one to turn to, and he expects the same of his people (Psalm 72:4; Matthew 25:31-46). He takes a special interest in children, often the most victimized members of a society...He stands opposed to the oppressor; by his very mission statement proclaimed at the beginning of his earthly ministry he demonstrates his love for the oppressed (Psalm 72:4; Luke 4:18-19). ***The Knowing Jesus Study Bible***

Christianity is a rescue religion. It declares that God has taken the initiative in Jesus Christ to deliver us from our sins. This is the main theme of the Bible. **John Stott**

Jesus didn't come to tell us the answers to the questions of life, he came to be the answer. **Timothy Keller**

Christ's Prayers

After saying all these things, Jesus looked up to heaven and said, "Father, the hour has come. Glorify your Son so he can give glory back to you. For you have given him authority over everyone. He gives eternal life to each one you have given him. And this is the way to have eternal life—to know you, the only true God, and Jesus Christ, the one you sent to earth. I brought glory to you here on earth by completing the work you gave me to do. Now, Father, bring me into the glory we shared before the world began." **John 17:1-5 NLT**

In the days of his flesh, Jesus offered up prayers and supplications, with loud cries and tears, to him who was able to save him from death, and he was heard because of his reverence. **Hebrews 5:7 ESV**

Jesus Christ taught his disciples to pray, healed people with prayers, denounced the corruption of the temple worship (which, he said, should be a "house of prayer"), and insisted that some demons could be cast out only through prayer. He prayed often and regularly with fervent cries and tears (Heb. 5:7), and sometimes all night. The Holy Spirit came upon him and anointed him as he was praying (Luke 3:21-22), and he was transfigured with the divine glory as he prayed (Luke 9:29). When he faced his greatest crisis, he did so with prayer. We hear him praying for his disciples and the church on the night before he died (John 17:1-26) and then petitioning God in agony in the Garden of Gethsemane. Finally, he died praying. **Timothy Keller**

What deep mysteries, my dearest brothers, are contained in the Lord's Prayer! How many and great they are! They are expressed in a few words but they are rich in spiritual powers so that nothing is left out; every petition and prayer we have to make is included. It is a compendium of heavenly doctrine. **Cyprian**

Jesus' pattern prayer, which is both crutch, road, and walking lesson for the spiritually lame like ourselves, tells us to start with God: for God matters infinitely more than we do. **J.I. Packer**

Even Jesus, the Savior of the world, had to take time each day to ask for his portion. **Lysa TerKeurst**

I can worry myself into a state of spiritual ennui over questions like "What good does it do to pray if God already knows everything?" Jesus silences such questions: he prayed, so should we. **Philip Yancey**

If I could hear Christ praying for me in the next room, I would not fear a million enemies. Yet the distance makes no difference; he is praying for me! **Robert Murray M'Cheyne**

Christ's Relationships

Jesus said to them, "If God were your Father, you would love Me, for I proceeded forth and have come from God, for I have not even come on My own initiative, but He sent Me." **John 8:42 NIV**

"The Father himself loves you because you have loved me and have believed that I came from God." **John 16:27 NIV**

People were bringing little children to Jesus for him to place his hands on them, but the disciples rebuked them. When Jesus saw this, he was indignant. He said to them, "Let the little children come to me, and do not hinder them, for the kingdom of God belongs to such as these. Truly I tell you, anyone who will not receive the kingdom of God like a little child will never enter it." And he took the children in his arms, placed his hands on them and blessed them. **Mark 10:13-16 NIV**

The hand that holds the seven stars is as loving as the hand that was laid in blessing upon the little children; the face that is as the sun shining in its strength beams with as much love as when it drew publicans and harlots to His feet. The breast that is girt with the golden girdle is the same breast upon which John leaned his happy head. **Alexander Maclaren**

The very fact that Jesus did attract hurting people to himself shows that he cannot have been forbidding in his manner. It suggests that the "man of sorrows" conception of his personality has been overrated in the past. Had he been a gloomy individual and a kill-joy, he would not have had such an appeal to common people and to children. **William Morrice**

Jesus was no ivory-tower theologian expounding abstract and abstruse theories; he was...able to talk to ordinary people in ordinary terms. **David Wenham**

Having spent time around "sinners" and also around purported saints, I have a hunch why Jesus spent so much time with the former group: I think he preferred their company. Because the sinners were honest about themselves and had no pretense, Jesus could deal with them. In contrast, the saints put on airs, judged him, and sought to catch him in a moral trap. In the end it was the saints, not the sinners, who arrested Jesus. **Philip Yancey**

Jesus is hungry but feeds others; He grows weary but offers others rest; He is the King Messiah but pays tribute; He is called the devil but casts out demons; He dies the death of a sinner but comes to save His people from their sins; He is sold for thirty pieces of silver but gives His life a ransom for many; He will not turn stones to bread for Himself but gives His own body as bread for people. **D.A. Carson**

Christ's Miracles

He went throughout all Galilee...healing every disease and every affliction among the people. So his fame spread throughout all Syria, and they brought him all the sick, those afflicted with various diseases and pains, those oppressed by demons, those having seizures, and paralytics, and he healed them. **Matthew 4:23-24 ESV**

Jesus answered, "Why are you afraid? You don't have enough faith." Then Jesus got up and gave a command to the wind and the waves, and it became completely calm. The men were amazed and said, "What kind of man is this? Even the wind and the waves obey him!" **Matthew 8:26-27 NCV**

He took the five loaves and the two fish, looked up to heaven, and gave thanks to God. He broke the loaves and gave them to the disciples, and the disciples gave them to the people. Everyone ate and had enough. Then the disciples took up twelve baskets full of what was left over. The number of men who ate was about five thousand, not counting the women and children. **Matthew 14:19-21 GNB**

When he had said this, Jesus called in a loud voice, "Lazarus, come out!" The dead man came out, his hands and feet wrapped with strips of linen, and a cloth around his face. Jesus said to them, "Take off the grave clothes and let him go." **John 11:43-44 NIV**

Jesus did many other miraculous signs in the presence of his disciples, which are not recorded in this book. But these are written that you may believe that Jesus is the Christ, the Son of God, and that by believing you may have life in his name. **John 20:26-31 NIV**

> Christ cannot be separated from the miraculous. His birth, His ministrations and His resurrection, all involve the miraculous, and the change which His religion works in the human heart is a continuing miracle. Eliminate the miracles and Christ becomes merely a human being and His gospel is stripped of divine authority. **William Jennings Bryan**

Attempts to strip the supernatural from Jesus' life can only produce a Jesus so radically different that he is unrecognizable and his impact on history unexplainable. **Robert Stein**

The healing acts of Jesus were themselves the message that he had come to set men free; they were not just to prove that his message was true. **Francis MacNutt**

Christ's miracles were parables in deeds, and his parables were miracles in words. **W. Graham Scroggie**

The miracles of Jesus were the ordinary works of his Father, wrought small and swift that we might take them in. **George MacDonald**

I believe in miracles, but I trust in Jesus. If you believe the Bible, you know that God is a miracle-working God. And God is not limited in any degree nor any respect. He is totally sovereign. Do you believe that? I hope you do. Believe in miracles, but don't put your faith in miracles. Put your faith and your trust in the Lord Jesus Christ. **Adrian Rogers**

If Jesus heals instantly, praise Him. If Jesus heals gradually, trust Him. When Jesus heals ultimately, you will understand. **Max Lucado**

Death, decay, entropy, and destruction are the true suspensions of God's laws; miracles are the early glimpses of restoration. **Philip Yancey**

Christ's Crucifixion

He was pierced for our transgressions, he was crushed for our iniquities; the punishment that brought us peace was on him, and by his wounds we are healed. We all, like sheep, have gone astray, each of us has turned to our own way; and the Lord has laid on him the iniquity of us all. He was oppressed and afflicted, yet he did not open his mouth; he was led like a lamb to the slaughter, and as a sheep before its shearers is silent, so he did not open his mouth. **Isaiah 53:5-7 NIV**

When they came to the place called "The Skull," they crucified Jesus there, and the two criminals, one on his right and the other on his left. **Luke 23:33 GNT**

"He himself bore our sins" in his body on the cross, so that we might die to sins and live for righteousness; "by his wounds you have been healed." For "you were like sheep going astray," but now you have returned to the Shepherd and Overseer of your souls. **1 Peter 2:24-25 NIV**

There is no doctrine more excellent in itself or more necessary to be preached and studied, than the doctrine of Christ, and him crucified. **John Flavel**

My entire theology can be condensed into four words, "JESUS DIED FOR ME." **Charles Spurgeon**

To know Jesus and Him crucified is my philosophy, and there is none higher. **Bernard of Clairvaux**

The gentle, compassionate Jesus is also the Jesus who drove the merchant-thieves from the Temple and spoke condemnation against self-righteous religious leaders. Were Jesus as meek and mild and utterly tolerant as many think, He never would have been crucified. But His less popular qualities so outraged people that they nailed Him to a cross. **Randy Alcorn**

Jesus was crucified not in a cathedral between two candles, but on a cross between two thieves. **George F. MacLeod**

The crucifixion was the shocking answer to the prayer that God's kingdom would come on earth as in heaven. **N.T. Wright**

Though many recent writers have spoken of God's vulnerability and weakness demonstrated on the cross, we must see this truth in the context of God's sovereignty. Christ chose this "weakness." His obedient death on the cross demonstrates it. "The reason my Father loves me," Jesus said, "is that I lay down my life—only to take it up again. No one takes it from me, but I lay it down of my own accord" (John 10:17-18). He willingly chose to suffer as a victim. Scripture portrays a God so strong He can take on weakness to overpower all opposition and accomplish His eternal purposes. **Randy Alcorn**

It was not the people or the Roman soldiers who put Jesus on the cross—it was your sins and my sins that made it necessary for Him to volunteer His death. **Billy Graham**

The true Son left his home with the Father and went to the cross so that we who had run from the Father could be welcomed as sons. **Trevor Laurence**

When God sent His only Son, Jesus, to this earth to bear your sin and mine on the cross, He put a price tag on us—He declared the value of our soul to be greater than the value of the whole world. **Nancy DeMoss Wolgemuth**

When Jesus went to the cross He didn't fall into Satan's trap—Satan fell into His. **Randy Alcorn**

Satan's motive in Jesus' crucifixion was rebellion; God's motive was love and mercy. Satan was a secondary cause behind the Crucifixion, but it was God who ultimately wanted it, willed it, and allowed Satan to carry it out. **Joni Eareckson Tada**

What looks like (and indeed was) the defeat of Goodness by evil is also, and more certainly, the defeat of evil by Goodness. Overcome there, he was himself overcoming. Crushed by the ruthless power of Rome, he was himself crushing the serpent's head (Genesis 3:15). The victim was the victor, and the cross is still the throne from which he rules the world. **John Stott**

God on a cross. Humanity at its worst. Divinity at its best. **Max Lucado**

Jesus knew He was being betrayed by one of His best friends at that very moment. He knew He was facing imminent arrest, trials, torture, crucifixion, and death. He bore the eternal weight of responsibility for fully completing His Father's will and redeeming mankind from sin. If ever there were multiple reasons for praise being interrupted, Jesus had them on that Thursday night. Yet Matthew 26:30 says that He sang! **Anne Graham Lotz**

Christ's Cross

Having disarmed the powers and authorities, he [God] made a public spectacle of them, triumphing over them by the cross. **Colossians 2:15 NIV**

The word of the cross is folly to those who are perishing, but to us who are being saved it is the power of God. **1 Corinthians 1:18 ESV**

It is at the cross that we see God most clearly. If history were the vastness of space, the cross would be its brightest star. **Chris Tomlinson**

The cross of Christ must be either the darkest spot of all in the mystery of existence or a searchlight by the aid of which we may penetrate the surrounding gloom. **Burnett H. Streeter**

The cross on which the Savior hung was not a tragic incident in the earth-life of the Son of God but rather the climax of a deliberate plan made in the councils of heaven before the creation of the present order of the cosmos. **Harold Rimmer**

Love was compressed for all history in that lonely figure on the cross, who said that he could call down angels at any moment on a rescue mission, but chose not to—because of us. **Philip Yancey**

The problem of how to reconcile evil people with a God who hates evil is the greatest problem of history. It calls for no less than the greatest solution ever devised, one so radical as to be nearly unthinkable, and to offend the sensibilities of countless people throughout history: the cross. **Randy Alcorn**

The cross of Christ is the hinge of history, the point of contact between BC and AD, where all time collides, where all human spectacles meet one unsurpassed, cosmic, divine spectacle...Our response to the ultimate spectacle of the cross of Christ defines us. **Tony Reinke**

The fact that a cross became the Christian symbol, and that Christians stubbornly refused, in spite of the ridicule, to discard it in favor of something less offensive, can have only one explanation. It means that the centrality of the cross originated in the mind of Jesus himself. It was out of loyalty to him that his followers clung so doggedly to this sign. **John Stott**

The cross stands as a reminder that God, in grace, takes very bad things and turns them into very good things. **Paul David Tripp**

Because of the cross, Christ's victory over Satan and death wasn't just possible, it was absolutely certain. **Randy Alcorn**

> The weapon with which Christ warred against the devil, and obtained a most complete victory and glorious triumph over him, was the cross, the instrument and weapon with which he thought he had overthrown Christ, and brought on him shameful destruction. **Jonathan Edwards**

The cross was not Christ's defeat but his triumph, his march of victory. **Tony Reinke**

Out of the worst evil imaginable, the sinless Son of God on the cross, God brought about the greatest good ever known. **Vaneetha Rendall Risner**

Until you see the cross as that which is done *by* you, you will never appreciate that it is done *for* you. **John Scott**

The cross of Christ doesn't show our worth, but God's. **Randy Alcorn**

Think lightly of hell, and you will think lightly of the cross. Think little of the sufferings of lost souls, and you will soon think little of the Savior who delivers you from them. **Charles Spurgeon**

The cross of Christ declares two things: first, God's infinite love of the world; second, God's infinite hatred of sin. **R.A. Torrey**

Any faith that rests short of the Cross is a faith that will land you short of heaven. **Charles Spurgeon**

All Christian preachers have to face this issue. Either we preach that human beings are rebels against God, under his just judgment and (if left to themselves) lost, and that Christ crucified who bore their sin and curse is the only available Saviour. Or we emphasize human potential and human ability, with Christ brought in only to boost them, and with no necessity for the cross except to exhibit God's love and so inspire us to greater endeavour. The former is the way to be faithful, the latter the way to be popular. It is not possible to be faithful and popular simultaneously. **John Stott**

If ever a person had room to complain for injustice, it was Jesus. He was the only innocent man ever to be punished by God. If we stagger at the wrath of God, let us stagger at the Cross. Here is where our astonishment should be focused. **R.C. Sproul**

When we think of Christ dying on the cross, we are shown the lengths to which God's love goes in order to win us back to himself. **Sinclair Ferguson**

There were no cords could have held him to the whipping-post but those of love; no nails have fastened him to the cross but those of love. **Thomas Goodwin**

On the cross divine mercy and justice were equally expressed and eternally reconciled. **John Stott**

Between the trees of the first and of the second Paradise there stands, silent and sublime, that other tree, the tree of shame, the accursed tree of the cross, upon which Christ once hung. From this cross God stretches out His hand to the lost wanderer in the wilderness, longing to bring him back for ever from his own ways to the heavenly homeland. **Erich Sauer**

Christ on our cross is the way Calvary really reads. For He died for us—in our place. We, then, are debtors. Strange, that so often we act like we owe nothing. **Neil Strait**

When I consider the cross of Christ, how can anything that I do be called sacrifice? **Amy Carmichael**

Men have said that the cross of Christ was not a heroic thing, but I want to tell you that the cross of Jesus Christ has put more heroism in the souls of men than any other event in human history. **John G. Lake**

The greatest and most effective remedy for navel gazing is cross surveying. **Scotty Smith**

Only humble, Christ-exalting thinking can survive in the presence of the cross...The cross does not nullify thinking, it purifies thinking. **John Piper**

Christ's Words from the Cross

Father, forgive them

> Jesus said, "Father, forgive them, for they know not what they do." And they cast lots to divide his garments. **Luke 23:34 ESV**

Even the excruciating pain could not silence his repeated entreaties: "Father, forgive them, for they do not know what they are doing."...The rulers sneered at him, shouting: "He saved others, but he can't save himself!" Their words, spoken as an insult, were the literal truth. He could not save himself and others simultaneously. He chose to sacrifice himself in order to save the world. **John Stott**

Whenever I see myself before God and realize something of what my blessed

Lord has done for me at Calvary, I am ready to forgive anybody anything. I cannot withhold it. I do not even want to withhold it. **Martyn Lloyd-Jones**

The victim was stripped of his clothing, beaten and in many instances nailed to the cross (John 19:1, 18, 23). It was dirty business, and the Romans were experts at it—known for lining the roads that led into a conquered city with people dying on crosses. The steady crack of their hammers could be heard above the screams of the victims. Each blow not only resulted in nearly intolerable agony but also reminded the victim that there was no hope left. But even in the middle of so horrific an ordeal, Jesus demonstrated his character. Unlike many others, he was no writhing, screaming, pleading victim, nor was he an angry, cursing man. Instead, as the hammers rang out, one voice could be heard to call out above the clamor, "Father, forgive them!" (Luke 23:34). ***The Knowing Jesus Study Bible***

Today you'll be with me in paradise

Then he said, "Jesus, remember me when you come into your kingdom!" And Jesus said to him, "I assure you, today you will be with me in paradise." **Luke 23:42-43 NLT**

To die is to be with the Lord. It is not just an idea; it is a reality. But at the same time, Christ, the same Christ, gives the promise just as definitely that when I have accepted Christ as my Savior, he lives in me. **Francis Schaeffer**

Woman, behold your son

When Jesus saw his mother and the disciple whom he loved standing nearby, he said to his mother, "Woman, behold, your son!" Then he said to the disciple, "Behold, your mother!" And from that hour the disciple took her to his own home. **John 19:26-27 ESV**

Jesus' mother, who almost certainly was widowed and probably in her early fifties with little or no personal income, was dependent on Jesus, her oldest son. In keeping with the biblical injunction to honor one's parents (Exod. 20:12; Deut. 5:16), Jesus makes here provision for his mother. It may be surprising that Jesus entrusts his mother to the "disciple Jesus loved" rather than to one of his brothers, but this may be explained by his brothers' unbelief. **Andreas J. Köstenberger**

My God, my God

Then at three o'clock Jesus called out with a loud voice, *"Eloi, Eloi, lama sabachthani?"* which means "My God, my God, why have you abandoned me?" **Mark 15:34 NLT**

God allowed his own Son, as our substitute, to be forsaken, in order that we might never be forsaken. ***The Knowing Jesus Study Bible***

The unrighteous damned have no right to ask God why He has forsaken them (the reasons are self-evident to all who understand His holiness and our sin), but God's Son, the Beloved One, was the only righteous one ever damned, and He had the right to ask...even knowing the answer. **Randy Alcorn**

Jesus' cries went unanswered so that my cries can always be heard. His loss is my gain. His sorrow is my rejoicing. **Melissa Kruger**

The amazing beautiful wonderful truth is that because Jesus was forsaken, I never will be. **Vaneetha Rendall Risner**

I thirst

Jesus knew that his mission was now finished, and to fulfill Scripture he said, "I am thirsty." **John 19:28 NLT**

Our Lord came down from life to suffer death;
the Bread came down, to hunger;

the Way came down, on the way to weariness;
the Fount came down, to thirst. **Augustine**

It is finished

When Jesus had received the sour wine, he said, "It is finished," and he bowed his head and gave up his spirit. **John 19:30 ESV**

After creation God said, "It is finished"—and he rested. After redemption Jesus said, "It is finished"—and we can rest. **Timothy Keller**

The concept of finished...can signal the realization of a goal or successful completion of an assignment...It can also mean fulfillment of a religious, legal or social obligation or accountability...One can also complete something in the same sense in which we finished a race...To finish might also signal the full repayment of a debt...When Jesus mouthed the three short words, "It is finished," from the cross, he was in effect declaring that he had fulfilled all meanings: He had completed his assigned task, kept God's law, finished the race and fully paid the debt for our sin. ***The Knowing Jesus Study Bible***

When Jesus said "it is finished," he used the Greek word *teleo*, which was commonly written over certificates of debt once they were fully paid. It's not that Christ paid for 99% of your sin and guilt and you must somehow pay the other 1%. He paid it all. **Randy Alcorn**

You can't imagine a more victimized person than Jesus. Yet when he died, he didn't say, "I am finished" but "It is finished." He did not play the victim, and thus he emerged the victor. **Joni Eareckson Tada**

The task Jesus had come to accomplish was indeed finished, but Jesus himself was not. The devastated disciples concluded that the mission into which they had poured their life energy had ended with Jesus' final breath (Matthew 26:56). The soldiers who had pierced Jesus' side with a spear assumed that the social upheaval caused by the activities of this rabble-rouser were "finished" and that they wouldn't have to deal any longer with this thorn in their side (John 19:33-34). The edgy religious leaders hoped that the influence of our Lord was "finished" but asked Pilate to seal Jesus' tomb to ensure that the disciples wouldn't steal his body (Matthew 27:62-66). Satan gleefully presumed that the threat from this sworn enemy had come to an end, and he gloated in the realization that Jesus was dead and buried (Colossians 2:15). But all of them were wrong. Three days later the Redeemer rose triumphant from the dead! ***The Knowing Jesus Study Bible***

All of salvation is from and about Jesus. No one can boast. He starts and finishes it. **Trillia Newbell**

Jesus' last word is our first word. It is finished. When he died, our life began. **Louie Giglio**

Father, I commit my spirit

Jesus shouted, "Father, I put myself in your hands!" Then he died. **Luke 23:46 CEV**

Jesus cried again with a loud voice and breathed his last. At that moment the curtain of the temple was torn in two, from top to bottom. The earth shook, and the rocks were split. The tombs also were opened, and many bodies of the saints who had fallen asleep were raised. **Matthew 27:50-52 NRSV**

As a true human being Jesus endured every kind of temptation and every kind of suffering a person can experience (Hebrews 2:18; 4:15), especially in those final, dying moments, and he could do nothing other than commit his life to the Father...His suffering, pain and death were all very real. He recognized, just as we must, that his "times" were secure in the hands of his loving and faithful Father (Psalm 31:15). ***The Knowing Jesus Study Bible***

Christ's Sufferings

Jesus went about a stone's throw away from them. He kneeled down and prayed, "Father, if you are willing, take away this cup of suffering. But do what you want, not what I want." Then an angel from heaven appeared to him to strengthen him. Being full of pain, Jesus prayed even harder. His sweat was like drops of blood falling to the ground. **Luke 22:41-44 NCV**

He was despised and rejected by mankind, a man of suffering, and familiar with pain. Like one from whom people hide their faces he was despised, and we held him in low esteem. Surely he took up our pain and bore our suffering, yet we considered him punished by God, stricken by him, and afflicted. **Isaiah 53:3-4 NIV**

I could never myself believe in God, if it were not for the cross. The only God I believe in is the One Nietzsche ridiculed as "God on the cross." In the real world of pain, how could one worship a God who was immune to it? **John Stott**

For whatever reason God chose to make man as he is—limited and suffering and subject to sorrows and death—God had the honesty and the courage to take his own medicine. Whatever game he is playing with his creation, he has kept his own rules and played fair. He can exact nothing from man that he has not exacted from himself. He has himself gone through the whole of human experience, from the trivial irritations of family life and the cramping restrictions of hard work and lack of money to the worst horrors of pain and humiliation, defeat, despair, and death. When he was a man, he played the man. He was born in poverty and died in disgrace and thought it well worthwhile. **Dorothy Sayers**

God may thunder His commands from Mount Sinai and men may fear, yet remain at heart exactly as they were before. But let a man once see his God down in the arena as a Man—suffering, tempted, sweating, and agonized, finally dying a criminal's death—and he is a hard man indeed who is untouched. **J.B. Phillips**

One look at Jesus—the second member of the triune God who suffered unimaginable torture on the cross—should silence the argument that God lacks feelings and has withdrawn to some far corner of the universe where he keeps his hands clean and maintains his distance from human suffering...In the suffering of Jesus, God himself suffered. No one who grasps this truth can say, "God doesn't understand my suffering." **Randy Alcorn**

When I consider my crosses, tribulations, and temptations, I shame myself almost to death, thinking what they are in comparison of the sufferings of my blessed Saviour Christ Jesus. **Martin Luther**

God's people have always put their own suffering in perspective by looking at Christ's. Can you gaze on the crucified Christ and still resent God for not doing enough to show you his love? **Randy Alcorn**

Man of sorrows! What a name
for the son of God, who came
ruined sinners to reclaim.
Hallelujah! What a Savior! **Philip Bliss**

He wore a crown of thorns, that thou mightest wear a crown of glory; and was nailed to the cross, with His arms wide open, to show with what freeness all His merits shall be bestowed on the coming soul; and how heartily He will receive it into His bosom. **John Bunyan**

Why did Jesus hang on the cross for six hours rather than six seconds or six minutes? Perhaps as a reminder that suffering is a process. God does not end our suffering as soon as we would like. He did not end his Son's suffering as soon as he would have liked. We stand in good company. **Randy Alcorn**

See from His head, His hands, His feet,
Sorrow and love flow mingled down!
Did e'er such love and sorrow meet,
Or thorns compose so rich a crown? **Isaac Watts**

Christ's Sacrifice

"I am the good shepherd. I know my own and my own know me, just as the Father knows me and I know the Father; and I lay down my life for the sheep." **John 10:14-15 ESV**

Greater love has no one than this: to lay down one's life for one's friends. **John 15:13 NIV**

God presented Christ as a sacrifice of atonement, through the shedding of his blood—to be received by faith. **Romans 3:25 NIV**

He who did not spare his own Son but gave him up for us all, how will he not also with him graciously give us all things? **Romans 8:32 ESV**

Let love be your guide. Christ loved us and offered his life for us as a sacrifice that pleases God. **Ephesians 5:2 CEV**

In all human history, who has paid the highest price for evil and suffering? Poll a hundred people on this question, and only a few would come up with the right answer: "Jesus." **Randy Alcorn**

In Abraham's case, God provided a substitute for Isaac, a ram caught by its horns in the bushes. But there could be no substitute when Jesus offered his life as the sacrifice for the sin of all humanity. On the cross, God's own Son took upon himself the Father's wrath against *all* sin for *all* time. ***The Knowing Jesus Study Bible***

For Christ to be the propitiation for our sins means that He became the sacrifice upon which God's wrath against sin was brought. Some object to this because they claim if the Father brought our punishment on Jesus it sounds like divine child abuse. But it isn't, because Jesus, God's Son, is not a helpless child but eternally God, and He fully consented to this plan. **Randy Alcorn**

Who delivered up Jesus to die? Not Judas, for money; not Pilate, for fear; not the Jews, for envy—but the Father, for love! **Octavius Winslow**

The fact that Jesus had to die for me humbled me out of my pride. The fact that Jesus was glad to die for me assured me out of my fear. **Timothy Keller**

Think as little of yourself as you want to, but always remember that our Lord Jesus Christ thought very highly of you—enough to give Himself for you in death and sacrifice. **A.W. Tozer**

He loves us in our sin. Only such a view of love correctly appreciates the sacrifice of Christ and respects the infinite chasm between what is deserved and mercy. **Jim Elliff**

Do not refuse the Lord Jesus who knocks at your door; for He knocks with a hand which was nailed to the tree for such as you are. **Charles Spurgeon**

Christ was utterly innocent, yet because He took our sins on Himself, He became temporarily damned on our behalf. Not damned forever, but damned on the cross so He experienced Hell on our behalf. Unthinkable. Inconceivable. And yet it happened...for us. **Randy Alcorn**

If we again ask the question: "Why does God allow evil and suffering to continue?" and we look at the cross of Jesus, we still do not know what the answer is. However, we know what the answer isn't. It can't be that he doesn't love us. It can't be that he is indifferent or detached from our condition. God takes our misery and suffering *so* seriously that he was willing to take it on himself. **Timothy Keller**

Christ's scars will remain forever. The only one who will appear less than perfect in eternity will be the eternally Perfect One. **Randy Alcorn**

Christ's Blood

Be shepherds of the church of God, which he bought with his own blood. **Acts 20:28 NIV**

When Christ appeared as a high priest of the good things to come, He entered through the greater and more perfect tabernacle...and not through the blood of goats and calves, but through His own blood, He entered the holy place once for all, having obtained eternal redemption. **Hebrews 9:11-12 ESV**

> How much more, then, will the blood of Christ, who through the eternal Spirit offered himself unblemished to God, cleanse our consciences from acts that lead to death, so that we may serve the living God! **Hebrews 9:14 NIV**

In fact, the law requires that nearly everything be cleansed with blood, and without the shedding of blood there is no forgiveness. **Hebrews 9:22 NIV**

If we walk in the light, as he is in the light, we have fellowship with one another, and the blood of Jesus, his Son, purifies us from all sin. **1 John 1:7 NIV**

Once you were far away from God, but now you have been brought near to him through the blood of Christ. **Ephesians 2:13 NLT**

Let us look upon a crucified Christ, the remedy of all our miseries. His cross hath procured a crown, his passion hath expiated our transgression. His death hath disarmed the law, his blood hath washed a believer's soul. This death is the destruction of our enemies, the spring of our happiness, and the eternal testimony of divine love. **Stephen Charnock**

One drop of Christ's blood is worth more than heaven and earth. **Martin Luther**

The wounds of Christ were the greatest outlets of his glory that ever were. **Robert Murray M'Cheyne**

God's love for us is soaked in divine blood. **Randy Alcorn**

Christ's blood has value enough to redeem the whole world, but the virtue of it is applied only to such as believe. **Thomas Watson**

Nothing in my hand I bring,
Simply to thy cross I cling;
Naked, come to thee for dress;
Helpless, look to thee for grace;
Foul, I to the fountain fly;
Wash me, Saviour, or I die. **Augustus Toplady**

When our conscience rises up and condemns us, where will we turn? We turn to Christ. We turn to the suffering and death of Christ—the blood of Christ. This is the only cleansing agent in the universe that can give the conscience relief in life and peace in death. **John Piper**

Be assured that there is no sin you have ever committed that the blood of Jesus Christ cannot cleanse. **Billy Graham**

I am ready to meet God face to face tonight and look into those eyes of infinite holiness, for all my sins are covered by the atoning blood. **R.A. Torrey**

Christ's blood is heaven's key. **Thomas Brooks**

Christ's Substitutionary Death and Atonement

It was necessary for him to be made in every respect like us, his brothers and sisters, so that he could be our merciful and faithful High Priest before God. Then he could offer a sacrifice that would take away the sins of the people. **Hebrews 2:17 NLT**

The atonement is the crucial doctrine of the faith. Unless we are right here, it matters little what we believe elsewhere. **Leon Morris**

The marvel of heaven and earth, of time and eternity, is the atoning death of Jesus Christ. This is the mystery that brings more glory to God than all creation. **Charles Spurgeon**

Moved by the perfection of his holy love, God in Christ substituted himself for us sinners. That is the heart of the Cross of Christ. **John Stott**

The merits of Jesus are enough! We are going to heaven on the merits of another—there is no question about that...We will be with God because another was rejected from the presence of God in the terror of the crucifixion. **A.W. Tozer**

Christ died for men precisely because men are not worth dying for; to make them worth it. **C.S. Lewis**

Theology has frequently confused redemption and the atonement. The atonement for sin offered by Christ on Calvary was universal, but redemption is limited to those that accept the conditions as specified in the Scriptures. Christ died for all, but, as a fact, only they that believe are saved. The atonement is God's provision for the salvation of the world, redemption of the sinner is the object God has in view. There could be no redemption without the atonement, but if redemption is not appropriated the atonement still remains. **R. Venting**

In the center of the kingdom of God, you do not find a gargantuan palace inhabited by an unapproachable king. No, in the center of the kingdom of God is a bloody cross, on which hung a broken King, who welcomes us as we are. **Paul David Tripp**

On the cross, by both demanding and bearing the penalty of sin and so simultaneously punishing and overcoming evil, God displayed and demonstrated his holy love. **John Stott**

The notion which the phrase "penal substitution" expresses is that Jesus Christ our Lord, moved by a love that was determined to do everything necessary to save us, endured and exhausted the destructive divine judgment for which we were otherwise inescapably destined, and so won us forgiveness, adoption and glory. To affirm penal substitution is to say that believers are in debt to Christ specifically for this, and that this is the mainspring of all their joy, peace and praise both now and for eternity. **J.I. Packer**

It was not for societies or states that Christ died, but for men. **C.S. Lewis**

Well might the sun in darkness hide,
And shut his glories in,
When God, the mighty Maker died
For man, the creature's sin. **Isaac Watts**

The beloved Son who had "well pleased" his Father (Matthew 3:17) became our sin (2 Corinthians 5:21). So the Father turned away. For the first time in all eternity, the oneness within the Godhead knew separation. In ways we cannot comprehend—ways that would amount to blasphemy had not God revealed it to us—the atonement somehow tore God apart. **Randy Alcorn**

The witness of the substitutionary atonement of Jesus is that God's most difficult promise has been kept. **Sheila Walsh**

The only way back to the tree of life is to trust in the one who hung upon the tree of death. **Trevor Laurence**

Christ's Resurrection: The Event

"He isn't here! He is risen from the dead, just as he said would happen. Come, see where his body was lying." **Matthew 28:6 NLT**

"This Jesus God raised up, and of that we all are witnesses." **Acts 2:32 ESV**

On the third day the friends of Christ coming at daybreak to the place found the grave empty and the stone rolled away. In varying ways they realized the new wonder; but even they hardly realized that the world had died in the night. What they were looking at was the first day of a new creation, with a new heaven and a new earth; and in a semblance of the gardener God walked again in the garden, in the cool not of the evening but of the dawn. **G.K. Chesterton**

When Christ died and was raised from death, a new day dawned, a new age began. **John Stott**

Christ is the "first fruits," the "pioneer of life." He has forced open a door that has been locked since the death of the first man. He has met, fought, and beaten the King of Death. Everything is different because He has done so. **C.S. Lewis**

Had Christ not risen we could not believe Him to be what He declared Himself when He "made Himself equal with God." But He has risen in the confirmation of all His claims. **B.B. Warfield**

The tomb of Christ is famous because of what it does not contain. **Sam Morris**

The son of God is dead: and it is believable, because it is folly. And having been buried, he rose again: it is certain, because it is impossible. **Tertullian**

How different is the epitaph on the tomb of Jesus! It is neither written in gold nor cut in stone. It is spoken by the mouth of an angel and is the exact reverse of what is put on all other tombs: "He is not here; for he is risen, as he said" (Matthew 28:6). **Billy Graham**

Christ the Lord is risen to-day,
Sons of men and angels say.
Raise your joys and triumphs high;
Sing, ye heavens, and earth reply. **Charles Wesley**

Our Lord has written the promise of resurrection, not in books alone, but in every leaf in springtime. **Martin Luther**

Christ's resurrection is not a matter of a "spirit appearance," but the utterly unprecedented, unique, world-transforming, heaven-anticipating, sovereign action of the Creator in the first installment of remaking the world. **Bruce Milne**

The resurrection of Christ is the Amen of all His promises. **John Boys**

Christ's Resurrection: The Importance

What I received I passed on to you as of first importance: that Christ died for our sins according to the Scriptures, that he was buried, that he was raised on the third day according to the Scriptures, and that he appeared to Peter, and then to the Twelve. After that, he appeared to more than five hundred of the brothers at the same time, most of whom are still living, though some have fallen asleep. Then he appeared to James, then to all the apostles, and last of all he appeared to me also, as to one abnormally born. **1 Corinthians 15:3-8 NIV**

"I am the resurrection and the life. Whoever believes in me, though he die, yet shall he live." **John 11:25-26 ESV**

"When I am raised to life again, you will know that I am in my Father, and you are in me, and I am in you." **John 14:20 NLT**

If Christ has not been raised, your faith is futile and you are still in your sins. **1 Corinthians 15:17 ESV**

Blessed be the God and Father of our Lord Jesus Christ! According to his great mercy, he has caused us to be born again to a living hope through the resurrection of Jesus Christ from the dead. **1 Peter 1:3 ESV**

No resurrection. No Christianity. **Michael Ramsey**

In the New Testament the Resurrection is that central miracle around which the Christian faith is gathered. The apostle Paul said that without believing the miracle of the Resurrection, faith was impossible (Romans 10:9; 1 Corinthians 15:17). **Calvin Miller**

Belief in the resurrection is not an appendage to the Christian faith; it is the Christian faith. **John S. Whale**

Christianity rises or falls on the resurrection. If this event is historically true, it makes all other religions false, because Jesus claimed to be the only way to God. To prove this, he predicted he would rise three days after his death. And he did. **Randy Alcorn**

Christianity is in its very essence a resurrection religion. The concept of resurrection lies at its heart. If you remove it, Christianity is destroyed. **John Stott**

If Christ be not risen, the dreadful consequence is not that death ends life, but that we are still in our sins. **Geoffrey Anketell Studdert-Kennedy**

Had He not emerged from the tomb all our hopes, all our salvation would be lying dead with Him unto this day. But as we see Him issue from the grave we see ourselves issue with Him in newness of life. Now we know that His shoulders were strong enough to bear the burden that was laid upon them, and that He is able to save to the uttermost all that come unto God through Him. The resurrection of Christ is thus the indispensable evidence of His completed work, His accomplished redemption. **B.B. Warfield**

If Christ has risen the Bible is true from Genesis to Revelation. The kingdom of darkness has been overthrown. Satan has fallen like lightning from heaven; and the triumph of truth over error, of good over evil, of happiness over misery, is forever secured. **Charles Hodge**

If Christ is risen, nothing else matters. And if Christ is not risen—nothing else matters. **Jaroslav Pelikan**

Christianity is realistic because it says that if there is no truth, there is also no hope; and there can be no truth if there is no adequate base. It is prepared to face the consequences of being proved false and say with Paul: If you find the body of Christ, the discussion is finished, let us eat and drink for tomorrow we die. It leaves absolutely no room for a romantic answer. **Francis Schaeffer**

If Jesus rose from the dead, then you have to accept all that he said; if he didn't rise from the dead, then why worry about any of what he said? The issue on which everything hangs is not whether or not you like his teaching but whether or not he rose from the dead. **Timothy Keller**

The sepulchre calls forth my adoring wonder,
for it is empty and thou art risen;
the four-fold gospel attests it,
the living witnesses prove it,

my heart's experience knows it.
The Valley of Vision: A Collection of Puritan Prayers and Devotions

Without the resurrection, at the name of Jesus every knee would not bow; more likely, people would say, "Jesus who?" **John Young**

In ancient times before the divine sojourn of the Savior took place, even to the saints death was terrible; all wept for the dead as though they perished. But now that the Savior has raised his body, death is no longer terrible; for all who believe in Christ trample on it as it were nothing and choose rather to die than deny their faith in Christ. **Athanasius of Alexandria**

Christ has turned all our sunsets into dawns. **Clement of Alexandria**

The power of Christ's resurrection is enough not only to remake us but also to remake every square inch of the universe. **Randy Alcorn**

Christ's Resurrection: The Evidence

"He has fixed a day in which he will judge the whole world with justice by means of a man he has chosen. He has given proof of this to everyone by raising that man from death!" **Acts 17:31 GNT**

There is more evidence that Jesus rose from the dead than there is that Julius Caesar ever lived or that Alexander the Great died at the age of thirty-three. **Billy Graham**

The resurrection of Jesus Christ from the dead is one of the best attested facts on record. There were so many witnesses to behold it, that if we do in the least degree receive the credibility of men's testimonies, we cannot and we dare not doubt that Jesus rose from the dead. **Charles Spurgeon**

As a lawyer I have made a prolonged study of the evidences for the events of the first Easter Day. To me the evidence is conclusive, and over and over again in the High Court I have secured the verdict on evidence not nearly so compelling.

Inference follows on evidence, and a truthful witness is always artless and disdains effect. The Gospel evidence for the Resurrection is of this class, and as a lawyer I accept it unreservedly as the testimony of truthful men to facts they were able to substantiate. **Edward Clarke**

About this time there lived Jesus, a wise man, if indeed one ought to call him a man. For he was one who wrought surprising feats and was a teacher of such people as accept the truth gladly. He won over many Jews and many of the Greeks. He was the Christ. When Pilate, upon hearing him accused by men of the highest standing among us, had condemned him to be crucified, those who had in the first place come to love him did not give up their affection for him. On the third day he appeared to them restored to life, for the prophets of God had prophesied these and countless other marvelous things about him. And the tribe of the Christians, so called after him, has still to this day not disappeared. **Flavius Josephus**

He appeared to every one of His friends, and to His best friends, but not a single one of His enemies got to see Him. I know that this story of the resurrection is true, because none but God would have had things happen in the order that they did, and in the way in which they occurred. Had the story been false the record would have made Jesus go to Pilate and the high priest, and to the others who had put Him to death, to prove that He was risen. **Elijah P. Brown**

I went to a psychologist friend and said if 500 people claimed to see Jesus after he died, it was just a hallucination. He said hallucinations are an individual event. If 500 people have the same hallucination, that's a bigger miracle than the resurrection. **Lee Strobel**

The least plausible of all explanations of the resurrection was that it was generated out of the despairing imagination of the disciples. For that does not explain why they were willing to risk their lives for it. Nor does it account for one of the most characteristic literary features of the Easter narratives: the report that the beholders were utterly surprised by the appearance of the risen Lord. The "surprise" element of the Easter narratives is too recurrent to be considered an anomaly. **Thomas Oden**

Perhaps the transformation of the disciples of Jesus is the greatest evidence of all for the resurrection. It was the resurrection which transformed Peter's fear into courage and James' doubt into faith...It was the resurrection which changed Saul the Pharisee into Paul the apostle and turned his persecuting into preaching. **John Stott**

I know the resurrection is a fact, and Watergate proved it to me. How? Because 12 men testified they had seen Jesus raised from the dead, then they proclaimed that truth for 40 years, never once denying it. Every one was beaten, tortured, stoned and put in prison. They would not have endured that if it weren't true. Watergate embroiled 12 of the most powerful men in the world—and they couldn't keep a lie for three weeks. You're telling me 12 apostles could keep a lie for 40 years? Absolutely impossible. **Charles Colson**

Ghosts, apparitions, and various psychological hallucinations may do a lot of things, but they don't fire up the charcoal grill and cook fish for breakfast. **Pheme Perkins**

The crowning evidence that he lives is not a vacant grave, but a spirit-filled fellowship. Not a rolled-away stone, but a carried-away church. **Clarence Jordan**

From the empty grave of Jesus the enemies of the cross turn away in unconcealable dismay. Those whom the force of no logic can convince, and whose hearts are steeled against the appeal of almighty love from the cross itself, quail before the irresistible power of this simple fact. Christ has risen from the dead! After two thousand years of the most determined assault upon the evidence which demonstrates it, that fact stands. And so long as it stands Christianity, too, must stand as the one supernatural religion. **B.B. Warfield**

The Saviour is working mightily among men, every day He is invisibly persuading numbers of people all over the world, both within and beyond the Greek-speaking world, to accept His faith and be obedient to His teaching. Can anyone, in face of this, still doubt that He has risen and lives, or rather that He is Himself the Life? Does a dead man prick the consciences of men? **Athanasius of Alexandria**

The evidence for Jesus' resurrection is so strong that nobody would question it except for two things: First, it is a very unusual event. And second, if you believe it happened, you have to change the way you live. **Wolfhart Pannenberg**

If Jesus rose from the dead, then there is no room for doubt that death is not the end of our journey. If Jesus truly rose, then there is for every person a heaven to embrace and a hell to shun. **Bruce Milne**

Christ's Ascension

"I came forth from the Father and have come into the world; I am leaving the world again and going to the Father." **John 16:28 NASB**

> "Why are you men from Galilee standing here and looking up into the sky? Jesus has been taken into heaven. But he will come back in the same way that you have seen him go." **Acts 1:11 CEV**

Hail the day that sees Him rise,
Ravished from our wistful eyes!
Christ, awhile to mortals given,
Re-ascends His native heaven.
There the glorious triumph waits,
Lift your heads, eternal gates!
Wide unfold the radiant scene,
Take the King of glory in! **Charles Wesley**

He ascended as a conqueror, in a way of triumph. **Thomas Watson**

The Lord, by his ascension into heaven, has opened up the access to the heavenly kingdom, which Adam had shut. For having entered it in our flesh, as it were in our name, it follows...that we are in a manner seated in heavenly places, not entertaining a mere hope of heaven, but possessing it in our covenantal Head. **John Calvin**

At the ascension, Jesus leaves the space-time continuum and passes into the presence of the Father. He is still human, still our second Adam...and still our Advocate—yet now he has been so glorified that everything he does has a cosmic scope...any time-space limitation passes away. **Timothy Keller**

The ascension of Jesus into heaven is designed to teach us that heaven does exist as a place in the space-time universe. **Wayne Grudem**

The ascension of Christ is his liberation from all restriction of time and space. It does not represent his removal from the earth, but his constant presence everywhere on earth. **William Temple**

What the ascension means is that Jesus Christ forever remains the Christ who is Jesus. He did not revert back to intangibility...The Incarnation is a miracle with no expiration date. **Jared C. Wilson**

Through the Ascension God exalted Christ in his human nature...Jesus received the power, authority, and glory that were not fully available to his human nature during his earthly ministry. Jesus' human nature was exalted in order that the purpose of ascension may be fulfilled so that Christ may rule and reign on the throne of heaven as the Mediator. **Nate Palmer**

The Ascension was from one standpoint the restoration of the glory that the Son had before the Incarnation, from another the glorifying of human nature in a way that had never happened before, and from a third the start of a reign that had not previously been exercised in this form. **J.I. Packer**

[As the ascended king] He controls all things for the church, and therefore you can face the world with peace in your heart…The man who died for you is not only at the right hand of the divine throne but he's there as the Executive Director of history, directing everything for the benefit of the church. **Timothy Keller**

> Without an ascended Christ, there is no High Priest ruling and reigning over all creation, our assurance of heaven is in serious doubt, and we would not be living temples in which God's Spirit resides helping us understand the things of God. In short, without an Ascension every book past John wouldn't exist and our union with Christ stops at an earthly resurrection. **Nate Palmer**

Christ's Return

> "In the same way, when you see all these things, you can know his return is very near, right at the door." **Matthew 24:33 NLT**

What we are teaching you now is the Lord's teaching: we who are alive on the day the Lord comes will not go ahead of those who have died. There will be the shout of command, the archangel's voice, the sound of God's trumpet, and the Lord himself will come down from heaven. Those who have died believing in Christ will rise to life first; then we who are living at that time will be gathered up along with them in the clouds to meet the Lord in the air. And so we will always be with the Lord. **1 Thessalonians 4:15-17 GNB**

Look, he is coming with the clouds and every eye will see him, even those who pierced him; and all the peoples of the earth will mourn because of him. So shall it be. Amen! **Revelation 1:7 NIV**

And now, little children, abide in him, so that when he appears we may have confidence and not shrink from him in shame at his coming. **1 John 2:28 ESV**

In his first coming he was wrapped in swaddling clothes. In his second coming he will be clothed royally in a robe dipped in blood. In his first coming he was surrounded by animals and shepherds. In his second coming he will be accompanied by saints and angels. In his first coming there was no room for him in the inn. In his second coming the door of the heavens will be opened to him. **Greg Laurie**

We are not a post-war generation; but a pre-peace generation. Jesus is coming. **Corrie ten Boom**

Believing in the second coming affirms that Jesus remains sovereign and will return at last to put everything right. This putting right (the biblical word for it is "justice") is the sort of sigh-of-relief event that the whole world, at its best and at many other times too, longs for most deeply...All sorts of things are still wrong with us, Jesus's followers; Jesus, when he comes, will put us right as well. That may not be comfortable, but it's what we need. **N.T. Wright**

The primitive church thought more about the Second Coming of Jesus Christ than about death or about heaven. The early Christians were looking not for a cleft in the ground called a grave but for a cleavage in the sky called Glory. They were watching not for the undertaker but for the uppertaker. **Alexander Maclaren**

Mighty Ruler and Counselor; Living Sacrifice and Friend...
He came as the child, born to die the spotless Lamb
But he'll be coming as the lion, proud and mighty he will stand,
On a day like today He'll come, breaking through the earthly skies

On a day like today we'll see the Son, with our own eyes;
We'll see him in all his glory, the angels will fill the skies,
And then up to glory we'll rise...
On a day just like today. **Paul Norquist**

Christ hath told us He will come, but not when, that we might never put off our clothes, or put out the candle. **William Gurnall**

The fact that Jesus Christ is to come again is not a reason for star-gazing, but for working in the power of the Holy Ghost. **Charles Spurgeon**

I never begin my work in the morning without thinking that perhaps He may interrupt my work and begin His own. I am not looking for death. I am looking for Him. **G. Campbell Morgan**

Jesus was very clear about one fact regarding his return: The date itself is not important. What matters is the manner in which we live our lives while we wait. ***The Knowing Jesus Study Bible***

We are to wait for the coming of Christ with patience. We are to watch with anticipation. We are to work with zeal. We are to prepare with urgency. **Billy Graham**

Let's trust Jesus to return when He is good and ready to do so, whether that is today, or a hundred years from now, or a thousand. Let's live as people who are indeed going to meet Jesus soon, either by His return or our deaths...and by His grace, hear those incredible words: "Well done, my good and faithful servant; enter into your Master's happiness" (Matthew 25:23). **Randy Alcorn**

In the first advent God veiled his divinity to prove the faithful; in the second advent he will manifest his glory to reward their faith. **John Chrysostom**

Christ's Eternal Reign

He must reign until he has put all his enemies under his feet. The last enemy to be destroyed is death. **1 Corinthians 15:25-26 ESV**

Then I heard something like the voice of a vast multitude...saying, "Hallelujah, because our Lord God, the Almighty, reigns!" **Revelation 19:6 CSB**

Everywhere there's a believer on this earth, there should be a taste of the victory that Christ will bring when he comes to reign on earth. **Nancy DeMoss Wolgemuth**

Jesus could have overpowered Jerusalem, but sovereignly chose not to. Jesus *will* reign over the New Jerusalem someday, filled with people who love and willingly bow to him. Christ's will shall *ultimately* prevail, even though he permitted it to be *immediately* resisted. Ironically, Jerusalem's rejection of his will was necessary to accomplish the fulfillment of his will through redemption. **Randy Alcorn**

He is Lord, and those who refuse him as Lord cannot use him as Savior...for to say we receive Christ when in fact we reject his right to reign over us is utter absurdity. **John MacArthur**

God and Satan are currently at war, but unlike human competitors, they are in no sense equals, and there is no possibility God will lose. **Randy Alcorn**

The kingdom must not be understood as merely the salvation of certain individuals or even as the reign of God in the hearts of his people; it means nothing less than the reign of God over his entire created universe. **Anthony Hoekema**

The angel Gabriel promised Mary concerning Jesus, "The Lord God will give him the throne of his father David, and he will reign over the house of Jacob forever; his kingdom will never end" (Luke 1:32-33). David's throne is not in Heaven but on Earth. It is God's reign on Earth, not in Heaven, that is the focus of the unfolding drama of redemption. That earthly reign will be forever established on the New Earth. **Randy Alcorn**

God could have set up a throne of strict justice, dispensing death to all who were convened before it...God has, instead, chosen to set up a throne of grace. There, at that throne, grace reigns, and acts with sovereign freedom, power, and bounty. **Joni Eareckson Tada**

The Bible's central storyline revolves around a question: Who will reign over the earth? Earth's destiny hangs in the balance. Because it is the realm where God's glory has been most challenged and resisted, it is therefore also the stage on which his glory will be most graphically demonstrated. By reclaiming, restoring, renewing, and resurrecting Earth—and empowering a regenerated mankind to reign over it—God will accomplish his purpose of bringing glory to himself. **Randy Alcorn**

Christ's Victory over Sin and Evil

Sin is the sting that results in death, and the law gives sin its power. But thank God! He gives us victory over sin and death through our Lord Jesus Christ. **1 Corinthians 15:56-57 NLT**

We know that since Christ was raised from the dead, he cannot die again...The death he died he died to sin once for all; but the life he lives, he lives to God. **Romans 6:9-10 NIV**

The wages of sin is death, but the free gift of God is eternal life in Christ Jesus our Lord. **Romans 6:23 ESV**

Wretched man that I am! Who will deliver me from this body of death? Thanks be to God through Jesus! **Romans 7:24-25 ESV**

There is no death of sin without the death of Christ. **John Owen**

The death of God's Son is a greater testimony to God's abhorrence of sin than if all humans had been damned forever. **John Piper**

No proposition can be more plain than this, that the power of Satan was destroyed by the death of Christ. **John Owen**

May we sit at the foot of the cross; and there learn what sin has done, what justice has done, what love has done. **John Newton**

Jesus is the only one who can heal you of the most deadly disease in your life—the disease of sin. **Nancy Guthrie**

It is a fact that the Lord Jesus has already died for you. It is also a fact that you have already died with the Lord Jesus. If you do not believe in your death with Christ, you will not be able to receive the effectiveness of death with Him—freedom from sin. **Watchman Nee**

Look to the cross, and hate your sin, for sin nailed your Well Beloved to the tree. Look up to the cross, and you will kill sin, for the strength of Jesus' love will make you strong to put down your tendencies to sin. **Charles Spurgeon**

I don't believe it is wise or truthful to the power of the gospel to identify oneself by the sins of one's past or the temptations of one's present but rather to only be defined by the Christ who's overcome both for those He calls His own. **Jackie Hill Perry**

Either the Lord Jesus Christ came to bring an end of self and reveal a new life in spiritual victory, or He came to patch and repair the old self—He certainly did not come to do both! **A.W. Tozer**

Ephesians 6 talks about God's armor...When you read closely you will see that the Lord Jesus Himself is our armor. He is peace. He is truth. He is in you; you are in Him. It might be a battle, but this time it is in a blessed circle. It is the Devil attacking you; you are falling, but you are lifted up, forgiven, cleansed. **Corrie ten Boom**

Make the victorious Christ, not the "victorious Christian life," your preoccupation. He's still Victor even when we're not. **Scotty Smith**

The gospel is boldly advancing under the contested reign and inevitable victory of Jesus the king. **D.A. Carson**

I need a battlefield Jesus at my side down here in the dangerous, often messy trenches of daily life. I need Jesus the rescuer, ready to wade through pain, death, and hell itself to find me, grasp my hand, and bring me safely through. **Joni Eareckson Tada**

The best answer to the problem of evil is a person—Jesus Christ. In fact, He is the only answer. **Randy Alcorn**

What do we find God "doing about" this business of sin and evil?...God did not abolish the fact of evil; He transformed it. He did not stop the crucifixion; he rose from the dead. **Dorothy Sayers**

What Jesus did about evil and suffering was so great and unprecedented that it shook the angelic realm's foundation. It ripped in half, from the top down, not only the temple curtain but the fabric of the universe itself. **Randy Alcorn**

No more let sins and sorrows grow
Nor thorns infest the ground;
He comes to make His blessings flow
Far as the curse is found. **Isaac Watts**

How far does Christ's redemptive work extend? *Far as the curse is found.* God won't be satisfied until every sin, sorrow, and thorn is reckoned with. **Randy Alcorn**

Christ's Triumph over Death

He will swallow up death forever! **Isaiah 25:8 NLT**

"I was dead, but look! Now I'm alive forever and always. I have the keys of Death and the Grave." **Revelation 1:18 CEB**

He will wipe away every tear from their eyes. There will be no more death or mourning or crying or pain, for the old order of things has passed away. **Revelation 21:4 NIV**

The life of Jesus is bracketed by two impossibilities: "a virgin's womb and an empty tomb." Jesus entered our world through a door marked "No Entrance" and left through a door marked "No Exit." **Peter Larson**

When Jesus was born in Bethlehem it was the dawn of death's destruction. **Jon Bloom**

Death has become like a tyrant who has been completely conquered by the legitimate monarch; bound hand and foot the passers-by sneer at him, hitting him and abusing him, no longer afraid of his cruelty and rage, because of the king who has conquered him. So has death been conquered. **Athanasius of Alexandria**

The death of Christ was the most dreadful blow ever given to the empire of darkness. **William Plumer**

Put Barabbas to death and it ends his revolution. Put Jesus to death and it launches his. **Scott Sauls**

Death stung himself to death when he stung Christ. **William Romaine**

We are told that Christ was killed for us, that His death has washed out our sins, and that by dying He disabled death itself. That is the formula. That is Christianity. That is what has to be believed. **C.S. Lewis**

Jesus didn't escape from death; he conquered it and opened the way to heaven for all who will dare to believe. The truth of this moment, if we let it sweep over us, is stunning. It means Jesus really is who he claimed to be, we are really as lost as he said we are, and he really is the only way for us to intimately and spiritually connect with God again. **Steven James**

Upon a life I did not live, upon a death I did not die; another's life, another's death, I stake my whole eternity. **Horatius Bonar**

If your hope is anchored in Jesus, the worst-case future scenario for you is resurrection and everlasting life. **Scott Sauls**

There was never any other way to escape death than for men to flee to Christ. **John Calvin**

Christ will by his death destroy the power of death, take away the sting of the first death, and prevent the second. **John Wesley**

When we see death, we see disaster. When Jesus sees death, he sees deliverance! **Max Lucado**

All life is a festival since the Son of God has redeemed you from death. **John Chrysostom**

Christ's Impact on World History

Now all glory to God, who is able to make you strong, just as my Good News says. This message about Jesus Christ has revealed his plan for you Gentiles, a plan kept secret from the beginning of time. But now as the prophets foretold and as the eternal God has commanded, this message is made known to all Gentiles everywhere, so that they too might believe and obey him. **Romans 16:25-26 NLT**

I am an historian, I am not a believer, but I must confess as a historian that this penniless preacher from Nazareth is irrevocably the very center of history. Jesus Christ is easily the most dominant figure in all history. **H.G. Wells**

Christus...suffered the extreme penalty during the reign of Tiberius at the hands of one of our procurators, Pontius Pilatus. **Cornelius Tacitus**

His birth and the history of His life; the profundity of His doctrine, which grapples the mightiest difficulties, and which is, of those difficulties, the most admirable solution; His Gospel, His apparition, His empire, His march across the ages and the realms, is for me a prodigy, a mystery insoluble, which plunges me into a reverence which I cannot escape, a mystery which is there before my eyes, a mystery which I cannot deny or explain. **Napoleon Bonaparte**

Comparing Jesus with history's greatest of human leaders is like comparing the sun to a flashlight with no batteries. **Ray Comfort**

In essentials the synoptic gospels agree remarkably well, and form a consistent portrait of Christ. No one reading these scenes can doubt the reality of the figure behind them. That a few simple men should in one generation have invented so powerful and appealing a personality, so lofty an ethic and so inspiring a vision of human brotherhood, would be a miracle far more incredible than any recorded in the Gospels. After two centuries of Higher Criticism the outlines of the life, character, and teachings of Christ, remain reasonably clear, and constitute the most fascinating feature in the history of Western man. **Will Durant**

The historian's test of greatness is not, "What did he accumulate?" It is not,

"What did he build up to tumble down on his head?"—not that at all, but this: Was the world different because he lived? Did he start men to think along fresh lines with a vigor and vitality that persisted after him? By this test Jesus stands first. **H.G. Wells**

All history is incomprehensible without Christ. **Ernest Renan**

Powerful regimes have often tried to establish their importance by dating the calendar around their existence...The idea of Jesus trying to impose a calendar on anyone was laughable...Yet today, every time we glance at a calendar or date a check, we are reminded that chronologically at least, this incredibly brief life has become somehow the dividing line of history. **John Ortberg**

Whatever you may believe about it, the birth of Jesus was so important that it split history into two parts. Everything that has ever happened on this planet falls into a category of before Christ or after Christ. **Philip Yancey**

Nazareth as a town turned its back on the one who would give them their only place in world history. **John Pollock**

Now it is interesting and significant, isn't it, that a historian, setting forth in that spirit, without any theological bias whatsoever, should find that he simply cannot portray the progress of humanity honestly, without giving a foremost place to a penniless teacher of Nazareth of Galilee? **H.G. Wells**

Nothing is more clear than that Christ cannot be explained by any humanistic system. He does not fit into any theory of natural evolution, for in that case the perfect flower of humanity should have appeared at the end of human history and not in the middle of it. **Loraine Boettner**

He stands absolutely alone in history; in teaching, in example, in character, an exception, a marvel, and He is Himself the evidence of Christianity. **A.T. Pierson**

Normally when someone dies, their impact on the world immediately begins to recede...But Jesus inverted this normal human trajectory, as he did so many others. Jesus' impact was greater a hundred years after his death than during his life; it was greater still after five hundred years; after a thousand years his legacy laid the foundation for much of Europe; after two thousand years he has more followers in more places than ever. **John Ortberg**

Certainly, no revolution that has ever taken place in society can be compared to that which has been produced by the words of Jesus Christ. **Mark Hopkins**

Him who, being the holiest among the mighty, and the mightiest among the holy, lifted with His pierced hands empires off their hinges, turned the stream of centuries out of its channels, and still governs the ages. **Jean Paul Richter**

When the drama of history is over, Jesus Christ will stand alone on the stage. All the great figures of history...will realize that they have been but actors in a drama produced by another. **Helmut Thielicke**

Christ's Superiority to Other Religious Leaders

For us, there is one God, the Father, by whom all things were created, and for whom we live. And there is one Lord, Jesus Christ, through whom all things were created, and through whom we live. **1 Corinthians 8:6 NLT**

Christianity is not a religion. Religion is humans trying to work their way to God through good works. Christianity is God coming to men and women through Jesus Christ. **Josh McDowell**

Every other religion in the world is the religion of "do," but...Christianity alone is the religion of "done." **Mark Dever**

Every religion, every program, every self-help book is about steps you have to take. Jesus is the only One who becomes the step—to take you. **Ann Voskamp**

The founders of every major religion said, "I'll show you how to find God." Jesus said, "I am God who has come to find you." **Timothy Keller**

Jesus' outlandish claim to being the only way to God puts Christianity in a class by itself. **Lee Strobel**

The Greek philosophers have compiled many works with persuasiveness and much skill in words; but what fruit have they to show for this such as has the cross of Christ? Their wise thoughts were persuasive enough until they died. **Athanasius of Alexandria**

Superficial minds see a resemblance between Christ and the founders of empires, and the gods of other religions...It is not so. **Napoleon Bonaparte**

I didn't get very far through the New Testament [as a professor at Brigham Young University] before I realized that the Christ in the Bible was not the Christ I knew in Mormonism. And I had sold this Christ short. This one was huge. This was the one that was real. This is the one that I wanted. This is the one that changed my life. **Lynn Wilder**

If you had gone to Buddha and asked him: "Are you the son of Brahma?" he would have said, "My son, you are in the vale of illusion." If you had gone to Socrates and asked, "Are you Zeus?" he would have laughed at you. If you had gone to Mohammed and asked, "Are you Allah?" he would first have rent his clothes and (might) then cut your head off. If you had asked Confucius, "Are you Heaven?" I think he would have probably replied, "Remarks which are not in accordance with nature are in bad taste."

The idea of a great moral teacher saying what Christ said is out of the question. In my opinion, the only person who can say that sort of thing is either God or a complete lunatic suffering from that form of delusion which undermines the whole mind of man. **C.S. Lewis**

Not once does the Quran apply the word *love* to God. Aristotle stated bluntly, "It would be eccentric for anyone to claim that he loved Zeus" or that Zeus loved a human being, for that matter. In dazzling contrast, the Christian Bible affirms that God is love and cites love as the main reason Jesus came to earth: "This is how God showed his love among us: He sent his one and only Son into the world that we might live through him" (1 John 4:9). **Philip Yancey**

So I cast my lot with Him—not the one who claimed wisdom, Confucius; or the one who claimed enlightenment, Buddha; or the one who claimed to be a prophet, Muhammad; but with the one who claimed to be God in human flesh. The one who declared, "Before Abraham was born, I am"—and proved it. **Norman Geisler**

Other religions invite us to worship their gods, allahs, creators, or metaphysical forces, but Christianity invites us to believe in a Son and to enter into an intimate family relationship with a loving Father. **Mary Kassian**

Jesus differs from all other teachers; they reach the ear, but he instructs the heart; they deal with the outward letter, but he imparts an inward taste for the truth. **Charles Spurgeon**

We know that all the various schemes of world reconstruction from the beginning of history to our time have failed. Christ's method of making a better world by making better men alone succeeds. **Max I. Reich**

If you think it takes courage to be with Jesus, consider that it took infinitely more courage for *him* to be with *you*. Only Christianity says one of the attributes of God is courage. No other religion has a God who needed courage. **Timothy Keller**

The other gods were strong, but Thou wast weak;
They rode, but Thou didst stumble to a throne;
But to our wounds only God's wounds can speak,
And not a god has wounds, but Thou alone. **Edward Shillito**

Christianity is the only religion whose God bears the scars of evil. **Os Guinness**

Christ's Kingdom

"Except a man be born again, he cannot see the kingdom of God." **John 3:3 KJV**

To him who loves us and has freed us from our sins by his blood, and has made us to be a kingdom and priests to serve his God and Father—to him be glory and power for ever and ever! Amen. **Revelation 1:5-6 NIV**

He has rescued us from the dominion of darkness and brought us into the kingdom of the Son he loves. **Colossians 1:13 NIV**

The seventh angel sounded his trumpet, and there were loud voices in heaven, which said: "The kingdom of the world has become the kingdom of our Lord and of his Messiah, and he will reign for ever and ever." **Revelation 11:15-17 NIV**

"My Kingdom is not an earthly kingdom. If it were, my followers would fight to keep me from being handed over to the Jewish leaders. But my Kingdom is not of this world." **John 18:36 NLT**

When Jesus said his kingdom isn't an earthly kingdom, he didn't mean his Kingdom wouldn't be *on* this Earth after it's transformed. He meant it isn't *of* this

Earth as it is now, under the curse. Although Christ's Kingdom isn't *from* the Earth, it extends *to* the Earth, and one day will be centered *on* the Earth. Christ's Kingdom touches this world now through his indwelling Spirit, the presence of the church, and his providential reign. **Randy Alcorn**

Those who would pretend to enforce the kingdom with tanks or guns or laws or edicts do not understand the nature of the kingdom Jesus preached. **Russell Moore**

It's hard to remember that Jesus did not come to make us safe, but rather to make us disciples, citizens of God's new age, a kingdom of surprise. **Jean Vanier**

Jesus made clear that the Kingdom of God is organic and not organizational. It grows like a seed and it works like leaven: secretly, invisibly, surprisingly, and irresistibly. **Os Guinness**

Christ is building His kingdom with earth's broken things. Men want only the strong, the successful, the victorious, the unbroken, in building their kingdoms; but God is the God of the unsuccessful, of those who have failed...He can lift earth's saddest failure up to heaven's glory. **J.R. Miller**

God's kingdom is built not on perpetual motion, one-liners, and flashbulbs but on Christ. **Carl F.H. Henry**

Consider this prophetic statement: "The kingdom of the world has become the kingdom of our Lord and of his Christ, and he will reign for ever and ever" (Revelation 11:15)...God won't obliterate earthly kingdoms but will *transform them into his own.* And it's that new earthly kingdom (joined then to God's heavenly Kingdom) over which "he will reign for ever and ever." **Randy Alcorn**

One day America and all its presidents will be a footnote in history, but the kingdom of Jesus will never end. **John Piper**

We need to think bigger, seeing Jesus as not just our personal Redeemer, but as the Redeemer of our families, our cities, our culture, and ultimately even the whole earth. That's the promise of the Gospel of the Kingdom. **Randy Alcorn**

Can you imagine living in a society where everyone is so happy with leadership decisions, they rejoice and celebrate? Can you imagine a world where no one ever again complains about government? Yes, it's possible! It's predicted. It's prepared. It's the kingdom of heaven. And it's real! **Larry Dick**

Christ's Church: His Body and Bride

Now you are the body of Christ, and individual members of it.
1 Corinthians 12:27 CSB

Husbands, love your wives, as Christ loved the church and gave himself up for her, that he might sanctify her, having cleansed her by the washing of water with the word, so that he might present the church to himself in splendor, without spot or wrinkle or any such thing, that she might be holy and without blemish.
Ephesians 5:25-27 ESV

Let us rejoice and exult and give him the glory, for the marriage of the Lamb has come, and his Bride has made herself ready. **Revelation 19:7 ESV**

> If you want to understand how committed Jesus is to the church, here's your answer. He doesn't just create it and let it be. He marries it...Church is not his hobby; it is his marriage. **Sam Allberry**

Jesus calls the church his bride. He died for her, and says that ultimately the gates of hell won't prevail against her. If you say you love Jesus but you don't want to be around the church, you're saying to Jesus, "I love you, but I can't stand your bride." If you said that to me, I'd say, "If you don't care for my wife, you and I won't have a relationship either." **Randy Alcorn**

He cannot possess the robe of Christ who rends and divides the Church of Christ. **Cyprian**

Christ is our temple, in which by faith all believers meet. **Matthew Henry**

The Church is not made up of whole people, rather of the broken people who find wholeness in a Christ who was broken for us. **Mike Yaconelli**

I saw that the church wasn't a museum for good people; it was a hospital for the broken. Jesus wasn't trying to create a place to show off his shiny employees; he wanted a place where his children could be healed. **Jefferson Bethke**

What if our churches weren't divided up by the same economic and racial and political and generational categories that would bind us together even if Jesus were not alive? What would it mean, in your church, if a minimum-wage janitor were mentoring the multimillionaire executive of the restaurant where he cleans toilets, because the janitor/mentor has the spiritual wisdom his boss/protégé needs? It would look awfully strange, but it would look no stranger than a crucified Nazarene governing the universe. **Russell Moore**

God created Adam and Eve to be king and queen over the earth, to rule the earth in righteousness, to the glory of God. They failed. Jesus Christ is the second and last Adam, and the church is his bride, the second Eve. Christ is the eternal King, the church his queen. Christ—with his beloved people as his bride and co-rulers—will accomplish on the New Earth what was entrusted to Adam and Eve on the old Earth. **Randy Alcorn**

Christ's Preeminence in Scripture

Beginning with Moses and all the Prophets, he interpreted for them the things concerning himself in all the Scriptures. **Luke 24:27 CSB**

The Bible is the cradle wherein Christ is laid. **Martin Luther**

Take Jesus out of the Bible—and it is like taking calcium out of lime, carbon out of diamonds, truth out of history, matter out of physics, mind out of metaphysics, numbers out of mathematics, cause and effect out of philosophy. Through this book the name of Jesus, the Revealed, the Redeeming, the Risen, the Reigning, the Returning Lord, runs like a line of glimmering light. The thought of Jesus, the Desire of all nations, threads this great book like a crystal river winds its way through a continent. **Robert G. Lee**

Take away the personal Christ from the gospels, leaving the same precepts and doctrines, and the whole aspect of Christianity would change, as the aspect of the earth changes when the sun goes down. The same eternal mountains lift their heads to heaven; the same rivers flow onward. But their animation is gone; they are cold, and gray, and dark. Thus would Christianity be without that central personage, around which all its glories cluster—from which they stream. **E.H. Chapin**

The Old Testament serves to point out our cavernous need for a better law keeper, a better judge, a better prophet, a better priest, a better king. On the Emmaus road Jesus must have looked at Cleopus and his companion in the eyes that day, and said, "That's me. I'm the one the whole of the Old Testament points to." **Nancy Guthrie**

It is impossible to revere the Scriptures more deeply or affirm them more completely than Jesus did. **Kevin DeYoung**

The temptation and baptism before Jesus's ministry warp into moralistic tales unless one relates these stories to Israel's past. The Sermon on the Mount is a beehive of misunderstanding unless one sees Jesus as the true and better Moses, David, and Solomon. And Jesus's death is merely a tragedy unless one sees that he fulfills all the Scriptures. **Patrick Schreiner**

If you wish to know God, you must know His Word. **Charles Spurgeon**

The New Testament completes the picture of Jesus Christ that was introduced in the prophecies, foreshadowings, and images of the Old Testament. Biblical terms like *Messiah, redeemer, shepherd, son of man* and *son of David* originate in the Old Testament and find their ultimate significance in the New Testament. The story begun in the Hebrew Bible is completed in the Greek New Testament. ***The Knowing Jesus Study Bible***

If you want to interpret Scripture well and confidently, set Christ before you, for He is the man to whom it all applies, every bit of it. **Martin Luther**

The Bible is the story of two gardens: Eden and Gethsemane. In the first, Adam took a fall. In the second, Jesus took a stand. In the first, God sought Adam. In the second, Jesus sought God. In Eden, Adam hid from God. In Gethsemane, Jesus emerged from the tomb. In Eden, Satan led Adam to a tree that led to his death. From Gethsemane, Jesus went to a tree that led to our life. **Max Lucado**

We know life, death, only through Jesus Christ. Except by Jesus Christ we know not what life is, what our death is, what God is, what we ourselves are. Thus, without Scripture, which has only Jesus Christ for its object, we know nothing, and we see not only obscurity and confusion in the nature of God, but in nature herself. **Blaise Pascal**

When the Bible says that Christ is God, it does not ask us to forget a single thing that it has said about the stupendous majesty of God. No, it asks us to remember every one of those things in order that we may apply them all to Jesus Christ. **J. Gresham Machen**

Christ is the Bible's fullness, the Bible's center, the Bible's fascination... The name of Jesus, the Supreme Personality, the center of a world's desire, is on every page—in expression, or symbol, or prophecy, or psalm, or proverb. **Robert G. Lee**

The Bible is one book, written by one Author, with one subject: Jesus Christ and the salvation God…provides through Him. **Alistair Begg**

Jesus loves me, this I know,
For the Bible tells me so;
Little ones to Him belong,
They are weak, but He is strong.
Yes, Jesus loves me,
Yes, Jesus loves me,
Yes, Jesus loves me,
The Bible tells me so. **Anne Bartlett Warner**

Christ's Misrepresentation by False Teachers

"Beware of false prophets who come disguised as harmless sheep but are really vicious wolves. You can identify them by their fruit, that is, by the way they act." **Matthew 7:15-16 NLT**

"False messiahs and false prophets will appear and perform great signs and wonders to deceive, if possible, even the elect." **Matthew 24:24 NIV**

"Keep watch over yourselves and all the flock of which the Holy Spirit has made you overseers. Be shepherds of the church of God, which he bought with his own blood. I know that after I leave, savage wolves will come in among you and will not spare the flock. Even from your own number men will arise and distort the truth in order to draw away disciples after them." **Acts 20:28-30 NIV**

It's rare for someone in church to openly deny Jesus. Movement away from the centrality of Christ is subtle. The false teacher will speak about how other people can help change your life, but if you listen carefully to what he is saying, you will see that Jesus Christ is not essential to his message. **Colin Smith**

Throughout the New Testament, the Apostles sought to fight false teaching and heresy. In fact, in nearly every letter, some false teaching or heresy is exposed and dealt with. For example, 1 Corinthians deals with teachers who denied the bodily resurrection of Jesus. Galatians argues against those who said that justification is by Jesus plus becoming a Jew, not faith alone in Jesus alone. In Colossians, Paul warns against a strange Jewish-mystical teaching that seemed to combine Jewish dietary laws with esoteric Greek philosophy. First John confronts many who denied that Jesus, the Son of God, came in a human body. **Sean Michael Lewis**

Whenever people are about to stab Christianity they often profess a great reverence for it. Beware of the sleek-faced hypocrisy that is the armorbearer of heresy and infidelity. **Charles Spurgeon**

Jesus warns us that false teachers will come from outside the community of believers, trying to hide their true intentions (Matt. 7:15-20). Peter tells us that false teachers can also arise from within the community of believers, bringing doctrine that is destructive and poisonous (2 Peter 2:1)...Simply put, false teaching is not just a problem for other people and churches out there; it is a problem about which all believers must be vigilant and against which they must be on guard. **Fred Greco**

Evangelical Christianity is often hesitant to confront false teachers with the seriousness and severity that Jesus and the apostles did. **John MacArthur**

...the true teacher asks, "What has God said in his Word?" The false teacher asks, "What do people want to hear? What will appeal to their flesh?" **Colin Smith**

PART 3:

The Names and Titles of Jesus

In these days we call children by the names, perhaps, of father or mother or some respected relative, but there is no special meaning, as a general rule, in our children's names. It was not so in the olden times. Then names meant something. Scriptural names, as a general rule, contain teaching, and especially is this the case in every name ascribed to the Lord Jesus. With him names indicate things. "His name shall be called Wonderful, Counsellor, the Mighty God, the everlasting Father, the Prince of Peace," because he really is all these. His name is called Jesus, but not without a reason. By any other name Jesus would not be so sweet, because no other name could fairly describe his great work of saving his people from their sins. When he is said to be called this or that, it means that he really is so.

Charles Spurgeon

The name *Jesus* comes from the transliteration of the Greek *IESOUS* (pronounced ee-ay-soos; there is no *J* in Greek) from the Hebrew name *Yeshua*, which means "Yahweh saves."

No matter how it is spelled or pronounced—whether Yeshua, Yēsū, Jesus, or something else—we are told that his name is above all names, and that one day every knee in the universe will bow to him (Philippians 2:9-10). Some will bow in humble adoring worship; others will bow with unrepentant hearts, subject to the King they have never recognized and do not want to know.

Christ is not his last name. (His stepfather's name was not Joseph Christ nor was his mother Mary Christ!) Christ is actually a title that means "anointed one," or "Messiah."

Jesus has many other names and titles. Each reveals something important about him. He is Immanuel, "God with us." He is our Savior, Redeemer, Creator, King of kings, and Lord of lords. He is the second person of the triune God, the Son of God and Son of Man, our Messiah, Judge, Advocate, High Priest, Mediator, Brother, and—incredibly—he calls himself our Friend! He is the Lamb of God, the Light of the World, our Good Shepherd, our Bridegroom, and our example. He is not *a* way, *a* truth and *a* life; he is *the* Way, *the* Truth and *the* Life, the only means of access to the Father and to Heaven, his dwelling place. He is the Bread of Life, the Living Water, the Rest-Giver, Word of God, and Prince of Peace.

We could spend eternity contemplating the meaning and implications and depths of these names and titles, and indeed we will! Wherever we go and whatever we do as resurrected beings walking on God's resurrected New Earth, we will never lose sight of Jesus. We will see the very face of God (Revelation 22:4). The conversations we have with brothers and sisters in Christ, the journeys and adventures we undertake, and the missions the Lord Jesus sends us on will all be centered on our desire to know and glorify and serve him.

But we don't have to wait until then to focus on knowing Jesus. If we had met Paul 2,000 years ago during his first Roman imprisonment and asked him, "How long have you known Jesus?," he might have replied, "I met him on the Damascus Road thirty years ago, but I am still getting to know him, and I will continue to know him better until I die, and forever afterward!" In Philippians 3:10, Paul declared his heart's desire: "I want to know Christ."

Though Paul knew Jesus thirty years later much better than at his conversion, he had barely scratched the surface of who Jesus is. It was the tip of an infinitely large iceberg. Now that I have known Jesus fifty years, I too "want to know Christ"! I thank God that today I don't just know and love Jesus as much as I used to; I know and love him more. That is to his credit, and I'm deeply grateful. He's what makes life exciting and worthwhile.

Jesus himself prayed, "Now this is eternal life: that they know you, the only true God, and Jesus Christ, whom you have sent" (John 17:3). Because our eternal life is wrapped up in knowing God through Jesus Christ, we are well-advised to *truly* know him!

One of many startling statements about Jesus is this: "No one has ever seen God; the only God, who is at the Father's side, he has made him known" (John 1:18 ESV). So Jesus is God and is at the Father's side, and he has come to make God known to us. Provided what we learn is true, the more we learn about Jesus, the more we know about the God that no one has seen, but in another sense can be truly seen in Jesus. He is the explanation and illustration of *who God really is.*

There is much to know about Jesus, but Scripture puts particular stress on grasping his love for us: "[I pray] that you, being rooted and grounded in love, may have strength to comprehend with all the saints what is the breadth and length and height and depth, and to know the love of Christ that surpasses knowledge, that you may be filled with all the fullness of God" (Ephesians 3:17-19 ESV).

As the hymn "Be Thou My Vision" puts so beautifully, Jesus is our "best thought, by day or by night." This book *It's All About Jesus* will succeed to the degree that it encourages you to better know and love Jesus and focus your heart and mind on him. May your worship be full and deep as you contemplate these names and titles of our Savior!

Jesus: Name Above All Names

Therefore God exalted him to the highest place and gave him the name that is above every name, that at the name of Jesus every knee should bow, in heaven and on earth and under the earth, and every tongue acknowledge that Jesus Christ is Lord, to the glory of God the Father. **Philippians 2:9-11 NIV**

You will conceive and give birth to a son, and you will name him Jesus. **Luke 1:31 NLT**

My favorite line of all: "you are to give him the name Jesus" (Luke 1:31). Do you realize this was the first proclamation of our Savior's personal name since the beginning of time? Jesus...A name by which I've made every single prayerful petition of my life. A name that has meant my absolute salvation, not only from eternal destruction, but from myself. A name with power like no other name. Jesus. **Beth Moore**

How sweet the name of Jesus sounds
In a believer's ear!
It soothes his sorrows, heals his wounds,
And drives away his fears. **John Newton**

It is in Jesus' name that desperate people pray, grateful people worship, and angry people swear. From christenings to weddings to sick-rooms to funerals, it is in Jesus' name that people are hatched, matched, patched, and dispatched. From the Dark Ages to postmodernity, he is the man who won't go away. **John Ortberg**

Out of all our Savior's names, there is not one which rings with such sweet music as this blessed name, "Jesus." I suppose the reason of this is that it answers to our own name, the name of sinner. **Charles Spurgeon**

Jesus! the name that charms our fears,
that bids our sorrows cease;
'tis music in the sinner's ears,
'tis life, and health, and peace. **Charles Wesley**

I have heard of ministers who can preach a sermon without mentioning the name of Jesus from beginning to end. If you ever hear such a sermon as that, mind that you never hear another from that man. **Charles Spurgeon**

What a beautiful name. I love to watch how it falls off the lips of those who love Him. I shudder as it falls off the lips of those who don't. Jesus. **Beth Moore**

For many the name of Jesus brings extraordinary comfort and hope. But others use his name to express anger, amazement or disgust; to them it is no more than a convenient expletive. The Name that is like no other stirs conflicting emotions in those who hear it, because Jesus is more than just a religious leader and teacher. He is more than simply a figure in world history. He is more than merely a moral influence. Jesus Christ is the Son of God. ***The Knowing Jesus Study Bible***

Jesus, whose name is not so much written as ploughed into the history of this world. **Ralph Waldo Emerson**

How sweet the Name of Jesus...
Dear Name, the Rock on which I build,
My Shield and Hiding Place,
My never failing treasury, filled
With boundless stores of grace!
John Newton

It is not merely in the name of a great teacher, not even the greatest teacher who ever lived, that Justinian built Hagia Sophia in Constantinople or Johann Sebastian Bach composed the Mass in B-Minor. There are no cathedrals in honor of Socrates. **Jaroslav Pelikan**

We write Jesus' name upon our banner, for it is hell's terror, heaven's delight and earth's hope. **Charles Spurgeon**

Tomorrow's history has already been written—at the name of Jesus every knee must bow. **Paul E. Kauffman**

Immanuel: "God with Us"

The Lord himself will give you a sign. Behold, the virgin shall conceive and bear a son, and shall call his name Immanuel. **Isaiah 7:14 ESV**

All this took place to fulfill what the Lord had spoken by the prophet: "Behold, the virgin shall conceive and bear a son, and they shall call his name Immanuel" (which means, God with us). **Matthew 1:22-23 ESV**

The implications of the name *Immanuel* are both comforting and unsettling. It is one thing to claim that God looks down upon us, from a safe distance, and speaks to us...But to say that He is right here, is to put ourselves and Him in a totally new situation. He is no longer the calm and benevolent observer in the sky, the kindly old caricature with the beard. His image becomes that of Jesus, who wept and laughed, who fasted and feasted, and who, above all, was fully present to those He loved. He was there with them. He is here with us. **Michael Card**

Christ, by highest heaven adored,
Christ, the everlasting Lord!
Late in time behold Him come,
Offspring of a virgin's womb.
Veiled in flesh the Godhead see,

Hail the incarnate Deity,
Pleased as man with man to dwell;
Jesus, our Emmanuel. **Charles Wesley**

"Immanuel, God with us." Satan trembles at the sound of it..."God with us" is eternity's sonnet, heaven's hallelujah, the shout of the glorified, the song of the redeemed, the chorus of the angels, the everlasting oratorio of the great orchestra of the sky. **Charles Spurgeon**

Oh holy Child of Bethlehem,
Descend to us, we pray;
Cast out our sin, and enter in;
Be born in us today.
We hear the Christmas angels
The great glad tidings tell;
O come to us, abide with us,
Our Lord Immanuel. **Phillips Brooks**

When Jesus ascended to Heaven in his resurrected body, he demonstrated that the Incarnation wasn't temporary. The New Earth will be Heaven incarnate, just as Jesus Christ, our Immanuel, is forever God incarnate who will happily live in our midst. **Randy Alcorn**

Someday God's chosen people will gather under the banner of Jesus the Messiah...Immanuel, "God with us," will reign over the nations, and his banner of love and grace will be unfurled and soar in triumph forever (Matthew 1:23). ***The Knowing Jesus Study Bible***

Redeemer

"Blessed be the Lord God of Israel, for he has visited us and accomplished redemption for his people." **Luke 1:68 ESV**

All have sinned and fall short of the glory of God, being justified as a gift by His grace through the redemption which is in Christ Jesus. **Romans 3:23-24 NASB**

In him we have redemption through his blood, the forgiveness of our trespasses, according to the riches of his grace. **Ephesians 1:7 ESV**

Christ redeemed us from the curse of the Law, having become a curse for us—for it is written, "cursed is everyone who hangs on a tree"—in order that in Christ Jesus the blessing of Abraham might come to the Gentiles, so that we would receive the promise of the Spirit through faith. **Galatians 3:13-14 NASB**

God undertook the most dramatic rescue operation in cosmic history. He determined to save the human race from self-destruction, and He sent His Son Jesus Christ to salvage and redeem them. **Billy Graham**

There was nothing that so annoyed people about the Lord Jesus Christ as when he said that he had come to seek and to save them. **Martyn Lloyd-Jones**

Leviticus 27 reminds us that there is always a price to pay when buying back someone or something...Jesus referred to his death as a "ransom for many" (Mark 10:45), and God reminds us throughout the New Testament that Jesus died as a payment for our sin. ***The Knowing Jesus Study Bible***

Jesus did not die to increase our self-esteem. Rather, Jesus died to bring glory to the Father by redeeming people from the curse of sin. **Edward Welch**

Because an eternal, unchangeable sentence of condemnation has passed upon sin—for God cannot and will not regard sin with favor, but his wrath abides upon it eternally and irrevocably—redemption was not possible without a ransom of such precious worth as to atone for sin, to assume the guilt, pay the price of wrath and thus abolish sin. This no creature was able to do. There was no remedy except for God's only Son to step into our distress and himself become man, to take upon himself the load of awful and eternal wrath and make his own body and blood a sacrifice for sin. **Martin Luther**

Sins that you thought were absolved by religion will always come back to haunt you. Only the Redeemer and Savior, Jesus Christ, can forgive and pardon and free from guilt—and the sins He has forgiven will never come back to haunt you as a child of God—never while the world stands! **A.W. Tozer**

Luther taught that every time you insist that I am a sinner, just so often do you call me to remember the benefit of Christ my Redeemer, upon whose shoulders, and not upon mine, lie all my sins. So, when you say that I am a sinner, you do not terrify, but comfort me immeasurably. **Thomas Oden**

> Jesus came because there is something broken inside us that can only be, will only be fixed by his person, presence, and redeeming work. **Paul David Tripp**

You couldn't make up a better story than God's unfolding drama of redemption. You can't find a greater hero than Jesus. **Randy Alcorn**

Jesus endured great pain, pain I can only imagine. But his pain was for a purpose—the redemption of the world. He did it on my behalf—and yours. **Trillia Newbell**

Redemption in Jesus Christ reaches just as far as the fall. The horizon of creation is at the same time the horizon of sin and of salvation. To conceive of either the fall or Christ's deliverance as encompassing less than the whole of creation is to compromise the biblical teaching of the radical nature of the fall and the cosmic scope of redemption. **Albert Wolters**

The total work of Christ is nothing less than to redeem this entire creation from the effects of sin. That purpose will not be accomplished until God has ushered in the new earth, until Paradise Lost has become Paradise Regained. **Anthony Hoekema**

Jesus has redeemed not only our souls, but our bodies. When the Lord shall deliver His captive people out of the land of the enemy He will not leave a bone of one of them in the adversary's power. The dominion of death shall be utterly broken. **Charles Spurgeon**

We were made for a better place and for a better person, and all the beauties of this world whisper that to our soul. We crave Christ. He has made this restoration possible and offers Himself to mankind as Savior, Redeemer, and Restorer. **Steve DeWitt**

King of Kings

Kingship belongs to the Lord, and he rules over the nations. **Psalm 22:28 ESV**

Rejoice greatly...See, your king comes to you, righteous and victorious, lowly and riding on a donkey, on a colt, the foal of a donkey...He will proclaim peace to the nations. His rule will extend from sea to sea and from the River to the ends of the earth. **Zechariah 9:9-10 NIV**

Jesus answered, "You say that I am a king. In fact, the reason I was born and came into the world is to testify to the truth." **John 18:37 NIV**

They will make war on the Lamb, and the Lamb will conquer them, for he is Lord of lords and King of kings, and those with him are called and chosen and faithful. **Revelation 17:14 ESV**

The Lord who vacated his tomb has not vacated his throne.
G.R. Beasley-Murray

Whenever Christ is enthroned as King, the kingdom of God is come, so that, while we cannot say that He is ruling over all in the world at the present time, He is certainly ruling in that way in the hearts and lives of all His people. **Martyn Lloyd-Jones**

Rejoice, the Lord is King:
Your Lord and King adore!
Rejoice, give thanks, and sing,
And triumph evermore. **Charles Wesley**

Crown Him with many crowns,
The Lamb upon His throne.
Hark! how the heavenly anthem drowns
All music but its own.
Awake, my soul, and sing
Of Him who died for thee,
And hail Him as thy matchless king
Through all eternity. **Matthew Bridges, Godfrey Thring**

That's the kind of king Jesus is—the kind of king who willingly walks into the wilderness to face down the Devil so that sinners like us can receive grace for all the ways that we've rebelled against God and chased after our temptations. **Trevor Laurence**

Death may be the King of terrors…but Jesus is the King of Kings! **Dwight L. Moody**

Crown the Savior, angels, crown him;
Rich the trophies Jesus brings;
In the seat of power enthrone him,
Whilst the vault of heaven rings.
Crown him! Crown him!
Crown the Savior King of kings! **Thomas Kelly**

Such as will not have Christ to be their King to rule over them shall never have his blood to save them. **Thomas Watson**

There's a throne in each life big enough for only one. Christ may be on that throne. Money may be on that throne. But both cannot occupy it. **Randy Alcorn**

If we come to God, it will be through one Jewish mediator-king, or it will not be at all. **Russell Moore**

Jesus was never against politics. He just wants us to recognize that there is a greater power above. We must all recognize there is a King of kings and a Lord of lords, Jesus Christ, who is above every political system. **Frederick Chiluba**

To meet an earthly king would be the ultimate experience. How much greater will it be to see King Jesus in his glory? There's no higher privilege, no greater thrill. **Randy Alcorn**

Isaiah described a king who would rule in splendor over the whole world—One who would be majestic and victorious beyond any of the historic kings of Israel and Judah. Isaiah described the glory and magnitude of this king's reign much as John depicted the glory of the new Jerusalem in Revelation 21:16-17. ***The Knowing Jesus Study Bible***

The King stepped from the great city, just outside the gate, and put his hand on my shoulder. I was aware of no one and nothing but him. I saw before me an aged, weathered King, thoughtful guardian of an empire. But I also saw a virile Warrior-Prince primed for battle, eager to mount his steed and march in conquest. His eyes were keen as sharpened swords yet deep as wells, full of the memories of the old and the dreams of the young. **Randy Alcorn**

We live in the kingdom of grace, where Christ rules by faith, but we wait for the kingdom of glory, when Christ will reign supreme over all. **Philip Graham Ryken**

Judge

"Not even the Father judges anyone, but He has given all judgment to the Son." **John 5:22 NASB**

"He gave Him authority to execute judgment, because He is the Son of Man." **John 5:27 NASB**

"He ordered us to preach to the people, and solemnly to testify that this is the One who has been appointed by God as Judge of the living and the dead." **Acts 10:42 NASB**

"He has fixed a day in which He will judge the world in righteousness through a Man whom He has appointed, having furnished proof to all men by raising Him from the dead." **Acts 17:31 NASB**

> We must all appear before the judgment seat of Christ, so that each one may be recompensed for his deeds in the body, according to what he has done, whether good or bad. **2 Corinthians 5:10 NASB**

Jesus is not only the merciful and ministering shepherd but the shepherd-judge. **Patrick Schreiner**

The meek and mild Jesus of progressive "tolerance" that so many of our contemporaries have come to prefer was nowhere to be found when he made a mess of the money-changers. **Jonathan Parnell**

Not only will Jesus be the judge, but the criterion of judgment will be men's attitude to him as shown in their treatment of his "brethren" or their response to his word. Those who have acknowledged him before men he will acknowledge before his Father: those who have denied him, he will deny. Indeed, for a man to be excluded from heaven on the last day, it will be enough for Jesus to say, "I never knew you." **John Stott**

Had Christ not gone to the cross, we would have borne the judgment for all our sins. Since he did go to the cross, the greatest sin is to choose not to trust him for his redemptive work. **Randy Alcorn**

God in his infinite mercy has devised a way by which justice can be satisfied, and yet mercy can be triumphant. Jesus Christ...offered unto Divine Justice that which was accepted as an equivalent for the punishment due to all his people. **Charles Spurgeon**

How much weightier our witness would be if we remembered to thunder God's justice, while always following with God's welcome, through the vision of a God who in the crucified Christ is both just and the justifier of the one who has faith in Jesus (Rom. 3:26). **Russell Moore**

The teaching of Christ on judgment is thus not an appendix to the good news of the gospel, an afterthought, but (strangely perhaps) it is part of the very texture of the good news. **Paul Helm**

Son of God

The angel answered, "The Holy Spirit will come on you, and the power of the Most High will overshadow you. So the holy one to be born will be called the Son of God." **Luke 1:35 NIV**

The reason the Son of God appeared was to destroy the works of the devil. **1 John 3:8 ESV**

The fact that the infinite, omnipotent, eternal Son of God could become man and join himself to a human nature forever, so that infinite God became one person with finite man, will remain for eternity the most profound miracle and the most profound mystery in all the universe. **Wayne Grudem**

Silent night! holy night!
Son of God, love's pure light.

Radiant beams from Thy holy face,
With the dawn of redeeming grace,
Jesus, Lord, at Thy birth. **Joseph Mohr**

Though the Son of God was incorporeal, he formed for himself a body like ours. He appeared as one of the sheep, yet he remained the Shepherd. He was esteemed a servant, yet he did not renounce being a Son. He was carried about in the womb of Mary, yet he was clothed in the nature of his Father. He walked on the earth, yet he filled heaven...He was standing before Pilate, and at the same time he was sitting with his Father. He was nailed on a tree, yet he was the Lord of all things. **Melito of Sardis**

God became man; the divine Son became a Jew; the Almighty appeared on earth as a helpless human baby, unable to do more than lie and stare and wriggle and make noises...And there was no illusion or deception in this: the babyhood of the Son of God was a reality. The more you think about it, the more staggering it gets. **J.I. Packer**

The baby of Bethlehem was Creator of the universe, pitching his tent on the humble camping ground of our little planet. God's glory now dwelt in Christ. He was the Holy of Holies. People had only to look at Jesus to see God, his permanent manifestation. **Randy Alcorn**

The beloved Son of God is the Father's most precious treasure, in which God's infinite riches, and infinite happiness and joy, from eternity to eternity, does consist. **Jonathan Edwards**

How can God be the eternal FATHER (not just God) without having an eternal Son? **M.R. DeHaan**

We believe...in one Lord Jesus Christ, the only-begotten Son of God, begotten of the Father before all the ages, Light of Light, true God of True God, begotten not made, of one substance with the Father, through whom all things were made; who for us men and for our salvation came down from the heavens, and was made flesh of the Holy Spirit and the Virgin Mary, and became a man, and was crucified for us under Pontius Pilate, and suffered and was buried, and rose again on the third day according to the Scriptures, and ascended in to the heavens, and sat down on the right hand of the Father, and will come again with glory to judge living and dead, of whose kingdom there shall be no end. **Nicene Creed**

> If the crucified Son of God is not at the very center of everything you believe about God, your theology has lost its balance, its anchor, and its meaning. **Marshall Segal**

Second Member of the Triune God

"Hear, O Israel: The LORD our God, the LORD is one." **Deuteronomy 6:4 ESV**

"I and the Father are one." The Jews picked up stones again to stone him. Jesus answered them, "I have shown you many good works from the Father; for which of them are you going to stone me?" The Jews answered him, "It is not for a good work that we are going to stone you but for blasphemy, because you, being a man, make yourself God." **John 10:30-33 ESV**

"Even though you do not believe me, believe the works, that you may know and understand that the Father is in me and I am in the Father." **John 10:38 ESV**

There is but one God, the Father, from whom all things came and for whom we live; and there is but one Lord, Jesus Christ, through whom all things came and through whom we live. **1 Corinthians 8:6 NIV**

The grace of the Lord Jesus Christ and the love of God and the fellowship of the Holy Spirit be with you all. **2 Corinthians 13:14 ESV**

Not all of the mystery of the Godhead can be known by man, but just as certainly, all that man can know of God in this life is revealed in Jesus Christ. **A.W. Tozer**

Some doctrines are deadly: those that alter the Deity of Christ, redefine the Trinity—or even deny the Trinity. Sometimes a charmer will lead the susceptible off into error that results in physical death—Jonestown and Waco come to mind. We must sharpen our awareness and be alert—not just for ourselves but for our loved ones who might otherwise be drawn to a false prophet. **Adrian Rogers**

The cross gives finite human beings a small taste of what it is like to be a member of the Trinity. In the moment of His sacrificial death, Jesus gave to us what He had given to the Father for all eternity: *everything*—the total surrender of self. **Steve DeWitt**

The Trinity had planned it. The Son had endured it. The Spirit enabled Him. The Father rejected the Son whom He loved. Jesus, the God-man from Nazareth, perished. The Father accepted His sacrifice for sin and was satisfied. The Rescue was accomplished. **Joni Eareckson Tada**

I Am

God said to Moses, "I AM WHO I AM." And he said, "Say this to the people of Israel: 'I AM has sent me to you.'" **Exodus 3:14 ESV**

"Father, glorify me in your own presence with the glory that I had with you before the world existed." **John 17:5 ESV**

Jesus answered, "...Your father Abraham rejoiced that he would see my day. He saw it and was glad." So the Jews said to him, "You are not yet fifty years old, and have you seen Abraham?" Jesus said to them, "Truly, truly, I say to you, before

Abraham was, I am." So they picked up stones to throw at him, but Jesus hid himself and went out of the temple. **John 8:54-59 ESV**

Jesus' declaration "Before Abraham was born, I am" (John 8:58) was a direct claim to be Yahweh, the God whose name is "I AM WHO I AM" (Exodus 3:14). We know those who heard him understood exactly what he was claiming, because "they picked up stones to stone him" (John 8:59). Blasphemy was a crime, and what Jesus said was blasphemy—unless, of course, it was true. **Randy Alcorn**

God's name, *Yahweh*, comes from the Hebrew verb *hayah*, meaning "to be." The name reminds us that God simply is—further description should be necessary. He is the God who transcends time so that past, present and future become irrelevant; he is eternal and unchanging. In many of our English Bibles his name is rendered as "LORD." It is the most sacred name for God; to this day it is not spoken aloud by Jewish people for fear of misusing God's name (see Exodus 20:7). When Jesus was on earth, he applied this most sacred name of God to himself. In this way he implicitly claimed to be the God who exists, eternal and unchanging. ***The Knowing Jesus Study Bible***

There is no clearer indication of Jesus' divine character in all the Gospel tradition than this. Jesus bears the divine name "I AM." The Scripture that underlies Jesus' claim is probably Exodus 3:14 where God tells Moses his name as "I am the I am" which is rendered in the Septuagint as ἐγὼ εἰμί ὁ ὢν "I am the one being." The meaning is, "I eternally was, I am now, and I will ever continue to be." **Leon Morris**

When Jesus said to "the Jews," "before Abraham was born, I am," he was identifying himself with God. Perhaps Jesus was also implying that Abraham, great though he was, had lived and died, but that he, Jesus, because he is one with God, remains forever as the "I am." **C.J. Kruse**

The Jews had committed the error of ascribing to Jesus a merely temporal existence. They saw only the historical *manifestation*, not the eternal *Person*; only the human, not the divine. Jesus, therefore, reaffirms his eternal, timeless, absolute essence...

Over against Abraham's fleeting span of life Jesus places his own timeless presence...He is therefore exalted infinitely above Abraham...The "I am" here (8:58) reminds one of the "I am" in 8:24. Basically the same thought is expressed in both passages; namely, that Jesus is God! **William Hendriksen**

The question of the Jews rests on a correct conclusion, namely that if Abraham actually saw the day of Jesus, Jesus must have seen Abraham. Does Jesus actually mean to say that he is so old? Not only does Jesus affirm what the question of the Jews asks, with the solemn formula of verity and authority he affirms vastly more. *Amen, amen, I say to you, before Abraham came to be, I am...*

What Jesus declares is that, although his earthly life covers less than fifty years, his existence as a person is constant and independent of any beginning in time...

Thus with the simplest words Jesus testifies to the divine, eternal pre-existence of his person. **R.C.H. Lenski**

Creator

All things were made through him, and without him nothing was made that was made. In him was life, and the life was the light of men. **John 1:3-4 ESV**

He was in the world, and the world was made through Him, and the world did not know Him. **John 1:10 NASB**

> By [Jesus] all things were created, things in heaven and on earth, visible and invisible, whether thrones or domimions or rulers or authorities—all things were created through him and for him. And he is before all things, and in him all things hold together. **Colossians 1:16-17 ESV**

About the Son he says, "Your throne, O God, will last for ever and ever; a scepter of justice will be the scepter of your kingdom."...He also says, "In the beginning, Lord, you laid the foundations of the earth, and the heavens are the work of your hands. They will perish, but you remain; they will all wear out like a garment. **Hebrews 1:8, 10-11 NIV**

Scripture identifies the pre-existent Jesus Christ as involved in the work of creation, and relates this to his work in redemption, by which a new creation is brought out of the ruins of the old. ***Dictionary of Bible Themes***

Jesus said, "Heaven and earth will pass away, but my words will never pass away" (Mk 13:31). He was claiming that his own word had a status and durability greater than the whole creation. And that meant that his word was on the same level as the creative word of God himself (Is 40:8). **Christopher Wright**

Jesus doesn't come into a foreign world and take it over for God...It is absolutely fitting that he have dominion over it because he created it in the first place. **Sean McDonaugh**

Christ's supreme sovereignty is in the foreground. He is the Lord of the creation, as He further demonstrated when He came to this earth: "Who can this be, that even the wind and the sea obey Him!" Answer? The Creator of them. **David Murray**

Capturing the beauty of the conversion of the water into wine, the poet Alexander Pope said, "The conscious water saw its Master and blushed." That sublime description could be reworked to explain each one of these miracles. Was it any different in principle for a broken body to mend at the command of its Maker? Was it far-fetched for the Creator of the universe, who fashioned matter out of nothing, to multiply bread for the crowd? Was it not within the power of the One who called all the molecules into existence to interlock them that they might bear His footsteps? **Ravi Zacharias**

Creation marks the beginning of his messianic dominion; he rules the world he made. **Sean McDonaugh**

Messiah (Christ)

> "But you," he asked them, "who do you say that I am?" Simon Peter answered, "You are the Messiah, the Son of the living God."
> **Matthew 16:15-16 CSB**

The first thing Andrew did was to find his brother Simon and tell him, "We have found the Messiah" (that is, the Christ). And he brought him to Jesus. **John 1:41-42 NIV**

The woman said, "I know that Messiah" (called Christ) "is coming. When he comes, he will explain everything to us." Then Jesus declared, "I, the one speaking to you—I am he." **John 4:25-26 NIV**

As was Paul's custom, he went to the synagogue service, and for three Sabbaths in a row he used the Scriptures to reason with the people. He explained the prophecies and proved that the Messiah must suffer and rise from the dead. He said, "This Jesus I'm telling you about is the Messiah." **Acts 17:2-3 NLT**

Come, thou long expected Jesus,
born to set thy people free;
from our fears and sins release us,
let us find our rest in thee.
Israel's strength and consolation,
hope of all the earth thou art;
dear desire of every nation,
joy of every longing heart. **Charles Wesley**

The prophets foretold the coming of Messiah. Yet centuries of oppression and suffering passed, and many lost hope. In every generation there were people like Simeon and Anna who longed for and prayed for Messiah's coming. And finally, when the Redeemer's absence became unbearable, he came. **Randy Alcorn**

By human standards, He didn't look like a Messiah. Isaiah 53:2 tells us that "he had no form or majesty that we should look at him, and no beauty that we should desire him." Significantly, the New Testament includes no description at all of Jesus' physical appearance…Scripture doesn't put a face on the Lord so that His real beauty can shine through. **Steve DeWitt**

When the gospel was manifested in Christ, God made sure the world had experienced enough of life without the Messiah to see their desperate need for the "good news of happiness" (Isaiah 52:7 NLV)…Nothing less than Jesus himself is that good news! **Randy Alcorn**

Jesus not only understood Himself to be the promised Messiah, He also says and does things throughout the Gospels that make it clear He understood Himself to be God incarnate. **Keith Mathison**

The most that one of Jewish faith can do—and some have gladly done it—is to say that Jesus was the greatest in the long succession of Jewish prophets. None can acknowledge that Jesus was the Messiah without becoming a Christian. **Kenneth Scott Latourette**

If He be not the Messiah, the world has not, and never can have, a Messiah. **Martin Luther**

Jesus is a messiah who wins his people back by redemption, rather than an enlightened philosopher who, by his therapeutic wisdom, guides us to higher and happier living. **Michael Horton**

If you are devastated or irate over the outcome of a presidential election, relax. Things will be okay. We only need, and already have, one Messiah. And he did not lose this election. If you are ecstatic about an election outcome, relax. Take inventory. We only need, and already have, one Messiah. And he did not win this election. **Scott Sauls**

Christianity must yet triumph in a renovated earth, and with the returned Messiah as universal king, or fail. There is no third alternative. **Anthony Buzzard**

Son of Man

I saw in the night visions, and behold, with the clouds of heaven there came one like a son of man, and he came to the Ancient of Days and was presented before him. **Daniel 7:13 ESV**

"I want you to know that the Son of Man has authority on earth to forgive sins." So he said to the paralyzed man, "Get up, take your mat and go home." Then the man got up and went home. **Matthew 9:6-7 NIV**

Jesus said to him, "You have said so. But I tell you, from now on you will see the Son of Man seated at the right hand of Power and coming on the clouds of heaven." **Matthew 26:64 ESV**

"No one has ascended into heaven except he who descended from heaven, the Son of Man." **John 3:13 ESV**

Son of man is a Messianic title used by Jesus to express his heavenly origin, earthly mission, and glorious future coming. It does not refer merely to his human nature or humanity...Rather, it reflects on the heavenly origin and divine dignity of Jesus, on the mystery of his manifestation in human form, and on his earthly mission which involved suffering and death. **W.A. Elwell**

God speaks to me not through the thunder and the earthquake, nor through the ocean and the stars, but through the Son of Man, and speaks in a language adapted to my imperfect sight and hearing.
William Lyon Phelps

Christ accomplished down here the work which the Father also gave Him to do as the Son of *Man*. As *man* He once wore the crown of thorns, which the soil, unredeemed and under the curse, yielded Him, and as *man* He will on the day of cosmic regeneration (Matthew 19:28), as the Head of His body, reign with all His saints over the same soil—now redeemed and free from the curse. **Erich Sauer**

In the Gospels, the term "Son of man" is used by Jesus some 80 times as a mysterious, indirect way of speaking about himself...The specific source of the term is Daniel 7:13, 14, with its vision of one "like a son of man" who "comes with the clouds" into the presence of "the Ancient of Days" who gives him the universal and eternal kingdom of God. Jesus repeatedly quoted parts of this text in teaching about his second coming...Clearly, Jesus understood this passage as a prophetic portrayal of his own person: his incarnation, ascension, and inheritance of the kingdom of God. **W.A. Elwell**

Lamb of God

"Behold, the Lamb of God, who takes away the sin of the world!" **John 1:29 ESV**

He was oppressed and treated harshly, yet he never said a word. He was led like a lamb to the slaughter. And as a sheep is silent before the shearers, he did not open his mouth. **Isaiah 53:7 NLT**

You know that God paid a ransom to save you from the empty life you inherited from your ancestors. And it was not paid with mere gold or silver, which lose their value. It was the precious blood of Christ, the sinless, spotless Lamb of God. **1 Peter 1:18-19 NLT**

The Lamb at the center of the throne will be their shepherd; "he will lead them to springs of living water." **Revelation 7:17 NIV**

I wept and wept because no one was found who was worthy to open the scroll or look inside. Then one of the elders said to me, "Do not weep! See, the Lion of the tribe of Judah, the Root of David, has triumphed. He is able to open the scroll and its seven seals." Then I saw a Lamb, looking as if it had been slain, standing at the center of the throne, encircled by the four living creatures and the elders...He went and took the scroll from the right hand of him who sat on the throne. And when he had taken it, the four living creatures and the twenty-four elders fell down before the Lamb. **Revelation 5:4-8 NIV**

The Israelites were expecting the Messiah as a powerful lion, bringing judgment on his enemies, and overlooked the passages showing him coming as a lamb (Isaiah 53:7). Appearing as a lamb seems a picture of weakness. But suddenly in Revelation, men are hiding themselves from the "wrath of the Lamb" (6:16). The magnificent Lamb of God is also the all-powerful Lion of Judah. **Randy Alcorn**

The most significant event of the centuries took place in...a stable...yes, Mary had a little lamb that night. And her precious little lamb was destined...for Golgotha's altar. **Charles R. Swindoll**

Why was so much blood needed for worship? (Exodus 29:11-21). A just and holy God could not ignore sin. But God allowed a substitute to take the place of the sinner. Anything less than blood would have devalued sin in the eyes of the people. In the New Testament Jesus became the sacrificial Lamb, removing the need for ongoing animal sacrifices. ***The Knowing Jesus Study Bible***

To continually behold the Lamb of God is life to our souls and death to our sins. **William Mason**

This is the solution to the world's problems? A lowly lamb? A weak, submissive sheep? Precisely. The answer to man's problems is the Lamb of God—Jesus Christ. The Lion-Lamb. The Sovereign Savior. What a combination of meekness and majesty! **Steven J. Lawson**

When you feel God's silence, or think him absent, look at Christ, the "lamb...silent before the shearers" (Acts 8:32). He shouts to us without opening his mouth: "Do these nail-scarred hands look like the hands of a God who does not care?" **Randy Alcorn**

He who had been a lamb in his passion became a lion in his resurrection. **Bernard of Clairvaux**

It was as a lamb that Jesus fought and conquered, and therefore it is as a lamb he appears in Heaven. I have read of certain military commanders, when they were conquerors, that on the anniversary of their victory they would never wear anything but the garment in which they fought...It seems as if the same feeling possessed the breast of Christ. "As a Lamb," says he, "I died and defeated Hell. As a Lamb I have redeemed my people, and therefore as a Lamb I will appear in Paradise." **Charles Spurgeon**

Mediator

We have been justified through faith, we have peace with God through our Lord Jesus Christ, through whom we have gained access by faith into this grace in which we now stand. **Romans 5:1-2 NIV**

There is one God and one Mediator who can reconcile God and humanity—the man Christ Jesus. He gave his life to purchase freedom for everyone. This is the message God gave to the world at just the right time. **1 Timothy 2:5-7 NLT**

Only Christ is that ladder between earth and heaven, the Mediator betwixt God and man; a mystery which the angels of heaven desire to pry into. **Isaac Ambrose**

The system of human mediation falls away in the advent to our souls of the living Christ. Who wants stars, or even the moon, after the sun is up? **A.B. Cave**

God became a man so that following a man—something you are able to do—you might reach God, which was formerly impossible to you. **Augustine**

Christ has taken our nature into heaven to represent us, and has left us on earth with his nature to represent him. **John Newton**

The Son of God, utterly clean of all fault, nevertheless took upon himself the shame and reproach of our iniquities, and in return clothes us with his purity...Christ was offered to the Father in death as an expiatory sacrifice that when he discharged all satisfaction through his sacrifice, we might cease to be afraid of God's wrath. **John Calvin**

Before any man can think to stand before the face of God's justice or be admitted to the secret chamber of God's mercy or partake of the riches of His grace, he must look to the Mediator, Christ Jesus. **Stephen Charnock**

Reality is not meant to be only creedal, though the creeds are important. Reality is to be experienced, and experienced on the basis of a restored relationship with God through that finished work of the Lord Jesus Christ on the cross. **Francis Schaeffer**

Thou hast chosen to transact all thy concerns
with us through a Mediator
in whom all fullness dwells
and who is exalted to be Prince and Saviour.
To him we look, on him we depend,
through him we are justified.
The Valley of Vision: A Collection of Puritan Prayers and Devotions

Now Christians can live with one another in peace; they can love and serve one another; they can become one. But they can continue to do so only by way of Jesus Christ. Only in Jesus Christ are we won, only through him are we bound together. To eternity he remains the one Mediator. **Dietrich Bonhoeffer**

Ultimate Prophet

"The LORD your God will raise up for you a prophet like me from among you, from your brothers—it is to him you shall listen...I will put my words in his mouth, and he shall speak to them all that I command him." **Deuteronomy 18:15, 18 ESV**

He said, "Young man, I say to you, get up!" The dead man sat up and began to talk, and Jesus gave him back to his mother. They were all filled with awe and praised God. "A great prophet has appeared among us," they said. "God has come to help his people." This news about Jesus spread throughout Judea and the surrounding country. **Luke 7:14-17 NIV**

"Jehovah thy God will raise up unto thee a prophet from the midst of thee, of thy brethren like unto me; unto him ye shall hearken."...This also demonstrates that Christ was to be a light and Savior after Moses, and no doubt better than Moses. **Martin Luther**

Jesus is not merely the new prophet; he is also the new mediator, the new servant, the new leader, the new miracle worker, the new teacher, and the new redeemer. He is all the things Moses was and more, and he leads the people on a greater exodus than Moses could have ever imagined. **Patrick Schreiner**

Jesus was not just a prophet but the fulfillment of all prophecy. **Kevin DeYoung**

Everything in the Hebrew worldview militated against the idea that a human being could be God. Jews would not even pronounce the name "Yahweh" nor spell it. And yet Jesus Christ—by his life, by his claims, and by his resurrection—convinced his closest Jewish followers that he was not just a prophet telling them how to find God, but God himself come to find us. **Timothy Keller**

Take Jesus for your king, and by baptism swear allegiance to him; take him for your prophet, and hear him; take him for your priest, to make atonement for you. **Matthew Henry**

Let us serve him faithfully as our Master. Let us obey Him loyally as our King. Let us study His teaching as our Prophet. Let us walk diligently after Him as our Example. Let us look anxiously for Him as our coming Redeemer of body as well as soul. But above all, let us prize Him as our sacrifice. **J.C. Ryle**

Jonah did not weep over the city, but Jesus, the true prophet, did...Jesus did not merely weep for us; he died for us. Jonah went outside the city, hoping to witness its condemnation, but Jesus Christ went outside the city to die on a cross to accomplish its salvation. **Timothy Keller**

High Priest

Jesus had to be made like his brothers and sisters in every way so he could be their merciful and faithful high priest in service to God. Then Jesus could die in their place to take away their sins. And now he can help those who are tempted, because he himself suffered and was tempted. **Hebrews 2:17-18 NCV**

We have confidence to enter the Most Holy Place by the blood of Jesus. **Hebrews 10:19 NIV**

Since we have a great high priest who has ascended into heaven, Jesus the Son of God, let us hold firmly to the faith we profess....Let us then approach God's throne of grace with confidence, so that we may receive mercy and find grace to help us in our time of need. **Hebrews 4:14, 16 NIV**

Jesus Christ, being a truly human high priest, perfectly represents humanity before God. He made atonement for sins by his own sacrificial death. Being a truly divine high priest, this act of Christ's was perfect, once for all and of eternal value. ***Dictionary of Biblical Themes***

The fact that Jesus did not need to offer sacrifices for his own sin makes him unique as a high priest (Hebrews 7:27). And rather than offering animals, he offered *himself* as the final sacrifice for our sins (Hebrews 7:27)—our high priest *became* the sacrifice. ***The Knowing Jesus Study Bible***

The striking thing in the Scriptural representations of the priestly work of Christ, is that Christ appears in them as both priest and sacrifice. **Louis Berkhof**

Do we work nothing for the obtaining of this righteousness? I answer: Nothing at all. For the nature of this righteousness is, to do nothing, to hear nothing, to know nothing whatsoever of the law or of works, but to know and to believe this only: that Christ is gone to the Father...that he sits in heaven at the right hand of his Father, not as a judge, but made unto us of God, wisdom, righteousness, holiness and redemption; briefly, that he is our high priest entreating for us, and reigning over us and in us by grace. **Martin Luther**

Sinless, he did not offer sacrifices for himself. Immortal, he never has to be replaced. Human, he could bear human sins...he offered himself as the final sacrifice. There will never be the need for another. There is one...priest. We need no other. Oh, how happy are those who draw near to God through Christ alone. **John Piper**

Advocate

Because Jesus lives forever, he has a permanent priesthood. Therefore he is able to save completely those who come to God through him, because he always lives to intercede for them. **Hebrews 7:24-25 NIV**

My dear children, I write this to you so that you will not sin. But if anybody does sin, we have an advocate with the Father—Jesus Christ, the Righteous One. **1 John 2:1 NIV**

The Greek word *paraklētos* for "advocate" means "one who appears in another's behalf; mediator, intercessor, helper."...In Christ's work as Advocate He pleads His own substitutionary atonement for the believer's sins and defends him against the attacks of Satan before God. **C.F. Pfeiffer**

How does it make you feel to know that Jesus is your advocate, your defense attorney? Can you imagine Jesus standing between you and your accuser, Satan (see Revelation 12:10)? The thought makes me worship, smile, rejoice, and praise God. **Randy Alcorn**

It is a source of joy to the Christian, that the Crucified is now the Glorified—that he rose triumphant from the grave and ascended into glory—that he is seated at God's right hand, to wield the scepter of the universe and to appear as the High Priest and Intercessor of his people. **John MacDuff**

Beyond His death and resurrection and ascension, the present work of Jesus Christ is twofold. It is to be an advocate above—a risen Savior with high priestly office at the throne of God; and the ministry of preparing a place for His people in the house of His Father and our Father, as well. **A.W. Tozer**

> If we cannot claim to live sinless lives, then the only thing that can keep us from despairing before a holy God is that we have an Advocate in heaven and he pleads our case not on the basis of our perfection but of his propitiation. **John Piper**

There is a charge against me, otherwise I should not want an advocate to meet it, and this implies that I have sinned. There is an adversary to press his suit against me, and he would hardly venture to do this if there were no sin...He who has a right to plead in court is the man who is accused, and the man who has some offence. Being brought up upon that charge, and having one who presses the charge against me, I have a right to reply, and that reply, through God's good grace, I have a right to make through my advocate.

Let us say concerning our advocate, that he is ordained with a special view to sinners; all his names and attributes prove him to be a suitable advocate for such. You and I, who though saved are still sinners, may safely put our case into his hands, for see who he is—"*Jesus Christ the righteous.*"

"*Jesus.*" Ah! then he is an advocate such as I want, for he loves me and takes an interest in me... **Charles Spurgeon**

God's hearing of our prayers doth not depend upon sanctification, but upon Christ's intercession; not upon what we are in ourselves, but what we are in the Lord Jesus. **Thomas Brooks**

Christ's intercession in heaven is a kind of powerful remembrance of His people, and of all their concerns, managed with state and majesty: not as a suppliant at the footstool, but as a crowned prince on the throne, at the right hand of the Father. **Robert Traill**

Friend

"I no longer call you slaves, because a master doesn't confide in his slaves. Now you are my friends, since I have told you everything the Father told me." **John 15:15 NLT**

The friendship of the LORD is for those who fear him, and he makes known to them his covenant. **Psalm 25:14 ESV**

A rule I have had for years is: to treat the Lord Jesus Christ as a personal friend. His is not a creed, a mere doctrine, but it is He Himself we have. **Dwight L. Moody**

The hymnist wrote, "What a friend we have in Jesus." This simple theme has been established throughout Christendom. Our immense fear of being alone has been answered...The Savior makes our friendship heaven's agenda. **Calvin Miller**

Jesus lived what he taught, and he was frequently criticized for being a friend of "sinners" (Matthew 11:19). But our Lord wasn't bothered by such accusations; then as now he stands ready to befriend *all* who need him. ***The Knowing Jesus Study Bible***

God has not left us on our own. Even though we have declared war on him deep in our hearts, he has declared peace with us. This friendship is made possible not because Jesus was born, but because Jesus would die. **Nancy Guthrie**

On the eve of the cross, Jesus made his decision. He would rather go to hell for you than go to heaven without you. **Max Lucado**

The saints must be honored as friends of Christ and children and heirs of God. **John of Damascus**

Those who walked with Jesus found they could not plumb the depths of His nature. They discovered in His friendship a quality enhanced by death, and a fathomless ocean of love. **George A. Buttrick**

The dearest friend on earth is a mere shadow compared to Jesus Christ. **Oswald Chambers**

I would sooner lie on a bed and ache in every limb, with the death sweat standing on my brow, by the month and year persecuted, despised, and forsaken...and have Christ for my friend, than I would sit in the palaces of wicked kings with all their wealth and luxury and pampering and sin. **Charles Spurgeon**

Occasionally when I'm praying, I pull out a chair for Jesus and envision him sitting there. It's not idolatry to imagine Jesus as a man. He was and is a man. He sat in chairs and made them, as He made the universe itself, so this is no big stretch. I talk to him. I'm not pretending Jesus is with me when I pray; I believe the God-Man really lived in this same world and is going to make us a better one. I really believe his promise that he's always with me and is my friend, and I seek to act in keeping with those incredible truths. **Randy Alcorn**

Christ says, "Give me all. I don't want so much of your time and so much of your money and so much of your work: I want You." **C.S. Lewis**

The whole outlook of mankind might be changed if we could all believe that we dwell under a friendly sky and that the God of heaven, though exalted in power and majesty, is eager to be friends with us. **A.W. Tozer**

Life without Jesus is like a dry garden, baking in the sun...What can the world give you without Jesus? His absence is hell; his presence, paradise...Poverty is life without Jesus, but close friendship with him is incalculable wealth. **Bernard Bangley**

People often say, "I like to think of Jesus as my friend, not my master." But he's all the things Scripture reveals him to be, including judge, father, friend, and master. His attributes aren't a smorgasbord for finicky Christians to choose what they want and leave the rest untouched. **Randy Alcorn**

Writing the history of Jesus is far more complicated than simply documenting the life of a figure from the past. It is more like writing the biography of a friend who is still very much alive and still liable to surprise us. **N.T. Wright**

Good Shepherd

As he went ashore, he saw a great crowd; and he had compassion for them, because they were like sheep without a shepherd. **Mark 6:34 NRSV**

"I am the good shepherd, and the good shepherd gives up his life for his sheep. Hired workers are not like the shepherd...Hired workers run away because they don't care about the sheep...My sheep know my voice and I know them. They follow me, and I give them eternal life, so that they will never be lost. No one can snatch them out of my hand. My Father gave them to me, and he is greater than all others. No one can snatch them from his hands, and I am one with the Father." **John 10:11-13, 27-30 CEV**

"What do you think? If a man owns a hundred sheep, and one of them wanders away, will he not leave the ninety-nine on the hills and go to look for the one that wandered off? And if he finds it, truly I tell you, he is happier about that one sheep than about the ninety-nine that did not wander off. In the same way, your Father in heaven is not willing that any of these little ones should perish." **Matthew 18:12-14 NIV**

When we give control of our lives to Jesus, he receives us as a gentle Shepherd and answers us that we "will dwell in the house of the Lord forever" (Psalm 23:6). ***The Knowing Jesus Study Bible***

The whole Christ seeks after each sinner, and when the Lord finds it, he gives himself to that one soul as if he had but that one soul to bless. How my heart admires the concentration of all the Godhead and humanity of Christ in his search after each sheep of his flock. **Charles Spurgeon**

In the Christian's life there is no substitute for the keen awareness that my Shepherd is nearby. There is nothing like Christ's presence to dispel the fear, the panic, the terror of the unknown. **Phillip Keller**

The best way to keep the enemy out is to keep Christ in. The sheep need not be terrified by the wolf; they have but to stay close to the shepherd. It is not the praying sheep Satan fears but the presence of the shepherd. **A.W. Tozer**

I am vile indeed, but Jesus is full of grace and truth. He leads and guides, he feeds and guards, he restores and heals. He is an all-sufficient Savior. **John Newton**

When Jesus takes your hand, He keeps you tight. When Jesus keeps you tight, He leads you through your whole life. When Jesus leads you through your life, He brings you safely home. **Corrie ten Boom**

Christ leads me through no darker rooms than he went through before. **Richard Baxter**

I know not the way He leads me, but well do I know my Guide. **Henrietta C. Mears**

Bridegroom

"The bride belongs to the bridegroom. The friend who attends the bridegroom waits and listens for him, and is full of joy when he hears the bridegroom's voice. That joy is mine, and it is now complete. He must become greater; I must become less." **John 3:29-30** NIV

They said to him, "John's disciples fast often and say prayers, and those of the Pharisees do the same, but yours eat and drink." Jesus said to them, "You can't make the wedding guests fast while the groom is with them, can you? But the time will come when the groom will be taken away from them—then they will fast in those days." **Luke 5:33-35 CSB**

"Let us rejoice and be glad and give the glory to Him, for the marriage of the Lamb has come and His bride has made herself ready." **Revelation 19:7 NASB**

Christ is not only good, but he is the best; and he is not only the best, but he is the best of the best...He is a Husband; but what a Husband! Was there ever such a Bridegroom as Christ Jesus the Lord? He is the Head; but Father Adam was a poor head compared with him. He is inexpressibly, unutterably, indescribably lovely; I might as well leave off talking about him, for I cannot hope to set him forth as he deserves. **Charles Spurgeon**

Every faithful Christian marriage points beyond itself to the perfect union we all share with the Lord Jesus Christ. Our little metaphorical marriages can always draw strength from the real marriage we share with our Savior. **Ray Ortlund Jr.**

Just as God presented Eve to Adam in the first wedding ceremony, so now the Father walks the church down the aisle to Jesus her bridegroom in the marriage celebration to which every other marriage points. **Trevor Laurence**

Then the church shall be brought to the full enjoyment of her bridegroom, having all tears wiped away from her eyes, and there shall be no more distance or absence. She shall then be brought to the entertainments of an eternal wedding feast, and to dwell forever with her bridegroom, yea, to dwell eternally in His embraces. Then Christ will give her His loves, and she shall drink her fill, yea, she shall swim in the ocean of His love. **Jonathan Edwards**

The day of Jesus's return will be a wedding feast—and Christians are invited to it not as guests, but as a bride. None of us will have to sneak into heaven through the back door—we'll be walking up the aisle. **Sam Allberry**

He who is coming is your Lord, your Friend, your Bridegroom...That day of Christ's appearing shall be to you a morning of the ringing out of harps, and a time of joyous shouts and blissful songs...it shall be your joy day, your wedding day, the brightest day in all your history. **Charles Spurgeon**

The heavens and the earth were created for the marriage of Adam and Eve. The new heavens and the new earth will be created for the marriage of Christ and his bride. The whole of cosmic reality exists as the venue for the eternal honeymoon of the perfect husband with his perfect bride in marital bliss forever and ever. **Ray Ortlund Jr.**

Light of the World

Simeon took him in his arms and praised God, saying: "Sovereign Lord, as you have promised, you may now dismiss your servant in peace. For my eyes have seen your salvation, which you have prepared in the sight of all nations: a light for revelation to the Gentiles, and the glory of your people Israel." **Luke 2:28-32 NIV**

The people living in darkness have seen a great light; on those living in the land of the shadow of death a light has dawned. **Matthew 4:16 NIV**

> The Word gave life to everything that was created, and his life brought light to everyone. The light shines in the darkness, and the darkness can never extinguish it. **John 1:4-5 NLT**

The true light, which gives light to everyone, was coming into the world. He was in the world, and the world was made through him, yet the world did not know him. **John 1:9-10 ESV**

"I have come as a light to shine in this dark world, so that all who put their trust in me will no longer remain in the dark." **John 12:46 NLT**

This is the message we heard from Jesus and now declare to you: God is light, and there is no darkness in him at all. **1 John 1:5 NLT**

"I am the light of the world. Whoever follows me will not walk in darkness, but will have the light of life." **John 8:12 ESV**

There was nothing dark and hidden about Jesus. He was and is the Light of the world, and He welcomed the light. **Samuel Logan Brengle**

Jesus didn't say, "I'll point you to the light," or "I'll give you the light." He said, "I am the light." Not one among many, but *the one and only.* **Randy Alcorn**

If I saw a wise man going into a blind asylum, laying on gas or making preparation for the electric light, I should feel sure that he had a view to people who can see; and if none but blind people could come into the building, I should conclude that he anticipated a time when the poor blind folks would find their eyes again, and would be able to use the light. So, as the Lord has set Jesus to be a light, you may be sure that He means to open blind eyes. **Charles Spurgeon**

I love John 1:9, which says that Jesus came as the light that "enlightens every man" (NASB) because it reflects the fact that all people in history have benefited from Christ's redemptive life and death—even those who reject him. The model of Christ, his grace and truth, his elevation of women and conciliatory words, created a reference point for bringing greater freedom and civil rights to many societies throughout history. **Randy Alcorn**

Don't shine so others can see you. Shine so that through you, others can see Him. **C.S. Lewis**

Christ is the morning star, who promises and reveals to the saints the eternal light of life, when the night of the world is past. **Venerable Bede**

The valley of the shadow of death holds no darkness for the child of God. There must be light, else there could be no shadow. Jesus is the light. **Dwight L. Moody**

Without Christ life is as the twilight with dark night ahead; with Christ it is the dawn of morning with the light and warmth of a full day ahead. **Philip Schaff**

Bread of Life

Jesus said to them, "I am the bread of life; whoever comes to me shall not hunger, and whoever believes in me shall never thirst." **John 6:35 ESV**

"Your ancestors ate manna in the desert, and later they died. But the bread from heaven has come down, so that no one who eats it will ever die. I am that bread from heaven!" **John 6:49-51 CEV**

Our Saviour Christ is both the first beginner of our spiritual life (who first begets us unto God his Father), and also afterward he is our lively food and nourishment. **Thomas Cranmer**

Jesus proclaimed that he is the "bread of life" (John 6:35). He had just satisfied more than 5,000 famished people with only five barley loaves and two small fish (John 6:1-14). But Jesus wanted the crowd to focus on a reality beyond the obvious that bread made from barley or any other grain will eventually spoil and that it cannot keep a person alive forever..."He who comes to me will never go hungry, and he who believes in me will never be thirsty" (John 6:35). ***The Knowing Jesus Study Bible***

> When we truly come to Christ, our thirst is quenched by the fountain of life and our hunger is filled with the bread of heaven. We discover that Jesus is the supreme source of satisfaction, and we want nothing apart from Him. We realize that He is better than all the pleasures, pursuits, plaudits, and possessions of this world combined. **David Platt**

Because the face of God is so lovely, my brothers and sisters, so beautiful, once you have seen it, nothing else can give you pleasure. It will give insatiable satisfaction of which we will never tire. We shall always be hungry and always have our fill. **Augustine**

Each time we partake of the bread and the cup in communion, we are reminded of the love and faithfulness of Christ. Every day in small ways God is at work to change us into the kind of people he wants us to be, and it is through the miracle of Jesus dying for our sins and rising again to new life that we see the consummate manifestation of God's power. ***The Knowing Jesus Study Bible***

Living Water

"Everyone who drinks this water will be thirsty again, but whoever drinks the water I give them will never thirst. Indeed, the water I give them will become in them a spring of water welling up to eternal life." **John 4:13-14 NIV**

Jesus made an offer to those who are frustrated and disillusioned with life: "If anyone is thirsty, let him come to me and drink. Whoever believes in me, as the Scripture has said, streams of living water will flow from within him" (John 7:37). Jesus not only promises to satisfy our deep inner longings, but he will also make us a source of refreshment for others. ***The Knowing Jesus Study Bible***

Christ is like a river…A river is continually flowing, there are fresh supplies of water coming from the fountain-head continually, so that a man may live by it, and be supplied with water all his life. So Christ is an ever-flowing fountain; he is continually supplying his people, and the fountain is not spent. They who live upon Christ, may have fresh supplies from him to all eternity; they may have an increase of blessedness that is new, and new still, and which never will come to an end. **Jonathan Edwards**

From time immemorial men have quenched their thirst with water without knowing anything about its chemical constituents. In like manner we do not need to be instructed in all the mysteries of doctrine, but we do need to receive the Living Water which Jesus Christ will give us and which alone can satisfy our souls. **Sadhu Sundar Singh**

God's people "drank from the spiritual rock that accompanied them, and that rock was Christ" (1 Corinthians 10:4). They quenched their thirst with water God had provided from the rock, just as we quench our spiritual thirst with "living water" from the real Rock—Jesus Christ. ***The Knowing Jesus Study Bible***

A dead Christ I must do everything for; a living Christ does everything for me. **Andrew Murray**

I spent half my life rebelling against the legalism of my childhood; when I tasted the first draught of the Living Water offered by Jesus, I knew I was changed forever. **Philip Yancey**

You weren't created for boredom or burnout or bondage to sexual lust or greed or ambition but for the incomparable pleasure and matchless joy that knowing Jesus alone can bring. Only then, in Him, will you encounter the life-changing, thirst-quenching, soul-satisfying delight that God, for His glory, created you to experience. **Sam Storms**

Desire is a signpost pointing to Heaven...Every thirst for beauty is a thirst for Christ. Every taste of joy is but a foretaste of a greater and more vibrant joy than can be found on Earth now. **Randy Alcorn**

Lord of Lords

What we proclaim is not ourselves, but Jesus Christ as Lord, with ourselves as your servants for Jesus' sake. **2 Corinthians 4:5 ESV**

At just the right time Christ will be revealed from heaven by the blessed and only almighty God, the King of all kings and Lord of all lords. **1 Timothy 6:15 NLT**

To him was given dominion and glory and a kingdom, that all peoples, nations, and languages should serve him; his dominion is an everlasting dominion, which shall not pass away, and his kingdom one that shall not be destroyed. **Daniel 7:14 ESV**

All glory to him who alone is God, our Savior through Jesus Christ our Lord. All glory, majesty, power, and authority are his before all time, and in the present, and beyond all time! Amen. **Jude 25 NLT**

Christ is called Lord in the New Testament with the same constancy and with the same preeminence that Jehovah is called Lord in the Old Testament. **Charles Hodge**

To the Jews, Jesus was a threat to their way of life and an ungodly man. To the crowds, one moment Jesus was a prophet and another moment he was a criminal. To Pilate, Jesus was an innocent man caught in the political crossfire. To Judas, Jesus was a rabbi, a teacher, a powerful man who was useful at one time, but he was never Lord... To the disciples, Jesus was the Christ, the son of the living God. He was their Savior and Lord and they spent their lives proclaiming the good news of what Jesus had done on the cross. **Vaneetha Rendall Risner**

The boundless realms of his Father's universe are Christ's by prescriptive right. As "heir of all things," he is the sole proprietor of the vast creation of God, and he has admitted us. **Charles Spurgeon**

...we need to preach again a whole Christ to the world—a Christ who does not need our apologies, a Christ who will not be divided, a Christ who will either be Lord of all or who will not be Lord at all! **A.W. Tozer**

To present Christ's lordship as an option leaves it squarely in the category of stereo equipment for a new car. **Dallas Willard**

It should not be surprising if people believe easily in a God who makes no demands, but this is not the God of the Bible. Satan has cleverly misled people by whispering that they can believe in Jesus Christ without being changed, but this is the Devil's lie. To those who say you can have Christ without giving anything up, Satan is deceiving you. **Billy Graham**

You cannot reject his lordship and still have him as your get-out-of-hell-free Savior. **David Mathis**

Everyone who receives Him must surrender to His authority, for to say we receive Christ when in fact we reject His right to reign over us is utter absurdity. **John MacArthur**

Jesus is not some puny religious teacher begging for an invitation from anyone. He is the all-sovereign Lord who deserves submission from everyone. **David Platt**

The devoted and committed person who takes the cross and follows the Lord does not ask what the consequences will be, neither does he argue about God's plan and God's wisdom. **A.W. Tozer**

The only way to spin free of the narrow confines of your little cubicle kingdom is to live in the big sky country of Christ-centered living. You will never win the battle with yourself simply by saying "no" to yourself. The battle only begins to be won when you say "yes" to the call of your King, the Lord Jesus Christ. **Paul David Tripp**

I cannot conceive it possible for anyone truly to receive Christ as Savior and yet not to receive him as Lord. A man who is really saved by grace does not need to be told that he is under solemn obligations to serve Christ. The new life within him tells him that. Instead of regarding it as a burden, he gladly surrenders himself—body, soul, and spirit—to the Lord who has redeemed him, reckoning this to be his reasonable service. **Charles Spurgeon**

Despite our constant talk about the lordship of Christ, we have narrowed its scope to a very small area of reality...The lordship of Christ over the whole of life means that there are no platonic areas in Christianity, no dichotomy or hierarchy between the body and the soul. God made the body as well as the soul, and redemption is for the whole man. **Francis Schaeffer**

Christ has been explained, humanized, demoted. Many professed Christians no longer expect Him to usher in a new order; they are not at all sure that He is able to do so; or if He does, it will be with the help of art, education, science and technology; that is, with the help of man. This revised expectation amounts to disillusionment for many. And of course no one can become too radiantly happy over a King of kings who has been stripped of His crown or a Lord of lords who has lost His sovereignty. **A.W. Tozer**

Jesus is not on a side. Jesus IS a side. Nobody owns Him. He owns us. **Janie B. Cheaney**

Christ is the final, complete, dominant, visible, manifest Lord of history. I want to be on *that* side. **John Piper**

Prince of Peace

A child is born to us! A son is given to us! And he will be our ruler. He will be called, "Wonderful Counselor," "Mighty God," "Eternal Father," "Prince of Peace." **Isaiah 9:6 GNT**

"I have told you these things, so that in me you may have peace. In this world you will have trouble. But take heart! I have overcome the world." **John 16:33 NIV**

He himself is our peace, who has made us both one and has broken down in his flesh the dividing wall of hostility...that he might create in himself one new man in place of the two, so making peace, and might reconcile us both to God in one body through the cross, thereby killing the hostility. And he came and preached peace to you who were far off and peace to those who were near. **Ephesians 2:14-17** ESV

Christ's life outwardly was one of the most troubled lives that was ever lived...but the inner life was a sea of glass. The great calm was always there. **Henry Drummond**

Jesus was napping in a boat when a storm came. Jesus' friends, the disciples, woke him because they were terrified...Jesus looked out at the storm and said, "Peace, be still." And it was...Peace doesn't come from finding a lake with no storms. It comes from having Jesus in the boat. **John Ortberg**

Our trouble is we want the peace without the prince. **Addison H. Leitch**

They think to order all things wisely; but having rejected Christ they will end by drenching the world with blood. **Fyodor Dostoevsky**

Would you have peace with God? Away, then, to God through Jesus Christ, who has purchased peace; the Lord Jesus has shed his heart's blood for this. He died for this; he rose again for this; he ascended into the highest heaven, and is now interceding at the right hand of God. **George Whitefield**

Peace is not automatic. It is a gift of the grace of God. It comes when hearts are exposed to the love of Christ. But this always costs something. For the love of Christ was demonstrated through suffering and those who experience that love can never put it into practice without some cost. **Festo Kivengere**

Peace is not the absence of trouble but the presence of Christ.
Sheila Walsh

I know the brutality and the cruelties of war better than many people. Now I want to work for peace. But how can mankind achieve a lasting peace? True peace of heart, mind, and soul can only come through Jesus Christ. **Mitsuo Fuchida (Japanese navy captain who commanded air strike against Pearl Harbor in 1941)**

Just think: Every promise God has ever made finds its fulfillment in Jesus. God doesn't just give us grace; he gives us Jesus, the Lord of grace. If it's peace, it's only found in Jesus, the Prince of Peace. Even life itself is found in the Resurrection and the Life. Christianity isn't all that complicated...it's Jesus. **Joni Eareckson Tada**

Peace is a person, and his name is Jesus...Peace came. Peace lived. Peace died. Peace rose. Peace reigns on your behalf. Peace indwells you by his Spirit. Peace graces you with everything you need. **Paul David Tripp**

The Way, the Truth, and the Life

"I am the way, and the truth, and the life. No one comes to the Father except through me." **John 14:6 ESV**

"I am the door. If anyone enters by me, he will be saved and will go in and out and find pasture." **John 10:9 ESV**

We know that the Son of God has come, and has given us understanding so that we may know Him who is true; and we are in Him who is true, in His Son Jesus Christ. This is the true God and eternal life. **1 John 5:20 NASB**

Christ is not one of many ways to approach God, nor is He the best of several ways; He is the only way. "*I am the way, the truth, and the life: no man cometh unto the Father, but by me.*" To believe otherwise is to be something less than a Christian. **A.W. Tozer**

No Christian has the right to claim on his own authority that Jesus is the only way to God. It is Jesus Himself who claimed this. He was either right or wrong...If Jesus was and is God, we had better trust what He said, not what we would prefer to believe or what our culture thinks. **Randy Alcorn**

Christ is a fixed meal. It is all or nothing with His claims. Everyone is invited, but only you can decide if you actually want to eat at His table. **Kent Weber**

The true gospel is radically exclusive. Jesus is not a way; He is the way, and all other ways are no way at all. If Christianity would only move one small step toward a more tolerant ecumenicalism and exchange the definite article *the* for the indefinite article *a*, the scandal would be over, and the world and Christianity could become friends. However, whenever this occurs, Christianity ceases to be Christianity, Christ is denied, and the world is without a Savior. **Paul Washer**

Fundamentally, our Lord's message was himself. He did not come merely to preach a gospel; he himself is that gospel. He did not come merely to give bread; he said, "I am the bread."...He did not come merely to show the door; he said, "I am the door." He did not come merely to name a shepherd; he said, "I am the shepherd." He did not come merely to point the way; he said, "I am the way, the truth, and the life." **J. Sidlow Baxter**

If there were more than one path to salvation then it would totally negate Jesus' sacrifice on the cross, his life, his teachings. **Josh McDowell**

God loves us enough to tell us the truth. There are two eternal destinations, not one, and we must choose the right path if we are to go to Heaven. All roads do not lead to Heaven. Only one does: Jesus Christ. **Randy Alcorn**

Be careful when you pursue truth, because you just might find him. **Jefferson Bethke**

"I know not the way!" despairing I cried.
"I am the Way," Jesus kindly replied.

"I'm searching for Truth!" was my heart's plaintive cry.
"I am the Truth," was His gentle reply.
"I'm longing for Life! Oh, where can it be?"
"I am the life. Thou shalt find it in Me!" **Flora Smith**

You and I are players, God's our coach, and we're playing the biggest game of all. We have a loving God that made us. We need to get on His team. It says in His word, there's only one way to Him and that's through Jesus Christ. **Joe Gibbs**

Christ's cross is Christ's way to Christ's crown. **William Penn**

What we believe about God is the most important truth we believe, and it's the one truth that does the most to shape us. God is the Sun too bright for us to see. Jesus is the Prism who makes the colors beautiful and comprehensible. **Michael Spencer**

Not only do we know God by Jesus Christ alone, but we know ourselves only by Jesus Christ. We know life and death only through Jesus Christ. Apart from Jesus Christ, we do not know what is our life, nor our death, nor God, nor ourselves. **Blaise Pascal**

To tie Jesus Christ to the very best human system is to tie a star, light years distant, to a dead horse here on earth. Neither star nor Christ will thus be bound. **Joseph Bayly**

We are called to be the people of the truth, even when the truth is not popular and even when the truth is denied by the culture around us. Christians have found themselves in this position before, and we will again. God's truth has not changed. The Holy Scriptures have not changed. The gospel of Jesus Christ has not changed. The church's mission has not changed. Jesus Christ is the same, yesterday, today, and forever. **Greg Laurie**

Rescuer from Hell

"Do not fear those who kill the body but cannot kill the soul. Rather fear him who can destroy both soul and body in hell." **Matthew 10:28 ESV**

"They will go away to eternal punishment, but the righteous to eternal life." **Matthew 25:46 NIV**

There is therefore now no condemnation for those who are in Christ Jesus. **Romans 8:1 ESV**

He has rescued us from the kingdom of darkness and transferred us into the Kingdom of his dear Son, who purchased our freedom and forgave our sins. **Colossians 1:13-14 NLT**

Jesus, the one who rescues us from hell, is also the one who speaks the most about it. **Edward Welch**

Let not anyone who thinks that fear of hell should be put out of the mind of unregenerate men ever suppose that he has the slightest understanding of what Jesus came into the world to say and do. **J. Gresham Machen**

By denying Hell's reality, we lower redemption's stakes and minimize Christ's work on the cross. If he didn't deliver us from a real and eternal Hell, then his work on the cross is less heroic, less potent, less consequential, and less deserving of our worship and praise. **Randy Alcorn**

There seems to be a kind of conspiracy to forget, or to conceal, where the doctrine of hell comes from. The doctrine of hell is not "mediaeval priestcraft" for frightening people into giving money to the church: it is Christ's deliberate judgment on sin...We cannot repudiate hell without altogether repudiating Christ. **Dorothy Sayers**

Who less than God could have carried your sins and mine and cast them all away? Who less than God could have interposed to deliver us from the jaws of hell's lions, and bring us up from the pit, having found a ransom? **Charles Spurgeon**

Thank God we DON'T get what we deserve. There's a four-letter word for that: Hell. Christ took upon Himself what He didn't deserve, so that we would not get what we deserved. **Randy Alcorn**

Jesus made this broken world his destination so that our final destination would be a place where every form of brokenness has ended. **Paul David Tripp**

Savior

"She will bear a son, and you shall call his name Jesus, for he will save his people from their sins." **Matthew 1:21 ESV**

"God did not send his Son into the world to be its judge, but to be its savior." **John 3:17 GNT**

"There is salvation in no one else! God has given no other name under heaven by which we must be saved." **Acts 4:12 NLT**

Here is a trustworthy saying that deserves full acceptance: Christ Jesus came into the world to save sinners—of whom I am the worst. **1 Timothy 1:15 NIV**

We have seen and testify that the Father has sent his Son to be the Savior of the world. **1 John 4:14 NIV**

All my theology is reduced to this narrow compass—Christ Jesus came into the world to save sinners. **Archibald Alexander**

Christ must be everything: the beginning, the middle, and the end of our salvation. **Martin Luther**

Whatever subject I preach, I do not stop until I reach the Savior, the Lord Jesus, for in Him are all things. **Charles Spurgeon**

In Hebrew the names Joshua and Jehoshua...Jesus in Greek, mean, "Jehovah is my help," or, "Jehovah is rescue," or, "The help of Jehovah." "You shall give him the name Jesus," the angel said, "for he will save his people from their sins" (Matt. 1:21). The very name stamps Jesus as Saviour. **William Barclay**

The essence of sin is man substituting himself for God, while the essence of salvation is God substituting himself for man. **John Stott**

God the Son knew his purpose, and he knew what was coming. He must soon be "lifted up" to die on a wooden cross, just as the replica of the snake had been lifted up on a wooden pole. By using that analogy [John 3:15], Jesus was explaining the only way to be saved from sin. Salvation is an act of faith. ***The Knowing Jesus Study Bible***

Bearing shame and scoffing rude,
In my place condemned He stood,
Sealed my pardon with His blood:
Hallelujah, what a Savior! **Philip Paul Bliss**

We have but one Saviour; and that one Saviour is Jesus Christ our Lord. Nothing that we are and nothing that we can do enters in the slightest measure into the ground of our acceptance with God. Jesus did it all. **B.B. Warfield**

Call on the coming judge to be your present Savior. As Judge, he is the law, but as Savior, he is the gospel. **J.I. Packer**

We are not saved by what Jesus taught, and we are certainly not saved by what we understand Jesus to have taught. We are saved by Jesus Himself. **Robert Farrar Capon**

Mankind intuitively places their hopes and allegiance in a perceived great one. We want someone we can look up to, believe in, and identify with. Image-bearers need a hero. More specifically, fallen humanity needs a Savior. All the beauty longings of our heart scream for just one beauty that restores, fulfills, and endures. Christianity heralds just such a beautiful one: Jesus Christ. **Steve DeWitt**

If I might comprehend Jesus Christ, I could not believe on Him. He would be no greater than myself. Such is my consciousness of sin and inability that I must have a superhuman Saviour. **Daniel Webster**

You may study, look, and meditate, but Jesus is a greater Savior than you think Him to be, even when your thoughts are at their highest. **Charles Spurgeon**

There is no better news, than the fact that Jesus can actually turn a life upside down and save it. **Cliff Richard**

He came to deliver us from our moral and spiritual disorders—but it must also be said He came to deliver us from our own remedies. **A.W. Tozer**

Christ died to save us, not from suffering, but from ourselves; not from injustice, far less than justice, but from being unjust. **George MacDonald**

You have trusted Christ as your dying Savior; now trust him as your living Savior. Just as much as he came to deliver you from future punishment, did he also come to deliver you from present bondage. **Hannah Whitall Smith**

Because the sinless Savior died,
My sinful soul is counted free;
For God, the just, is satisfied
To look on him and pardon me. **Charitie Lees Smith**

On Christ, and what he has done, my soul hangs for time and eternity. And if your soul also hangs there, it will be saved as surely as mine shall be. And if you are lost trusting in Christ, I will be lost with you and will go to hell with you. I must do so, for I have nothing else to rely upon but the fact that Jesus Christ, the Son of God, lived, died, was buried, rose again, went to heaven, and still lives and pleads for sinners at the right hand of God. **Charles Spurgeon**

Although my memory's fading, I remember two things very clearly: I am a great sinner and Christ is a great Savior. **John Newton**

Giver of Rest

"Come to me, all you who are weary and burdened, and I will give you rest. Take my yoke upon you and learn from me, for I am gentle and humble in heart, and you will find rest for your souls. For my yoke is easy and my burden is light." **Matthew 11:28-30 NIV**

Jesus doesn't participate in the rat race. He's into the slower rhythms of life, like abiding, delighting, and dwelling—all words that require us to trust Him with our place and our pace. **Lysa TerKeurst**

The atonement of Jesus Christ is the only remedy and rest for my soul. **Martin Van Buren**

Whatever you will complete or not today, rest in the only work that will never need to be done again. Rest in the fact that Jesus has done the most impossible job in the world, done it perfectly, and made it available. Take it. Enjoy it. Build your life on it. **David Murray**

He came when all things were growing old, and made them new...He came both to console you in the midst of present troubles, and to promise you everlasting rest. Do not choose then to cleave to this aged world, and to be unwilling to grow young in Christ. **Augustine**

Jesus calls upon us to carry our crosses, yet as we do so paradoxically promises a light burden and rest for our souls. **Randy Alcorn**

Only the man who follows the command of Jesus single-mindedly, and unresistingly lets his yoke rest upon him, finds his burden easy... The command of Jesus is hard, unutterably hard, for those who try to resist it. But for those who willingly submit, the yoke is easy, and the burden is light. **Dietrich Bonhoeffer**

Thou art the Lord who slept upon the pillow,
Thou art the Lord who soothed the furious sea,
What matters beating wind and tossing billow
If only we are in the boat with Thee?
Hold us quiet through the age-long minute
While Thou art silent and the wind is shrill. **Amy Carmichael**

In the ark, the weary dove
Found a welcome resting-place;
Thus my spirit longs to prove
Rest in Christ, the Ark of grace:
Tempest-tossed I long have been,
And the flood increases fast;
Open, Lord, and take me in,
Till the storm be overpast. **John Newton**

I need to be quieted. What will quiet me is God's love. Mary knew this, when she sat at Jesus' feet. Jesus said only one thing was necessary, and Mary had chosen it. Despite my to-do list, I have only one thing to do: worship Him, love Him, listen to Him, rest in Him. **Randy Alcorn**

The Word of God

In the beginning was the Word, and the Word was with God, and the Word was God. He was in the beginning with God. All things were made through him, and without him was not any thing made that was made. **John 1:1-3 ESV**

The Word became flesh and dwelt among us, and we have seen his glory, glory as of the only Son from the Father, full of grace and truth. **John 1:14 ESV**

He is dressed in a robe dipped in blood, and his name is the Word of God. **Revelation 19:13 NIV**

Let us read the Bible as the Word of God and never apologize for finding Jesus Christ throughout its pages, for Jesus Christ is what the Bible is all about! **A.W. Tozer**

For Jesus, Scripture is powerful, decisive, and authoritative because it is nothing less than the voice of God. **Kevin DeYoung**

Get into God's Word, and you will get a heart for Jesus. Get passionate about Scripture, and your passion for him will increase. **Joni Eareckson Tada**

And so the Word had breath, and wrought with human hands the creed of creeds in loveliness of perfect deeds, more strong than all poetic thought. **Alfred, Lord Tennyson**

God has given them a share in His own Image...Why? Simply in order that through this gift of Godlikeness in themselves they may be able to perceive the Image Absolute, that is the Word Himself, and through Him to apprehend the Father; which knowledge of their Maker is for men the only really happy and blessed life. **Athanasius of Alexandria**

It is as if God the Father is saying to us: "Since I have told you everything in My Word, Who is My Son, I have no other words that can at present say anything or reveal anything to you beyond this. Fix your eyes on Him alone, for in Him I have told you all, revealed all, and in Him you will find more than you desire or ask...for He is My whole word and My reply, He is My whole vision and My whole revelation." **Anthony M. Coniaris**

Jesus is a living book—"the Word"—which we will continue to "read" for eternity, but which we will never finish and never exhaust, and whose depths we will never reach. **Randy Alcorn**

PART 4:

Jesus, in and with His Disciples

Jesus does not seem to choose his followers on the basis of native talent or perfectibility or potential for greatness. When he lived on earth he surrounded himself with ordinary people who misunderstood him, failed to exercise much spiritual power, and sometimes behaved like churlish schoolchildren. Three followers in particular (the brothers James and John, and Peter) Jesus singled out for his strongest reprimands—yet two of these would become the most prominent leaders of the early Christians. I cannot avoid the impression that Jesus prefers working with unpromising recruits. Once, after he had sent out seventy-two disciples on a training mission, Jesus rejoiced at the successes they reported back. No passage in the Gospels shows him more exuberant. "At that time Jesus, full of joy through the Holy Spirit, said, 'I praise you, Father, Lord of heaven and earth, because you have hidden these things from the wise and learned, and revealed them to little children.'"

Philip Yancey

Jesus, who came to us in successive acts of love that neither started nor ended with his time on earth, became a man in order to rescue us from sin and suffering and transform us into the people we were meant to be. As the saying goes, he loves us just as we are, but he loves us too much to let us stay that way. He wants to make us clean, pure, and radiant, and in the process, grant us the joy we can find only in Him. He came to make us better and happier than we could have ever imagined.

Lost until he finds us, broken until he fixes us, and rebels until he transforms us into allies, Jesus makes us his beloved ambassadors. He delegates tasks to us and gives us meaningful and fulfilling work to do. He invites us to the banquet table not as servants but as honored members of his royal family. He makes us his brothers and sisters and together, his bride.

He chose us though we have nothing to offer and redeems and reconciles and renews us, empowering us to live honorable lives that are pleasing to him and to us. He came to seek and to save and to serve the lost.

He gives us not only eternal life after we die, but abundant life now. He came to us from Heaven's palaces and gardens to meet us in our slums of desperate need. He invites us to believe and trust in him, to follow him in an adventure that may at times be perilous but will also be rewarding beyond measure. He calls us to confess and repent, to become his disciples, to live the radical life of faith, to depend on him, to focus on him, and to find freedom in him.

It is impossible to talk about Jesus without pondering who he is in relationship to his people. In short, the universe, the plan of God, and we who know him are ultimately *All About Jesus*!

All disciples of Jesus are to find their identity in relationship with Him. That's what this final section is all about.

Our Forgiveness and Salvation in Jesus

When the goodness and loving kindness of God our Savior appeared, he saved us, not because of works done by us in righteousness, but according to his own mercy. **Titus 3:4-5 ESV**

If our greatest need had been information, God would have sent an educator. If our greatest need had been technology, God would have sent us a scientist. If our greatest need had been money, God would have sent us an economist. But since our greatest need was forgiveness, God sent us a Saviour. **Source Unknown**

Forgiveness is the greatest miracle that Jesus ever performs. It meets the greatest need; it costs the greatest price; and it brings the greatest blessing and the most lasting results. **Warren Wiersbe**

The sinner can no more raise himself from the deadness of sin than Lazarus, who had been dead four days, until Jesus came. **George Whitefield**

The gospel is for us, not about us. It isn't about anything that we do, feel, or choose. It is the Good News about Jesus Christ and what he has accomplished for us. **Michael Horton**

If we think we are not all that bad, the idea of grace will never change us. Change comes by seeing a need for a Savior and getting one. **Timothy Keller**

We will never be cleansed until we confess we are dirty. **Max Lucado**

If I had an hour to share my faith with someone, I'd spend 45 minutes convincing them that they were lost...Only when we are honest with ourselves about our sinful state will we be ready to accept Jesus' work on our behalf and respond in lives of grateful service. **Francis Schaeffer**

This I will ever preach, that all, under pain of damnation, are obliged to come to him. **Thomas Boston**

It is important to make your peace with Christ while the opportunity exists. Life is so fragile...It could be over in the blink of an eye, and then it's too late to accept God's gift of salvation. **Chuck Norris**

> The thief had nails through both hands, so that he could not work; and a nail through each foot, so that he could not run errands for the Lord; he could not lift a hand or a foot toward his salvation, and yet Christ offered him the gift of God; and he took it. **Dwight L. Moody**

There never was a sinner half as big as Christ is as a Savior. Come and measure the sinner from head to foot and all around. Make him out to be an elephantine sinner, yet there is room for him in the ark, Christ Jesus. **Charles Spurgeon**

The man who dies out of Christ is said to be lost, and hardly a word in the English tongue expresses his condition with greater accuracy. He has squandered a rare fortune and at the last he stands for a fleeting moment and looks around, a moral fool, a wastrel who has lost in one overwhelming and irrecoverable loss, his soul, his life, his peace, his total, mysterious personality, his dear and everlasting all. **A.W. Tozer**

Jesus suffered for our sins so we would not have to. By refusing to accept His provision, we imply that He died in vain. By inflicting suffering on ourselves, we imply that we are good enough to pay our own way. **Randy Alcorn**

Morality is a neat cover for foul venom...Men will be damned with good works as well as without them, if they make them their confidence [rather than Jesus]. **Charles Spurgeon**

Jesus himself is the main argument for why we should believe Christianity. **Timothy Keller**

The Bible never says you have to believe in Christians to be saved. It says you have to believe in Jesus. He's the One we're invited to come and see (John 1:46), and the only One who can save and transform us. **Randy Alcorn**

Jesus Christ loves to see poor sinners coming to Him, He is pleased to see them lie at His feet pleading His promises; and if you thus come to Christ, He will not send you away without His Spirit; no, but will receive and bless you. **George Whitefield**

Our Faith and Trust in Jesus

To all who did receive him, who believed in his name, he gave the right to become children of God. **John 1:12 ESV**

By grace you have been saved through faith. And this is not your own doing; it is the gift of God. **Ephesians 2:8 ESV**

Without faith it is impossible to please God, because anyone who comes to him must believe that he exists and that he rewards those who earnestly seek him. **Hebrews 11:6 NIV**

There are three primary forms of the word "faith" in Greek...Each form's meaning is a variation of the word "trust."...Therefore, biblically, trust and faith have the same meaning. **Marten Visser**

This is faith: a renouncing of everything we are apt to call our own, and relying wholly upon the blood, righteousness, and intercession of Jesus. **John Newton**

A man can eat his dinner without understanding exactly how food nourishes him. A man can accept what Christ has done without knowing how it works: indeed, he certainly would not know how it works until he has accepted it.
C.S. Lewis

"Twant me, 'twas the Lord. I always told him, 'I trust to you. I don't know where to go or what to do, but I expect you to lead me,' and He always did."
Harriet Tubman, born a slave and rescued hundreds of slaves through the Underground Railroad; died free at age 93

According to Jesus, what I think about him and how I respond will determine my destiny for all eternity. **Philip Yancey**

The Christian clings to the doctrine of the deity of Christ. He does not approach it as a cold academic matter, but he comes to it as a drowning man lays hold of a plank that may save him from the abyss. **J. Gresham Machen**

We must hide our unholiness in the wounds of Christ as Moses hid himself in the cleft of the rock while the glory of God passed by. We must take refuge from God in God. **A.W. Tozer**

All self-effort is but sinking sand. Christ alone is the Rock of our salvation.
Henry Allen Ironside

Faith speaks in an entirely different manner and makes a man say, "Yes I have sinned grievously, I have lived a life of sin, yet I know that I am a child of God because I am not resting on any righteousness of my own." **Martyn Lloyd-Jones**

Faith is rest, not toil. It is the giving up all the former weary efforts to do or feel something good, in order to induce God to love and pardon...and relying implicitly upon the free love of Him who so loved the world that He gave His only begotten Son. **Horatius Bonar**

It is not, strictly speaking, even faith in Christ that saves, but Christ that saves through faith. The saving power resides exclusively, not in the act of faith or the attitude of faith or nature of faith, but in the object of faith. **B.B. Warfield**

> It is not the strength of your faith that saves you, but the strength of Him upon whom you rely! **Charles Spurgeon**

Wherever Jesus sees faith, he has forgiveness on a hair trigger. **Glen Scrivener**

"Lord, I believe; help my unbelief" is the best any of us can do really, but thank God it is enough. **Frederick Buechner**

Till men have faith in Christ, their best services are but glorious sins. **Thomas Brooks**

True faith always produces real conformity to Christ. **R.C. Sproul**

True faith brings a spiritual and moral transformation and an inward witness that cannot be mistaken. These come when we stop believing in belief and start believing in the Lord Jesus Christ indeed. **A.W. Tozer**

Faith is a confidence in the person of Jesus Christ and in His power, so that even when His power does not serve my end, my confidence in Him remains because of who He is. **Ravi Zacharias**

If you truly believe in Jesus, it is for life. Saving faith is a life-long act. **Charles Spurgeon**

Christ is our fortress; patience our defense; the word of God our sword; and our victory is a candid, firm, unfeigned faith in Jesus Christ. **Menno Simons**

It won't be long before your faith will be rewarded with the sight of the One who has promised to be with you to the end. **Nancy DeMoss Wolgemuth**

Our Repentance Before Jesus

From that time Jesus began to preach his message: "Turn away from your sins, because the Kingdom of heaven is near!" **Matthew 4:17 GNT**

"They that are whole need not a physician; but they that are sick. I came not to call the righteous, but sinners to repentance." **Luke 5:31-32 KJV**

If we confess our sins, [Jesus] is faithful and just and will forgive us our sins and purify us from all unrighteousness. **1 John 1:9 NIV**

When the hand of faith opens to lay hold of Christ, it drops the sin it had grasped before. You must part with your sin—or Christ. **John Angell James**

After Jesus rebuked the Pharisees who were ready to stone a woman for adultery (John 8:1-11), he could have told the woman, "Go burn for your sins" *or* "Go and feel free to sin some more." Instead he said, "Go now and leave your life of sin." Jesus didn't deny truth. He affirmed it. She needed to repent. And change. Jesus didn't deny grace. He offered it. He sent her away, forgiven and cleansed, to new life. **Randy Alcorn**

Jesus is the God whom we can approach without pride and before whom we can humble ourselves without despair. **Blaise Pascal**

Arise my soul, and review your deeds which have preceded from you. Scrutinize them closely, and shed the rain of your tears, declaring openly to Christ your thoughts and deeds, so that you may be justified. **Andrew of Crete**

When our Lord and Master Jesus Christ said, "Repent," he willed the entire life of believers to be one of repentance. **Martin Luther**

A gospel which is only about the moment of conversion but does not extend to every moment of life in Christ is too small. A gospel that gets your sins forgiven but offers no power for transformation is too small. A gospel that isolates one of the benefits of union with Christ and ignores all the others is too small. A gospel that must be measured by your own moral conduct, social conscience, or religious experience is too small. A gospel that rearranges the components of your life but does not put you personally in the presence of God is too small. **Fred Sanders**

If the man does not live differently from what he did before, both at home and abroad, his repentance needs to be repented of, and his conversion is a fiction. Not only action and language, but spirit and temper must be changed. **Charles Spurgeon**

True repentance will entirely change you; the bias of your souls will be changed, then you will delight in God, in Christ, in His Law, and in His people. **George Whitefield**

Scripture considers repentance a path to liberation, not condemnation. **Edward Welch**

Our Righteousness in Jesus

Since we have been declared righteous by faith, we have peace with God through our Lord Jesus Christ. **Romans 5:1 CSB**

God made him who had no sin to be sin for us, so that in him we might become the righteousness of God. **2 Corinthians 5:21 NIV**

You can't kneel before the manger of One who is righteousness and hold to your own righteousness at the same time. **Paul David Tripp**

True conversion means turning not only from sin but also from depending on self-made righteousness. Those who trust in their own righteousness for conversion hide behind their own good works. This is the reason that self-righteous people are so angry with gospel preachers, because the gospel does not spare those who will not submit to the righteousness of Jesus Christ! **George Whitefield**

Nothing will do except righteousness; and no other conception of righteousness will do except Christ's. **Matthew Arnold**

He died on the cross in our place and then rose from the dead to prove that the dire situation brought about by our sinfulness need not prove terminal...God no longer sees the chasm of sin that has separated us from himself; instead he views us just as he sees Jesus—as pure and untarnished. ***The Knowing Jesus Study Bible***

This is the mystery of the riches of divine grace for sinners; for by a wonderful exchange our sins are now not ours but Christ's, and Christ's righteousness is not Christ's but ours. **Martin Luther**

Jesus Christ does not just offer us salvation as though it is a decoration or a bouquet or some addition to our garb. He says plainly: "Throw off your old rags; strip to the skin! Let Me dress you in the fine, clean robes of My righteousness—all Mine." **A.W. Tozer**

There, poor sinner, take my garment, and put it on; you shall stand before God as if you were Christ, and I will stand before God as if I had been the sinner; I will suffer in the sinner's stead, and you shall be rewarded for works that you did not do, but which I did for you. **Charles Spurgeon**

Learn to know Christ and him crucified. Learn to sing to him, and say, "Lord Jesus, you are my righteousness, I am your sin...You have become what you were not so that I might become what I was not." **Martin Luther**

Behold, then, beloved, the high vantage-ground on which a saint of God stands, with regard to his hope of heaven. He stands "outside" of his own righteousness, in the righteousness of another. **Octavius Winslow**

The Lord our Righteousness is a sweet name to a convinced sinner; to one that has felt the guilt of sin in his conscience; seen his need of that righteousness, and the worth of it. **Matthew Henry**

Our Transformation in Jesus

If anyone is in Christ, he is a new creation. The old has passed away; behold, the new has come. **2 Corinthians 5:17 ESV**

We were buried therefore with him by baptism into death, in order that, just as Christ was raised from the dead by the glory of the Father, we too might walk in newness of life. **Romans 6:4 ESV**

Jesus changes everything about a person's life, from the obvious to the unseen. He shatters black and white into brilliant color and shakes the asleep until they're wide awake. **Jaquelle Crowe**

The Bible teaches us that God offers us a brand-new start when we give over our lives to him...the only determining factor in our being made right with our Maker is the rebirth which he offers us through Jesus Christ, a transformation so revolutionary, so radical, that it can only be termed a "new creation" (Galatians 6:15). ***The Knowing Jesus Study Bible***

You can laugh at Christianity; you can mock and ridicule it. But it works. A relationship with Jesus changes lives. **Josh McDowell**

The same Jesus who turned water into wine can transform your home, your life, your family, and your future. He is still in the miracle-working business, and His business is the business of transformation. **Adrian Rogers**

Faith in Jesus leads to a life transformed by Jesus—any other message isn't gospel truth. **Melissa Kruger**

Preach Christ and show the love of God to the most primitive, most neglected, most illiterate people in the world; be patient and make them understand. Their hearts will awake, the Spirit will illuminate their minds. Those who believe on Jesus will be transformed. This is a beautiful thing that is being demonstrated over and over again in the world today. **A.W. Tozer**

Jesus is about growth not death, sanctification not stagnation. That's the key to a Christian life, and it's not boring but adventurous. Jesus, who spun the galaxies into being, paints the sunsets, and taught the humpback whales to migrate, can be comforting and rest-giving, but he is *never* boring! **Randy Alcorn**

The more we let God take us over, the more truly ourselves we become—because He made us. He invented us…It is when I turn to Christ, when I give up myself to His personality, that I first begin to have a real personality of my own. **C.S. Lewis**

Grace is the work of the Holy Spirit in transforming our desires so that knowing Jesus becomes sweeter than illicit sex, sweeter than money and what it can buy, sweeter than every fruitless joy. Grace is God satisfying our souls with His Son so that we're ruined for anything else! **Sam Storms**

The heart that has really tasted the grace of Christ, will instinctively hate sin. **J.C. Ryle**

All change comes from deepening your understanding of the salvation of Christ and living out the changes that understanding creates in your heart. **Timothy Keller**

When we receive Jesus Christ, our perspective changes, and with it our attitude. The trivial and the important change places. **William L. Stidger**

By a miracle of grace, Jesus touched me deeply when I was a teenager, gave me a new heart, and utterly transformed my life. Fifty years later, he's still unveiling himself and changing me into his image and likeness. I couldn't be happier that he's every bit as real to me now as the moment I met him—but now I know him better, and therefore worship him more deeply. Jesus didn't just change everything back then. He still changes everything today. **Randy Alcorn**

When I came to believe in Christ's teaching, I ceased desiring what I had wished for before…What was good and bad had changed places. **Leo Tolstoy**

When you accept His gift of grace, you are transformed, not only for today, but also for all eternity. **Joni Eareckson Tada**

Did Christ finish His work for us? Then there can be no doubt but He will also finish His work in us. **John Flavel**

Our Holiness in Jesus

Since we have these promises, beloved, let us cleanse ourselves from every defilement of body and spirit, bringing holiness to completion in the fear of God. **2 Corinthians 7:1 ESV**

He has saved us and called us with a holy calling, not according to our works, but according to his own purpose and grace, which was given to us in Christ Jesus before time began. **2 Timothy 1:9 CSB**

We could not take one step in the pursuit of holiness if God in His grace had not first delivered us from the dominion of sin and brought us into union with His risen Son. Salvation is by grace and sanctification is by grace. **Jerry Bridges**

Remember holiness is a flower, not a root; it is not sanctification that saves, but salvation that sanctifies. **Charles Spurgeon**

God sees us perfect in His Son while He disciplines and chastens and purges us that we may be partakers of His holiness. **A.W. Tozer**

The holiest Christians are not those most concerned about holiness as such, but whose minds and hearts and goals and purposes and love and hope are most fully focused on our Lord Jesus Christ. **J.I. Packer**

Holiness is not some lofty experience, unattainable except to those who can leap the stars, but it is rather a lowly experience, which lowly people in the lowly walks of life can share with Jesus, by letting His mind be in them. **Samuel Logan Brengle**

The best way to overcome the world is not with morality or self-discipline. Christians overcome the world by…seeing something more attractive than the world: Christ. **Thomas Chalmers**

Preferring anything above Christ is the very essence of sin. It must be fought. **John Piper**

The world and you must part, or Christ and you will never meet. **Thomas Brooks**

There must be a divorce between you and sin, or there can be no marriage between you and Christ. **Charles Spurgeon**

If we truly think of Christ as our source of holiness, we shall refrain from anything wicked or impure in thought or act and thus show ourselves to be worthy bearers of his name. For the quality of holiness is shown not by what we say but by what we do in life. **Gregory of Nyssa**

I cannot trifle with the evil that killed my best Friend. I must be holy for His sake. How can I live in sin when He has died to save me from it? **Charles Spurgeon**

Wonderful are the effects when a crucified, glorious Savior is presented to the eye of Faith. This sight destroys the love of sin. **John Newton**

There is no detour to holiness. Jesus came to the resurrection through the cross, not around it. **Leighton Ford**

Can Christ be in thy heart, and thou not know it? Can one king be dethroned and another crowned in thy soul, and thou hear no scuffle? **William Gurnall**

There will be three effects of nearness to Jesus, all beginning with the letter *h*—humility, happiness, and holiness. **Charles Spurgeon**

Our Discipleship Under Jesus

"If anyone would come after me, let him deny himself and take up his cross and follow me. For whoever would save his life will lose it, but whoever loses his life for my sake will save it." **Matthew 16:24-25 ESV**

"Those of you who do not give up everything you have cannot be my disciples." **Luke 14:33 NIV**

"If you want to be my disciple, you must, by comparison, hate everyone else—your father and mother, wife and children, brothers and sisters—yes, even your own life. Otherwise, you cannot be my disciple." **Luke 14:26 NLT**

"Whoever serves me must follow me; and where I am, my servant also will be. My Father will honor the one who serves me." **John 12:26 NIV**

Our Lord had only one desire, and that was to do the will of his Father, and to have this desire is characteristic of a disciple. **Oswald Chambers**

Live for God. Obey the Scriptures. Think of others before yourself. Be holy. Love Jesus. And as you do these things, do whatever else you like, with whomever you like, wherever you like, and you'll be walking in the will of God. **Kevin DeYoung**

Peter, James and John relinquished their careers, their boats (apparently still laden with fish!), their families, *everything* to follow in the footsteps of their new-found Master. It may seem as though we are called on to give up a great deal to follow our Lord, but the blessings we will receive from such a commitment will go beyond what we could ever have imagined (Luke 18:28-30; 1 Corinthians 2:9). ***The Knowing Jesus Study Bible***

There is no other way except the way of the cross. Jesus made it so crystal clear. He simply said, "If you want to be my disciple…," and that stands just exactly the same way today. He is saying that to each of us, "Do you want to be my disciple?" **Elisabeth Elliot**

…discipleship never consists in this or that specific action: it is always a decision, either for or against Jesus Christ. **Dietrich Bonhoeffer**

Jesus…taught that if we make our life on earth so important and all-possessing that we cannot surrender it gladly to Him, we will lose it at last. **A.W. Tozer**

If Jesus is who he says he is, and if his promises are as rewarding as the Bible claims they are, then we may discover that satisfaction in our lives and success in the church are not found in what culture deems most important but in radical abandonment to Jesus. **David Platt**

If we are serious about our discipleship, Jesus will eventually request each of us to do those very things which are most difficult for us to do. **Neal A. Maxwell**

The disciples were with Jesus. They heard Jesus, saw Jesus, touched Jesus. Their life in Christ was being with Jesus...We are with Jesus when we spend time in the Word, prayer, and practice his continual presence with us. Who is responsible for developing your relationship with Jesus Christ? It's not your pastor, your mentor or your discipler. It's you! **Steve Keels**

Have the courage to have your wisdom regarded as stupidity. Be fools for Christ. And have the courage to suffer the contempt of the sophisticated world. **Antonin Scalia**

The decision to grow always involves a choice between risk and comfort. This means that to be a follower of Jesus, you must renounce comfort as the ultimate value of your life. **John Ortberg**

Christ's followers cannot expect better treatment in the world than their Master had. **Matthew Henry**

Our Mission in Jesus

By this my Father is glorified, that you bear much fruit and so prove to be my disciples. **John 15:8 ESV**

My life is worth nothing to me unless I use it for finishing the work assigned me by the Lord Jesus—the work of telling others the Good News about the wonderful grace of God. **Acts 20:24 NLT**

Jesus didn't save you so you could cruise to heaven in a luxury liner. He wants you to be useful in His kingdom! **David Wilkerson**

How many there are...who imagine that because Jesus paid it all, they need pay nothing, forgetting that the prime object of their salvation was that they should follow in the footsteps of Jesus Christ in bringing back a lost world to God. **Lottie Moon**

I have loved to hear my Lord spoken of; and wherever I have seen the print of His shoe in the earth, there have I coveted to set my foot too. **John Bunyan (Mr. Stand-fast in *The Pilgrim's Progress*)**

Never forget what Jesus did for you. Never take lightly what it cost Him. And never assume that if it cost Him His very life, that it won't also cost you yours. **Rich Mullins**

If Jesus bore the cross, and died on it for me, ought I not to be willing to take it up for Him? **Dwight L. Moody**

If we think the main mission of the church is to improve life in Adam and add a little moral strength to this fading evil age, we have not yet understood the radical condition for which Christ is such a radical solution. **Michael Horton**

Jesus didn't come to make us safe. He came to make us dangerous to the kingdom of darkness. **Christine Caine**

If sinners be damned, at least let them leap to Hell over our bodies. If they will perish, let them perish with our arms about their knees. Let no one go there unwarned and unprayed for. **Charles Spurgeon**

The church tends to become very preoccupied with its own affairs, obsessed with petty, parochial trivia, while the needy world outside is waiting. So the Son sends us out into the world, as the Father had sent him into the world. **John Stott**

The spirit of Christ is the spirit of missions. The nearer we get to Him, the more intensely missionary we become. **Henry Martyn**

As soon as a man has found Christ, he begins to find others. **Charles Spurgeon**

Sometimes it may seem to us that there is no purpose in our lives, that going day after day for years to this office or that school or factory is nothing else but waste and weariness. But it may be that God has sent us there because but for us, Christ would not be there. If our being there means that Christ is there, that alone makes it worthwhile. **Caryll Houselander**

You want to honor Jesus, you desire to put many crowns upon His head, and this you can best do by winning souls for Him. These are the spoils that He covets, these are the trophies for which He fights, these are the jewels that shall be His best adornment. **Charles Spurgeon**

The greatest cause in the world is joyfully rescuing people from hell, meeting their earthly needs, making them glad in God, and doing it with a kind, serious pleasure that makes Christ look like the Treasure he is. **John Piper**

Looking to Christ gives us a goal to pursue, a person to enjoy, a passion to feed. Looking to Christ orients the direction...of our entire lives. **Nancy Guthrie**

God can use anyone who loves Jesus. **George Verwer**

Oh how I wish the people would awake up from their lethargy and come out soul and body for Christ. **George Washington Carver**

You see, the root cause of our lack of engagement in God's mission is not a missions problem but a gospel problem. We demonstrate by our inaction that we no longer marvel at grace. We are unaffected by the beauty of what God has done for us in Christ. **Trevin Wax**

The preaching that this world needs most is the sermons in shoes that are walking with Jesus Christ. **Dwight L. Moody**

For years I thought my assignment or the Church's assignment was to articulate the Gospel and nothing more. Now I believe that if we don't support the verbal expression of the Gospel with physical demonstration of compassion, we are not imitating Jesus. **Max Lucado**

I live as though Jesus Christ was crucified yesterday, arose today and is coming again tomorrow. **Martin Luther**

Our Sacrifice for Jesus

Jesus told his disciples, "If anyone would come after me, let him deny himself and take up his cross and follow me. For whoever would save his life will lose it, but whoever loses his life for my sake will find it." **Matthew 16:24-25 ESV**

Through Jesus, therefore, let us continually offer to God a sacrifice of praise—the fruit of lips that openly profess his name. And do not forget to do good and to share with others, for with such sacrifices God is pleased. **Hebrews 13:15-16 NIV**

Jesus now has many lovers of his Heavenly Kingdom, but few bearers of his cross. **Thomas à Kempis**

Christians are meant to have the same vocation as their King, that of cross-bearers. It is this consciousness of a high calling and of partnership with Jesus which brings gladness in tribulations, which makes Christians enter prisons for their faith with the joy of a bridegroom entering the bridal room. **Richard Wurmbrand**

What our Lord said about cross-bearing and obedience is not in fine type. It is in bold print on the face of the contract. **Vance Havner**

To take up your cross is to consider it better to die than to live for something other than Jesus. **Richard Chin**

You will not get to steal quietly into heaven, into Christ's company, without a conflict and a cross. I find crosses to be Christ's carved work that he marks out for us and that with crosses he portraits us to his own image. **Samuel Rutherford**

Let fire and cross; let the crowds of wild beasts; let tearings…let shatterings of the whole body; and let all the evil torments of the Devil come upon me: only let me attain to Jesus Christ. **Ignatius of Antioch**

The paradox of our faith is that acceptance of the Lord Christ Jesus is not a pathway to an easy life but a call to do hard things if we are to live in the image of our Lord. "Love my enemies?" "Give my riches to the poor and take up the cross?" "Die so that I might live?" Jesus has a disruptive set of teachings…often tough on his followers, and yet compassionate with those in need. **Condoleezza Rice**

When Christ calls a man, he bids him come and die. **Dietrich Bonhoeffer**

A crucified Savior will never be content to have a self-pleasing, self-indulging, worldly-minded people. **J.C. Ryle**

For the sake of each of us he laid down his life—worth no less than the universe. He demands of us in return our lives for the sake of each other. **Clement of Alexandria**

Something about Jesus keeps prodding people to do what they would rather not: Francis of Assisi gives up his possessions, Augustine gives up his mistress, John Newton gives up his slave trade, and Father Damien gives up his health. **John Ortberg**

Please take all of me, Lord, that I may be wholly yours. Help me to hold loosely those things, even those blessings, that I have here, that I may be available for service to you at any time. **Amy Carmichael**

I will place no value on anything I have or may possess except in relation to the Kingdom of Christ. **David Livingstone**

Vacate the throne room of your heart and enthrone Jesus there...Dedicate your entire life to His honor alone and shift the motives of your life from self to God. Let the reason back of your daily conduct be Christ and His glory, not yourself, not your family nor your country nor your church. In all things let Him have the preeminence. **A.W. Tozer**

Die to self. Live for Christ. And then do what you want, and go where you want, for God's glory. **Kevin DeYoung**

If you cling to your own plans and desires you will never discover the freedom and joy found in losing your life for Jesus. **Nancy Guthrie**

When we meet Jesus face to face, behold His nail-scarred hands reaching out to us, and see the look in His eyes when He says, "Enter into your Master's happiness" (Matthew 25:23), I believe we will gain a new perspective on this life. Quite simply, we'll see that when it came to following Jesus, the benefits always far outweighed the costs...each and every time. **Randy Alcorn**

Our Knowledge of Jesus

"This is eternal life, that they may know You, the only true God, and Jesus Christ whom You have sent." **John 17:3 NASB**

I want to know Christ—yes, to know the power of his resurrection and participation in his sufferings, becoming like him in his death...Not that I have already obtained all this, or have already arrived at my goal, but I press on to take hold of that for which Christ Jesus took hold of me. **Philippians 3:10-12 NIV**

Continue to grow in the grace and knowledge of our Lord and Savior Jesus Christ. To him be the glory, now and forever! Amen. **2 Peter 3:18 GNT**

By this we know that we have come to know Him, if we keep His commandments. **1 John 2:3 NASB**

We weren't meant to be somebody—we were meant to know Somebody. **John Piper**

Today the greatest single deterrent to knowledge of Jesus is His familiarity. Because we think we know Him, we pass Him by. **Winifred Kirkland**

I may know all the doctrines in the Bible, but unless I know Christ, there is not one of them that can save me. **Charles Spurgeon**

Christianity is not a doctrine, not truth as truth, but the knowledge of a Person; it is knowing the Lord Jesus. You cannot be educated into being a Christian. **T. Austin-Sparks**

What were we made for? To know God. What aim should we have in life? To know God. What is the eternal life that Jesus gives? To know God. What is the best thing in life? To know God. What in humans gives God most pleasure? Knowledge of himself. **J.I. Packer**

The longer you know Christ, and the nearer you come to him, still the more do you see of his glory. Every farther prospect of Christ entertains the mind with a fresh delight. He is as it were a new Christ every day, and yet the same Christ still. **John Flavel**

If you know Christ and him crucified, you know enough to make you happy…And without this, all your other knowledge cannot keep you from being everlastingly miserable. **George Whitefield**

The Fort Knox of faith is Christ. Fellowshipping with him. Walking with him. Pondering him. Exploring him. The heart-stopping realization that in him you are part of something ancient, endless, unstoppable, and unfathomable. **Max Lucado**

I do not believe that I have a wish in all the world except to know more of my Master, and to win more souls for him. **Charles Spurgeon**

Our Identity in Jesus

He makes the whole body fit together perfectly. As each part does its own special work, it helps the other parts grow, so that the whole body is healthy and growing and full of love. **Ephesians 4:16 NLT**

You are a chosen race, a royal priesthood, a holy nation, a people for his own possession, that you may proclaim the excellencies of him who called you out of darkness into his marvelous light. **1 Peter 2:9 ESV**

I have been crucified with Christ; it is no longer I who live, but Christ lives in me; and the life which I now live in the flesh I live by faith in the Son of God, who loved me and gave Himself for me. **Galatians 2:20 NKJV**

The gospel brings me explosive news: my search for approval is over. In Christ I already have all the approval I need. **Dave Harvey**

Outside of Christ, I am only a sinner, but in Christ, I am saved. Outside of Christ, I am empty; in Christ, I am full. Outside of Christ, I am weak; in Christ, I am strong. Outside of Christ, I cannot; in Christ, I am more than able. Outside of Christ, I have been defeated; in Christ, I am already victorious. **Watchman Nee**

All men and women, including myself, that are well acquainted with sexual temptation are ultimately not what our temptation says of us. We are what Christ had done for us; therefore, our ultimate identity is very simple: We are Christians. **Jackie Hill Perry**

Look for yourself, and you will find in the long run only hatred, loneliness, despair, rage, ruin, and decay. But look for Christ and you will find Him, and with Him everything else thrown in. **C.S. Lewis**

The idea of a spiritual heart transplant is a vivid image to me...Jesus' heart is inside me, and my heart is gone. So if God were to place a stethoscope against my chest, he would hear the heart of Jesus Christ beating. **Max Lucado**

Thou hast made us for thyself, O Lord, and our heart is restless until it finds its rest in thee. **Augustine**

Should anyone knock at my heart and say, "Who lives here?" I should reply, "Not Martin Luther, but the Lord Jesus Christ." **Martin Luther**

My faith rests not upon what I am or shall be or feel or know, but in what Christ is, in what He has done, and in what He is now doing for me. Hallelujah! **Charles Spurgeon**

Oneness with Christ means to be identified with Christ...in crucifixion. But we must go on to be identified with Him in resurrection as well, for beyond the cross is resurrection and the manifestation of His Presence. **A.W. Tozer**

To be in Christ is the source of the Christian life; to be like Christ is the sum of his excellence; to be with Christ is the fullness of his joy. **Charles Hodge**

In our present condition, Jesus sees us as the acorns that will become oak trees, the apple seeds that will become orchards, the caterpillars that will become butterflies, and the random cacophonies of words and notes that will become musical masterpieces. **Scott Sauls**

Christ has made my soul beautiful with the jewels of grace and virtue. I belong to Him Whom the Angels serve. **Agnes of Rome**

All that I am I owe to Jesus Christ, revealed to me in His divine Book. **David Livingstone**

Our Need for Jesus

"You are worried and troubled over so many things, but just one is needed. Mary has chosen the right thing, and it will not be taken away from her." **Luke 10:41-42 GNT**

God, you are my God; I eagerly seek you. I thirst for you; my body faints for you in a land that is dry, desolate, and without water. **Psalm 63:1 CSB**

My God will supply every need of yours according to his riches in glory in Christ Jesus. **Philippians 4:19 ESV**

There is only one Being who can satisfy the last aching abyss of the human heart and that is the Lord Jesus Christ. **Oswald Chambers**

The biggest need in your life, and in mine, is to see the glory of God in the face of Jesus Christ. **Kevin DeYoung**

Until Jesus Christ is the obsession of your heart, you'll always be looking to mere men to meet your needs that only He can fill. **Leslie Ludy**

You were made for him (Romans 11:36). He is ultimately all that you need...If lasting love is what you're looking for anywhere else, you are chasing the wind, seeking what you will never find, slowly being destroyed by your pursuit. But in Jesus, there is fullness of joy. In Jesus, there is a relationship worth everything, because he is everything. Run to him. **Jackie Hill Perry**

Jesus Christ is God's everything for man's total needs. **Richard Halverson**

God's greatest gift is Himself. We don't need just salvation; we need Jesus, the Savior. It is He who graciously offers us Heaven—a place purchased by His blood. **Randy Alcorn**

Everything you need is found in Jesus Christ the Son of God! **A.W. Tozer**

No other person and nothing else in this world can meet our deepest needs. Jesus is the incarnation of all the fullness of God, a God we can know personally. We know the great "I AM"! Every day is a burning-bush day in Jesus Christ! ***The Knowing Jesus Study Bible***

What the sun is to the flower, so Jesus is to me. **Alfred, Lord Tennyson**

Jesus is presented too often much as "Someone who will meet your need." That's the throbbing heart of modern evangelism...He's the Need-meeter. Well, He is that indeed; but, ah, He's infinitely more than that. **A.W. Tozer**

I need Christ, not something that resembles Him. **C.S. Lewis**

It is not opinions that man needs: it is TRUTH. It is not theology; it is God. It is not religion; it is Christ. **Horatius Bonar**

It is tragic to go through our days making Christ the subject of our study but not the sustenance of our souls. **Vance Havner**

The irony is that while God doesn't need us but still wants us, we desperately need God but don't really want Him most of the time. **Francis Chan**

People who are rich, successful, and beautiful may well go through life relying on their natural gifts. People who lack such natural advantages, hence underqualified for success in the kingdom of this world, just might turn to God in their time of need. Human beings do not readily admit desperation. **Philip Yancey**

You may never know that JESUS is all you need, until JESUS is all you have. **Corrie ten Boom**

Our Dependence on Jesus

"I am the true vine...Remain in me, as I also remain in you. No branch can bear fruit by itself; it must remain in the vine. Neither can you bear fruit unless you remain in me...apart from me you can do nothing. If you do not remain in me, you are like a branch that is thrown away and withers...If you remain in me and my words remain in you, ask whatever you wish, and it will be done for you. This is to my Father's glory, that you bear much fruit, showing yourselves to be my disciples." **John 15:1-8 NIV**

I can do all things through him who strengthens me. **Philippians 4:13 ESV**

He has said to me, "My grace is sufficient for you, for power is perfected in weakness." Most gladly, therefore, I will rather boast about my weaknesses, so that the power of Christ may dwell in me. **2 Corinthians 12:9 NASB**

Do not become self-sufficient. Self-sufficiency is Satan's net where he catches men, like poor silly fish...God pours no power into man's heart till man's power is all poured out. Live, then, daily, a life of dependence on the grace of God. **Charles Spurgeon**

Jesus Christ is not a crutch; He is the ground to walk on. **Leighton Ford**

God…doesn't intend to help us live the Christian life. Immaturity considers the Lord Jesus a Helper. Maturity knows Him to be life itself. **Miles J. Stanford**

Jesus Christ is indeed a crutch for the lame, to help us walk upright, just as he is also medicine for the spiritually sick, bread for the hungry and water for the thirsty. We do not deny this; it is perfectly true. But then all human beings are lame, sick, hungry and thirsty. The only difference between us is not that some are needy, while others are not. It is rather that some know and acknowledge their need, while others either don't through ignorance or won't through pride. **John Stott**

When you realize just how dependent you are on Jesus for your salvation—his death for your sin, his life for your righteousness—you understand why the Bible is so insistent that salvation comes only through faith in him. **Greg Gilbert**

Christianity does not begin with our pursuit of Christ, but with Christ's pursuit of us. **David Platt**

Abide in Jesus. Let the Holy Ghost in you keep you abiding in Jesus, so that when Satan comes to knock at your door, Jesus will go and open it, and as soon as the devil sees the face of Christ looking through the door, he will turn tail... **F.B. Meyer**

Neither theological knowledge nor social action alone is enough to keep us in love with Christ unless both are preceded by a personal encounter with Him…The Holy Hour becomes like an oxygen tank to revive the breath of the Holy Spirit in the midst of the foul and fetid atmosphere of the world. **Fulton J. Sheen**

Christ went more willingly to the cross than we do to the throne of grace. **Thomas Watson**

Our Focus on Jesus

I decided to know nothing among you except Jesus Christ and him crucified. **1 Corinthians 2:2 ESV**

Whatever you do, whether in word or deed, do it all in the name of the Lord Jesus, giving thanks to God the Father through him. **Colossians 3:17 NIV**

There have been men before who got so interested in proving the existence of God that they came to care nothing for God himself, as if the good Lord had nothing to do but to exist. **C.S. Lewis**

Miss Christ and you miss all. **Thomas Brooks**

Doctrine without Christ will be nothing better than his empty tomb. Doctrine with Christ is a glorious high throne, with the King sitting on it. **Charles Spurgeon**

Too often we argue about Christianity instead of marveling at Jesus. **John Ortberg**

We are distracted by our self-focus. All our boasting and pompous self-talk would be so utterly vain if we were to see Christ fully with our eyes of faith. **Tony Reinke**

> The key...to loving God is to see Jesus, to hold him before the mind with as much fullness and clarity as possible. It is to adore him. **Dallas Willard**

A man may take the measure of his growth and decay in grace according to his thoughts and meditations upon the person of Christ. **John Owen**

The great cause of neglecting the Scriptures is not want of time, but want of heart, some idol taking the place of Christ. **Robert Chapman**

The mark of a life governed by the Holy Spirit is that such a life is continually and ever more and more occupied with Christ, that Christ becomes greater and greater as time goes on. **T. Austin-Sparks**

I like to hear a man dwell much on the same essentials of Christianity. For we have but one God, and one Christ, and one faith to preach; and I will not preach another Gospel to please men with variety, as if our Saviour and our Gospel had grown stale. **Richard Baxter**

If I had only one more sermon to preach before I died, it would be about my Lord Jesus Christ. And I think that when we get to the end of our ministry, one of our regrets will be that we did not preach more of him. I am sure no minister will ever repent of having preached him too much. **Charles Spurgeon**

The Christian's whole desire, at its best and highest, is that Jesus Christ be praised. **D.A. Carson**

Paul preached on various "real-life" topics, but he did so in such a way that Jesus wasn't seen as just another (albeit better) life coach, self-help expert, Mr. Fix It, or success guru. In Paul's preaching, Jesus is the crucified and risen Lord. There is no other option, because there is no other Jesus. **Yancey Arrington**

Preach Christ or nothing: don't dispute or discuss except with your eye on the cross. **Charles Spurgeon**

To be a Christian is to be a Jesus person—one whose life is based on his priorities, not on the priorities of subsequent theologians. **Andrew Wilson**

If you wish to be disappointed, look to others. If you wish to be downhearted, look to yourself. If you wish to be encouraged...look upon Jesus Christ. **Eric Sauer**

Are you tempted? Look unto Jesus. Are you afflicted? Look unto Jesus. Do all speak evil of you? Look unto Jesus. Do you feel cold, dull, and backsliding? Look unto Jesus. **J.C. Ryle**

In the greatest temptations, a single look to Christ, and the barely pronouncing his name, suffices to overcome the wicked one, so it be done with confidence and calmness of spirit. **John Wesley**

Christ is a jewel worth more than a thousand words, as all know who have Him. Get Him, and get all; miss Him and miss all. **Thomas Brooks**

Life in Christ is simple, it's just not easy—love God, love your neighbor. How? Focus on Jesus: look up at Him on the cross and once you make that vertical focus on God your habit, notice how His outstretched arms bring your horizontal relationships back into order. **Doreen Button**

Our Freedom in Jesus

It is for freedom that Christ has set us free. Stand firm, then, and do not let yourselves be burdened again by a yoke of slavery. **Galatians 5:1** NIV

To the Jews who had believed him, Jesus said, "If you hold to my teaching, you are really my disciples. Then you will know the truth, and the truth will set you free." **John 8:31-32** NIV

If the Son sets you free, you will be free indeed. **John 8:36** ESV

The law of the Spirit of life has set you free in Christ Jesus from the law of sin and death. **Romans 8:2** ESV

In him and through faith in him we may approach God with freedom and confidence. **Ephesians 3:12 NIV**

Live as free people, but do not use your freedom as a cover-up for evil; live as God's slaves. **1 Peter 2:16 NIV**

The farther we wander from God and the more we try to break free from him, the more enchained we become. Every step we take away from him leads us farther from the freedom of Jesus and closer to the cruelty of Cain. **Steven James**

I feel so sorry that many Christians live in bondage even though Jesus has signed their release form with His own blood. **Liu Zhenying**

> You have to stop loving and pursuing Christ in order to sin. When you are pursuing love, running toward Christ, you do not have opportunity to wonder, "Am I doing this right?" or "Did I serve enough this week?" When you are running toward Christ, you are freed up to serve, love, and give thanks without guilt, worry or fear. **Francis Chan**

More than anything else, we crave deep intimacy with Jesus; and we are most alive and free when we realize and pursue it. **Scotty Smith**

Don't follow a defeated foe. Follow Christ. It is costly. You will be an exile in this age. But you will be free. **John Piper**

Our Devotion and Surrender to Jesus

Nor must you surrender any part of yourselves to sin to be used for wicked purposes. Instead, give yourselves to God, as those who have been brought from death to life, and surrender your whole being to him to be used for righteous purposes. **Romans 6:13 GNT**

Surely you know that when you surrender yourselves as slaves to obey someone, you are in fact the slaves of the master you obey—either of sin, which results in death, or of obedience, which results in being put right with God. **Romans 6:16 GNT**

No one else holds or has held the place in the heart of the world which Jesus holds. Other gods have been as devoutly worshipped; no other man has been so devoutly loved. **John Knox**

Many of us are missing something in life because we are after the second best, I put before you what I have found to be the best—one who is worthy of all our devotion—Jesus Christ. He is the Saviour for the young and the old. Lord, here I am. **Eric Liddell**

Jesus Christ demands more complete allegiance than any dictator who ever lived. The difference is, He has a right to it. **Vance Havner**

Christ...will never go into partnership as a part Saviour of men. If He be something He must be everything, and if He be not everything He is nothing to you. **Charles Spurgeon**

Come away, my dear brethren, fly, fly, fly for your lives to Jesus Christ; fly to a bleeding God, fly to a throne of grace; and beg of God to break your heart; beg of God to convince you of your actual sins; beg of God to convince you of your original sin; beg of God to convince you of your self-righteousness; beg of God to give you faith, and to enable you to close with Jesus Christ. **George Whitefield**

Oh that Christ were All and Enough for me. He is supposed to be...but oh, to be swept away in a flood of consuming passion for Jesus, that all desire must be sublimated to him. **Jim Elliot**

Stir up the fire of your faith! Christ is not a figure of the past. He is not a memory lost in history. He lives! **Josemaría Escrivá**

Jesus is there for us in the Scriptures. How often do we ignore Him? We must shake off this indifference...but it requires men and women, warriors ready to risk their good names, even their very lives to stand up for the truth. **Jim Caviezel**

Leave it all in the Hands that were wounded for you. **Elisabeth Elliot**

Our Worship of Jesus

Behold, Jesus met them and said, "Greetings!" And they came up and took hold of his feet and worshiped him. **Matthew 28:9 ESV**

Anna never left the temple but worshiped night and day...She gave thanks to God and spoke about the child to all who were looking forward to the redemption of Jerusalem. **Luke 2:37-38 NIV**

Jesus was born of a virgin, suffered under Pontius Pilate, died on the cross, and rose from the grave to make worshippers out of rebels! **A.W. Tozer**

The real issue...is this: is Jesus to be worshipped or only admired? **John Stott**

Ten thousand worlds, and the glory of them all, is but the dust of the balance, if weighed with Christ. These things are but poor creatures, but he is God over all, forever praised (Rom. 9:5). **John Flavel**

Depend on it, my hearer, you never will go to heaven unless you are prepared to worship Jesus Christ as God. **Charles Spurgeon**

While we worship the enthroned and inner Christ, we cannot be intrigued by negative preoccupations with sin. Rules, instead of limiting our sin, define sin, rivet our attention to it and lead us to desire it. Worship, on the other hand, avoids all interest in sin, pointing our hearts and minds in a totally different direction. **Calvin Miller**

Praise is a contradiction of pride. Pride says "looks at me," but praise longs for people to see Jesus. **Matt Redman**

We are saved to worship God. All that Christ has done in the past and all that He is doing now leads to this one end. **A.W. Tozer**

Whenever the method of worship becomes more important than the Person of worship, we have already prostituted our worship. There are entire congregations who worship praise and praise worship but who have not yet learned to praise and worship God in Jesus Christ. **Judson Cornwall**

The purpose of God in sending His Son...was...that He might restore to us the missing jewel...of worship; that we might come back and learn to do again that which we were created to do in the first place—worship the Lord in the beauty of holiness, to spend our time in awesome wonder and adoration of God, feeling and expressing it, and letting it get into our labors and doing nothing except as an act of worship to Almighty God through His Son Jesus Christ. **A.W. Tozer**

When we eat, we taste the emblem of our heavenly food—the Bread of Life. And when we fast we say, "I love the Reality above the emblem." In the heart of the saint both eating and fasting are worship. Both magnify Christ. **John Piper**

Each time, before you intercede, be quiet first, and worship God in His glory. Think of what He can do, and how He delights to hear the prayers of His redeemed people. Think of your place and privilege in Christ, and expect great things! **Andrew Murray**

Without worship, we go about miserable. **A.W. Tozer**

Our Need for Sound Teaching About Jesus

A time is coming when people will no longer listen to sound and wholesome teaching. They will follow their own desires and will look for teachers who will tell them whatever their itching ears want to hear. **2 Timothy 4:3 NLT**

The Jesus that men want to see is not the Jesus they really need to see. **G. Campbell Morgan**

> It is all too easy to believe in a Jesus who is largely a construction of our own imagination—an inoffensive person whom no one would really trouble to crucify. **F.F. Bruce**

Much of the history of Christianity has been devoted to domesticating Jesus—to reducing that elusive, enigmatic, paradoxical person to dimensions we can comprehend, understand, and convert to our own purposes. So far it hasn't worked. **Andrew Greeley**

We refuse to present a picture of "gentle Jesus, meek and mild," a portrait that tugs at your sentiments or pulls at your heartstrings. That's because we deal with so many people who suffer, and when you're hurting hard, you're neither helped nor inspired by a syrupy picture of the Lord, like those sugary, sentimental images many of us grew up with. You know what I mean? Jesus with His hair parted down the middle, surrounded by cherubic children and bluebirds. **Joni Eareckson Tada**

The people who hanged Christ never, to do them justice, accused him of being a bore—on the contrary, they thought him too dynamic to be safe. It has been left for later generations to muffle up that shattering personality and surround him with an atmosphere of tedium. We have very efficiently pared the claws of the Lion of Judah, certified him "meek and mild," and recommended him as a fitting household pet for pale curates and pious old ladies. **Dorothy Sayers**

We make Jesus Christ a convenience. We make Him a Lifeboat to get us to shore, a Guide to find us when we are lost. We reduce Him simply to Big Friend to help us when we are in trouble. **A.W. Tozer**

Our prayers and expectations for Jesus usually involve making our lives easy. But Jesus isn't our genie who grants our wishes. While he sometimes doesn't give us what we want, he *always* gives us what we need. **Randy Alcorn**

Why do we try so hard to make Jesus cool?! He doesn't need a makeover. **Matt Chandler**

One of the greatest distinguishing marks of a false prophet is that he will always tell you what you want to hear, he will never rain on your parade...he will keep you entertained, and he will present a Christianity to you that will make your church look like a six flags over Jesus. **Paul Washer**

A cheap Christianity, without a cross, will prove in the end a useless Christianity, without a crown. **J.C. Ryle**

God hates the lukewarm gospel of half-truths that is now spreading over the globe. This gospel says, "Just believe in Jesus and you'll be saved. There's nothing more to it." It ignores the whole counsel of God, which speaks of repenting from former sins, of taking up your cross, of being conformed to the image of Christ by the refining work of the Holy Spirit. It is totally silent about the reality of hell and an after-death judgment. **David Wilkerson**

Whenever you find a preacher who takes the Bible allegorically and figuratively...that preacher is preaching an allegorical gospel which is no gospel. I thank God for a literal Christ, for a literal salvation. There is literal sorrow, literal death, literal Hell, and, thank God, there is a literal Heaven. **J. Frank Norris**

If I profess with the loudest voice and clearest exposition every portion of the truth of God except precisely that little point which the world and the devil are at that moment attacking, I am not confessing Christ, however boldly I may be professing Christ. **Martin Luther**

Just so take Christ away, and the whole arch of truth becomes a heap of rubbish. **Robert Murray M'Cheyne**

The soul is in danger when knowledge of doctrine outsteps intimate touch with Jesus. **Oswald Chambers**

Our Need to Grasp True Salvation

Hold on to the pattern of wholesome teaching you learned from me—a pattern shaped by the faith and love that you have in Christ Jesus. **2 Timothy 1:13 NLT**

The nature of Christ's salvation is woefully misrepresented by the present-day evangelist. He announces a Saviour from Hell rather than a Saviour from sin. And that is why so many are fatally deceived, for there are multitudes who wish to escape the Lake of fire who have no desire to be delivered from their carnality and worldliness. **A.W. Pink**

Lukewarm people...don't genuinely hate sin and aren't truly sorry for it; they're merely sorry because God is going to punish them. Lukewarm people don't really believe that this new life Jesus offers is better than the old sinful one. **Francis Chan**

> Cheap grace is grace without discipleship, grace without the cross, grace without Jesus Christ, living and incarnate. **Dietrich Bonhoeffer**

Jesus did not go willingly to the cross so we could have an easy life or offer a faith built on easy-believism. As someone once said, "Salvation is free, but not cheap." It cost Jesus His life. **Billy Graham**

For too long, we've called unbelievers to "invite Jesus into your life." Jesus doesn't want to be in your life. Your life is a wreck. Jesus calls you into his life. And his life isn't boring or purposeless or static. It's wild and exhilarating and unpredictable. **Russell Moore**

Everyone goes around asking, "Will you accept Jesus? Will you accept Him?" This makes a brush salesman out of Jesus Christ, as though He meekly stands waiting to know whether we will patronize Him or not. Although we desperately need what He proffers, we are sovereignly deciding whether we will receive Him or not. **A.W. Tozer**

What the world needs is not "a little bit of love," but major surgery. If you think you are helping lost people with your sympathy and understanding, you are a traitor to Jesus Christ. You must have a right-standing relationship with Him yourself, and pour your life out in helping others in His way—not in a human way that ignores God. **Oswald Chambers**

Self-righteousness exclaims, "I will not be saved in God's way; I will make a new road to heaven…I will enter heaven by my own strength, and glorify my own merits." The Lord is very wroth against self-righteousness. I do not know of anything against which His fury burneth more than against this, because this touches Him in a very tender point, it insults the glory and honor of His Son Jesus Christ. **Charles Spurgeon**

Satan has obvious motives for fueling our denial of eternal punishment: He wants unbelievers to reject Christ without fear; he wants Christians to be unmotivated to share Christ; and he wants God to receive less glory for the radical nature of Christ's redemptive work. **Randy Alcorn**

Our Obedience to Jesus

Jesus said to the Jews who had believed Him, "If you abide in my word, you are truly my disciples." **John 8:31 ESV**

Jesus answered and said to him, "If anyone loves Me, he will keep My word; and My Father will love him, and We will come to him and make Our abode with him. He who does not love Me does not keep My words; and the word which you hear is not Mine, but the Father's who sent Me." **John 14:23-24 NASB**

"If you keep My commandments, you will abide in My love; just as I have kept My Father's commandments and abide in His love. These things I have spoken to you so that My joy may be in you, and that your joy may be made full. This is My commandment, that you love one another, just as I have loved you." **John 15:10-12 NASB**

The one who keeps His commandments abides in Him, and He in him. We know by this that He abides in us, by the Spirit whom He has given us. **1 John 3:24 NASB**

This is the love of God, that we keep His commandments; and His commandments are not burdensome. **1 John 5:3 NASB**

It is altogether doubtful whether any man can be saved who comes to Christ for His help with no intention to obey Him. **A.W. Tozer**

There would be no sense in saying you trusted a person if you would not take his advice...if you have really handed yourself over to Jesus Christ, it must follow that you are trying to obey Him. But trying in a new way, a less worried way. Not doing these things in order to be saved, but because He has begun to save you already...because a first faint gleam of Heaven is already inside you. **C.S. Lewis**

If you do not plan to live the Christian life totally committed to knowing your God and to walking in obedience to Him, then don't begin, for this is what Christianity is all about. **Kay Arthur**

If for you, the Christian life is all about feeling good and having everything go your way, then you won't like being a disciple. Being a follower of Christ is the most joyful and exciting life there is. But it also can be the most challenging life there is. It's a life lived out under the command of someone other than yourself. **Greg Laurie**

A passion to obey Christ is born out of our relationship with him. The more we love him, the more we want him to be a part of our affairs. **Calvin Miller**

According to Jesus, every call to obey hangs on the foundational command to love God and others. Any righteousness not firmly hung on love is filthiness and rags, just so many sodden garments on the floor of a flooded closet. **Jen Wilkin**

...God does not require great achievements but a heart that holds back nothing for self. **Rose Philippine Duchesne**

As Elisabeth Elliot points out, not even dying a martyr's death is classified as extraordinary obedience when you are following a Savior who died on a cross. Suddenly a martyr's death seems like normal obedience. **David Platt**

When He tells us to love our enemies, He gives, along with the command, the love itself. **Corrie ten Boom**

You become a disciple in the biblical sense only when you are totally and completely committed to Jesus Christ and His Word. **Greg Laurie**

Whosoever will reign with Christ in heaven, must have Christ reigning in him on earth. **John Wesley**

> The question remains, as it will always remain, one of ultimate authority. Who are you going to follow in your life? Who will command your allegiance? Christ...or culture? You really can't have it both ways.
> **Stu Weber**

Our Love for Jesus

He answered, "You shall love the Lord your God with all your heart and with all your soul and with all your strength and with all your mind, and your neighbor as yourself." **Luke 10:27 ESV**

"Whoever has my commandments and keeps them, he it is who loves me. And he who loves me will be loved by my Father, and I will love him and manifest myself to him." **John 14:21 ESV**

We love because he first loved us. **1 John 4:19 ESV**

Forgiven souls LOVE CHRIST. This is that one thing they can say, if they dare say nothing else...His name, His cross, His blood, His words, His example, His ordinances—all, all are precious to forgiven souls. He is their Redeemer...their King...their hope, their joy, their All. **J.C. Ryle**

I had rather be blind and deaf and dumb, and lose my taste and smell, than not love Christ. To be unable to appreciate him is the worst of disabilities, the most serious of calamities. It is not the loss of a single spiritual faculty, but it proves the death of the soul. **Charles Spurgeon**

Like my relationship with my wife, if I want to love her well, I need to know her well. I need to study her, and understand what makes her tick. If we want to love Jesus we need to know him. **Jeremy Adelman**

There is excitement in true love, and...we Christians who love our Savior ought to be more excited about who He is and what He is! **A.W. Tozer**

All to Jesus I surrender,
All to him I freely give;
I will ever love and trust him,
In his presence daily live. **Judson W. Van DeVenter**

If I had my choice of all the lives that I could live, I certainly would not choose to be an emperor, nor to be a millionaire, nor to be a philosopher, for power and wealth and knowledge bring with them sorrow. But I would choose to have nothing to do but to love my Lord Jesus—nothing, I mean, but to do all things for his sake, and out of love to him. **Charles Spurgeon**

We come, Lord Jesus; we have no service to offer now; we do not come to ask for anything not even for guidance. We come just to love Thee. **Amy Carmichael**

If you make doctrine the main thing, you are very likely to grow narrow-minded. If you make your own experience the main thing, you will become gloomy and critical of others. If you make ordinances the main thing, you will be apt to grow merely formal. But you can never make too much of the living Christ Jesus...Doctrines and ordinances are the planets, but Christ is the sun. Get to love *him* best of all. **Charles Spurgeon**

There is a vast difference between devotion to a person and devotion to principles or to a cause. Our Lord never proclaimed a cause—He proclaimed personal devotion to Himself. **Oswald Chambers**

They do not love Christ who love anything more than Christ.
Thomas Brooks

Anything that cools my love for Christ is the world. **John Wesley**

Our estimate of Christ is the best gauge of our spiritual condition...When pride of self fills up the soul, there is little room for Jesus; but when Jesus is fully loved, self is subdued, and sin driven off the throne. **Charles Spurgeon**

Give me 100 men that hate nothing but sin, and love Jesus Christ, and we'll shake England for God. **John Wesley**

The question is not: How many people take you seriously? How much are you going to accomplish? Can you show some results? but: Are you in love with Jesus? **Henri Nouwen**

Our Fellowship with Jesus

"Behold, I am with you always." **Matthew 28:20 ESV**

"Here I am! I stand at the door and knock. If anyone hears my voice and opens the door, I will come in and eat with that person, and they with me." **Revelation 3:20 NIV**

Become so intimate with Jesus, so full of Him, that it does not matter what challenges in life present themselves to you. You will be so spiritually full that you can feed a multitude of other people's needs. Jesus will give you more than enough. **Heidi Baker**

I am born for God only. Christ is nearer to me than father, or mother, or sister—a near relation, a more affectionate Friend; and I rejoice to follow Him, and to love Him. Blessed Jesus! Thou art all I want—a forerunner to me in all I ever shall go through as a Christian, a minister, or a missionary. **Henry Martyn**

Remember: He WANTS your fellowship, and He has done everything possible to make it a reality. He has forgiven your sins, at the cost of His own dear Son. He has given you His Word, and the priceless privilege of prayer and worship. **Billy Graham**

The Christian who is truly intimate with Jesus will never draw attention to himself but will only show the evidence of a life where Jesus is completely in control. This is the outcome of allowing Jesus to satisfy every area of life to its depth. **Oswald Chambers**

Jesus taught that your highest priority must be your relationship with Him. If anything detracts you from that relationship, that activity is not from God. God will not ask you to do something that hinders your relationship with Christ.
Henry Blackaby

Talking about my relationship with Jesus Christ is as natural as breathing for me. I say relationship because it's a day-by-day, night-by-night, ongoing communication between Jesus and me. I'm not saying that any person can use the name of Jesus and beat every opponent. If that were true, I could skip all my practices, and forget about my weight training and conditioning. But I do want to live and breathe Jesus Christ so much that when people see me, they see Him.
Reggie White

Rose early to seek God and found Him whom my soul loveth. Who would not rise early to meet such company? **Robert Murray M'Cheyne**

There's not a single fear, thought, feeling or need that's too big or too small for Jesus. He wants you to tell Him what's on your heart. **Jeremy Camp**

I urge upon you communion with Christ; a growing communion. There are curtains to be drawn aside in Christ that we never saw, and newfoldings of love in him. I despair that I shall ever win to the far end of that love, there are so many aspects to it. **Samuel Rutherford**

What have you been doing with your life? Is Christ living in your home and yet you have not spoken to him for months? Do not let me condemn you or judge; only let your conscience speak. **Charles Spurgeon**

When life caves in, you do not need reasons—you need comfort. You do not need some answers—you need someone. And Jesus does not come to us with an explanation—He comes to us with His presence. **Bob Benson**

I don't worry over the future, for I know what Jesus said; so today I'll walk beside Him, for He knows what is ahead. **Ira Stanphill**

> The closer we draw to the Lord Jesus and the more we set our hearts and minds on heavenly glories above, the better prepared we shall be for heaven's perfection. **Joni Eareckson Tada**

O my Lord Jesus Christ, if I could be in heaven without thee, it would be a hell; and if I could be in hell, and have thee still, it would be a heaven to me, for thou art all the heaven I want. **Samuel Rutherford**

Fellowship in Heaven won't mean sitting at the feet of Jesus and fighting back boredom while everyone else is enraptured. No. Fellowship will be the best of what earthly friendship merely hinted at. **Joni Eareckson Tada**

Our Suffering in and for Jesus

They went on their way from the presence of the Council, rejoicing that they had been considered worthy to suffer shame for His name. **Acts 5:41 NASB**

To you it has been granted for Christ's sake, not only to believe in Him, but also to suffer for His sake. **Philippians 1:29 NASB**

Join with me in suffering, like a good soldier of Christ Jesus. **2 Timothy 2:3 NIV**

After you have suffered for a little while, the God of all grace, who called you to His eternal glory in Christ, will Himself perfect, confirm, strengthen and establish you. **1 Peter 5:10 NASB**

Think Jesus came to remove our pains? Wherever did you get that notion? The Lord came, not to remove our suffering, but to show us the way through it to the glory beyond. **Stephen R. Lawhead**

Jesus promised his disciples three things—that they would be completely fearless, absurdly happy, and in constant trouble. **Attributed to G.K. Chesterton**

If you are going to walk with Jesus Christ, you are going to be opposed...In our days, to be a true Christian is really to become a scandal. **George Whitefield**

The manger at Christmas means that, if you live like Jesus, there won't be room for you in a lot of inns. **Timothy Keller**

How do we know that our suffering is not punishment for our sin? Because someone has already been punished for our sin...Hardship will either distract our focus from Christ or intensify our focus on him. If we give in to grumbling and complaining about the hardships and difficulties in our lives, we will miss out on what there is to learn from them. **Nancy Guthrie**

Afflictions cannot sanctify us, except as they are used by Christ as his mallet and his chisel. **Charles Spurgeon**

If God gives you an abundant harvest of trials, it is a sign of great holiness which He desires you to attain. **Ignatius of Loyola**

Once we agree with God that we exist for His pleasure and His glory, we can accept whatever comes into our lives as a part of His sovereign will and purpose...designed by God to make us more like Jesus and to bring glory to Himself. **Nancy DeMoss Wolgemuth**

When it comes to the cross you daily bear, it is not one inch too large nor one ounce too heavy, for the Lord especially hand-tailored it so that Christ's kingdom might be advanced through you. That alone is the highest of honors. **Joni Eareckson Tada**

Life is not a straight line leading from one blessing to the next and then finally to heaven. Life is a winding and troubled road. Switchback after switchback. And the point of biblical stories like Joseph and Job and Esther and Ruth is to help us feel in our bones (not just know in our heads) that God is for us in all these strange turns. God is not just showing up after the trouble and cleaning it up. He is plotting the course and managing the troubles with far-reaching purposes for our good and for the glory of Jesus Christ. **John Piper**

A test of a Christian's character is what he does after he comes to the blockade in the road and what his attitude is after everything has left him except Jesus. **Lester Roloff**

There is nothing—no circumstance, no trouble, no testing—that can ever touch me until, first of all, it has gone past God and past Christ right through to me. If it has come that far, it has come with a great purpose, which I may not understand at the moment. **Alan Redpath**

When you're in great pain, it helps to personalize "God so loved the world." Christ didn't die for the world or the church in general, but for people in particular. Each believer's individual name is written in the Book of Life. When you are suffering most, his eyes are on you and he cares deeply about you—not just the world in general but you in particular. **Randy Alcorn**

You will never find Jesus so precious as when the world is one vast howling wilderness. Then he is like a rose blooming in the midst of the desolation, a rock rising above the storm. **Robert Murray M'Cheyne**

I know now, Lord, why you utter no answer. You are yourself the answer. **C.S. Lewis**

Glorify the Lord in your sufferings, and take his banner of love and spread it over you. Others will follow you, if they see you strong in the Lord...Look up and see who is coming! Lift up your head, he is coming to save, in garments dyed in blood, and traveling in the greatness of his strength. I laugh, I smile, I leap for joy to see Christ coming to save you so quickly. Oh, such wide steps Christ taketh! Three or four hills are but a step to him. **Samuel Rutherford**

If you had never known physical pain in your life, how could you appreciate the nail-scarred hands with which Jesus Christ will meet you? **Joni Eareckson Tada**

I would not trade my cancer journey for anything because of the growth in my love, adoration and trust in Jesus and God's perfect plan. **Nanci Alcorn**

No pit is so deep that He is not deeper still; with Jesus even in our darkest moments, the best remains and the very best is yet to be. **Corrie ten Boom**

Our Hope in Jesus

God wanted to make known among the Gentiles the glorious wealth of this mystery, which is Christ in you, the hope of glory. **Colossians 1:27 CSB**

We look forward with hope to that wonderful day when the glory of our great God and Savior, Jesus Christ, will be revealed. **Titus 2:13 NLT**

> We know that when Christ appears, we shall be like him, because we shall see him as he really is. Everyone who has this hope in Christ keeps himself pure, just as Christ is pure. **1 John 3:2-3 GNT**

There is hope for a ruined humanity—hope of pardon, hope of peace with God, hope of glory—because at the Father's will Jesus Christ became poor and was born in a stable so that thirty years later he might hang on a cross. **J.I. Packer**

Hope for the Christian isn't just confidence in a certain, glorious future. It's hope in a present providence. It's hope that God's plans can't be thwarted by local authorities or irate mobs, by unfriendly bosses or unbelieving husbands, by Supreme Court rulings or the next election. The Christian hope is that God's purposes are so unassailable that a great thunderstorm of events can't drive them off course. Even when we're wave-tossed and lost at sea, Jesus remains the captain of the ship and the commander of the storm. **Elliot Clark**

When Christ is my hope, he becomes the one thing in which I have confidence. I act on his wisdom and bank on his grace. I trust his promises and I rely on his presence. And I pursue all the good things that he has promised me simply because I trust him. So, I am not manipulating, controlling, or threatening my way through life to get what I want, because I have found what I want in Christ. **Paul David Tripp**

The answer to all your doubts and failures begins here: You are not the answer. He is. **N.D. Wilson**

I know, perhaps as well as anyone, what depression means, and what it is to feel myself sinking lower and lower. Yet at the worst, when I reach the lowest depths, I have an inward peace which no pain or depression can in the least disturb. Trusting in Jesus Christ my Savior, there is still a blessed quietness in the deep caverns of my soul. **Charles Spurgeon**

We can be sure that the place Christ is preparing for us will be ready when we arrive, because with Him nothing is left to chance. Everything He promised He will deliver. **Billy Graham**

Through Jesus, your past is explained, your present has a purpose, and your future is secure. What more could you really want in life? **Jase Robertson**

Our Resemblance to Jesus

We were buried therefore with him by baptism into death, in order that, just as Christ was raised from the dead by the glory of the Father, we too might walk in newness of life. **Romans 6:4 ESV**

Those whom he foreknew he also predestined to be conformed to the image of his Son. **Romans 8:29 ESV**

Don't let the world around you squeeze you into its own mould, but let God re-mould your minds from within, so that you may prove in practice that the plan of God for you is good, meets all his demands and moves towards the goal of true maturity. **Romans 12:2 PHILLIPS**

Whoever says he abides in him ought to walk in the same way in which he walked. **1 John 2:6 ESV**

As the business of the soldier is to fight, so the business of the Christian is to be like Christ. **Jonathan Edwards**

The gospel-centered teacher understands that the unsaved need the gospel in order to come to know Christ, while the saved need the gospel in order to become more like Christ. **Trevin Wax**

The Christian life is simply a process of having your natural self changed into a Christ self, and that this process goes on very far inside. **C.S. Lewis**

The Christian should take nothing short of Christ for his model. **Charles Spurgeon**

Character in a saint means the disposition of Jesus Christ persistently manifested. **Oswald Chambers**

A disciple is one who thinks, feels and acts like Jesus Christ...God's No. 1 purpose in our lives is to make us like Jesus. **Rick Warren**

How do we bring glory to God? The Bible's short answer is: by growing more and more like Jesus Christ. **Sinclair Ferguson**

While Martha is busy trying to be *like* Jesus, Mary spends her energy being *with* him. And in being with him, Mary becomes like him. **Scott Sauls**

You are either becoming more like Christ every day or you are becoming less like Him. There is no neutral position in the Lord. **Stormie Omartian**

Jesus shows us exactly what God looks like. Problems arise when we trust our own subjective picture of Jesus, including that he was always nice. By our standards of niceness, the Jesus of Scripture who called people hypocrites and overturned tables in the temple wasn't Christlike. Sometimes the Jesus people believe in is less like the Jesus of Scripture and more like Mister Rogers or Barney the dinosaur than the bold, powerful and controversial Jesus of Scripture. **Randy Alcorn**

God is reordering and reshaping our loves to make us increasingly like Jesus (2 Cor. 3:18). He is at work in us, teaching us to discern and mature in our affections (Matt. 6:33). He's chiseling our superficial longings for ease, comfort, and anything else we prefer over taking up our crosses daily, and making us solid, rooted, and strong "oaks of righteousness" (Is. 61:3). **Bethany Jenkins**

A Christian should be a striking likeness of Jesus Christ...Oh! My brethren, there is nothing that can so advantage you, nothing can so prosper you, so assist you, so make you walk towards heaven rapidly, so keep your head upwards towards the sky, and your eyes radiant with glory, like the imitation of Jesus Christ. **Charles Spurgeon**

Humility is not a character trait to develop, it's the natural by-product of being with Jesus. **Louie Giglio**

Those whose hearts are warm but who lack sound doctrine will trample the truth of Jesus. Those whose doctrine is sound but who lack the grace of Jesus will trample people. Christ's heart is equally grieved by grace-twisting and truth-twisting. To honor Jesus, grace and truth are both essential. **Randy Alcorn**

I have just put my soul, as a blank, into the hand of Jesus, my Redeemer, and desired Him to write on it what He pleases; I know it will be His image. **George Whitefield**

God is concerned with teaching us and changing us to be more like Jesus, and it is his good pleasure to concentrate more on the beauty he is fashioning into our lives than on the amount of time the process requires. ***The Knowing Jesus Study Bible***

If I am not today all that I hope to be, yet I see Jesus...that assures me that I shall one day be like Him. **Charles Spurgeon**

Our Joy in Jesus

The LORD is my strength and shield. I trust him with all my heart. He helps me, and my heart is filled with joy. I burst out in songs of thanksgiving. **Psalm 28:7 NLT**

Let all who take refuge in you rejoice; let them ever sing for joy, and spread your protection over them, that those who love your name may exult in you. **Psalm 5:11 ESV**

I will celebrate in the LORD; I will rejoice in the God of my salvation! **Habakkuk 3:18 CSB**

"Go quickly and tell his disciples that he has risen from the dead, and he is going ahead of you to Galilee. You will see him there. Remember what I have told you." The women ran quickly from the tomb. They were very frightened but also filled with great joy, and they rushed to give the disciples the angel's message. **Matthew 28:7-8 NLT**

The early Christians did not say in dismay, "look what the world has come to," but in delight, "look what has come into the world." **E. Stanley Jones**

Christ came to take away our sins, to roll off our curse, to unbind our chains, to open our prison-house, to cancel our debt...Is not this joy?...There is every element of joy—deep, ecstatic, satisfying, sanctifying joy—in the gospel of Christ. The believer in Jesus is essentially a happy man. **Octavius Winslow**

Christ is not only a remedy for your weariness and trouble, but he will give you an abundance of the contrary, joy and delight. They who come to Christ, do not only come to a resting-place after they have been wandering in a wilderness, but they come to a banqueting-house where they may rest, and where they may feast. They may cease from their former troubles and toils, and they may enter upon a course of delights and spiritual joys. **Jonathan Edwards**

No created powers can mar our Lord Jesus' music, nor spill our song of joy. **Samuel Rutherford**

When we search for happiness apart from Christ, we find loneliness, confusion, and misery. When we focus on Jesus and others, we find untold happiness. **Randy Alcorn**

Christ is that ocean in which all true delights and pleasures meet. **John Flavel**

The sense of the joy in anything is the sense of Christ. **Caryll Houselander**

The Lord Jesus is a deep sea of joy; my soul shall dive therein, shall be swallowed up in the delights of his society. **Charles Spurgeon**

Ah! dear friend, wherever we journey, union to Jesus and holiness from his Spirit flowing into us, is our chief and only happiness. **Robert Murray M'Cheyne**

Jesus invites us to come to him, the Source of happiness, and sit at the feet of him who wired us to want happiness. **Randy Alcorn**

There is nothing dreary or doubtful about this life [in Christ]. It is meant to be continually joyful...We are called to a settled happiness in the Lord whose joy is our strength. **Amy Carmichael**

Enjoyment of Jesus is not like icing on the cake; it's like powder in the shell. **John Piper**

I have been listed under Jesus' banner only for a few years, but I have enjoyed more solid pleasure in one moment's communion with my God than I should or could have enjoyed in the ways of sin, though I had continued to have gone on in them for thousands of years. **George Whitefield**

A person who is in real communion with God and with the Lord Jesus Christ is happy. It does not matter whether he is in a dungeon, or whether he has his feet fast in the stocks, or whether he is burning at the stake; he is still happy if he is in communion with God...Whenever we are unhappy it means that in some way or other we are looking at ourselves and thinking about ourselves, instead of communing with God. **Martyn Lloyd-Jones**

True Joy is not the absence of pain but the sanctifying, sustaining presence of the Lord Jesus in the midst of the pain. **Nancy DeMoss Wolgemuth**

If you live gladly to make others glad in God, your life will be hard, your risks will be high, and your joy will be full...Some of you will die in the service of Christ. That will not be a tragedy. Treasuring life above Christ is a tragedy. **John Piper**

The greatest joy of a Christian is to give joy to Christ. **Charles Spurgeon**

No man has made much progress in the school of Christ who does not look forward with joy to the day of death and final resurrection. **John Calvin**

When Christ calls me home, I shall go with the gladness of a boy bounding away from his school. **Adoniram Judson**

I see myself now at the end of my journey, my toilsome days are ended. I am going now to see that Head that was with thorns and that Face that was spit upon for me. I have formerly lived by hearsay and faith, but now I go where I shall live by sight, and shall be with him in whose company I delight myself. **John Bunyan (Mr. Stand-fast in *The Pilgrim's Progress*)**

When Jesus wipes away tears with his gentle, omnipotent hand, I believe our eyes will fall on the scars that made our suffering his so that his eternal joy could become ours. **Randy Alcorn**

Our Call to Follow Jesus

"I pray for these followers, but I am also praying for all those who will believe in me because of their teaching. Father, I pray that they can be one. As you are in me and I am in you, I pray that they can also be one in us. Then the world will believe that you sent me." **John 17:20-21 NCV**

He said to all, "If anyone would come after me, let him deny himself and take up his cross daily and follow me." **Luke 9:23 ESV**

Jesus said to them, "Come with me! I will teach you how to bring in people instead of fish." **Matthew 4:19 CEV**

I know God's call for your life. It's to be an ever-growing disciple of Jesus. **Matt Chandler**

Those who aren't following Jesus aren't his followers. It's that simple. **Scot McKnight**

If Jesus Christ is not controlling all of me, the chances are very good that He is not controlling any of me. **A.W. Tozer**

Let us be wary of praying to Christ with our mouths but remaining mute in our life. **Augustine**

Spiritual transformation is not a matter of trying harder, but of training wisely…Following Jesus simply means learning from him how to arrange my life around activities that enable me to live in the fruit of the Spirit. **John Ortberg**

Jesus is notoriously uncooperative with all attempts to repackage and market him. He's not looking for image-enhancers. We're to follow him as servants, not walk in front of him as a PR entourage. **Randy Alcorn**

Struggling against the legalism of simple obedience, we end by setting up the most dangerous law of all, the law of the world and the law of grace…The only way of overcoming this legalism is by real obedience to Christ when he calls us to follow him; for in Jesus the law is at once fulfilled and cancelled. **Dietrich Bonhoeffer**

It is only after we yield to Jesus Christ and begin to follow Him that we…begin to grieve about the way we have been living and we become convicted by aimlessness and futility and carelessness in our Christian walk. **A.W. Tozer**

When Christ came into my life, I came about like a well-handled ship. **Robert Louis Stevenson**

Let the laying hold of Christ as my propitiation be the unvarying initial act of every morning. **Thomas Chalmers**

Do little things as though they were great, because of the majesty of Jesus Christ who does them in us, and who lives our life; and do the greatest things as though they were little and easy, because of His omnipotence. **Blaise Pascal**

Don't overcomplicate God's will. Just stay connected to Jesus. Love Him. Look into His eyes. He will lead. Follow. Repeat. **Louie Giglio**

Our Servanthood in Jesus

Jesus called the Twelve and said, "Anyone who wants to be first must be the very last, and the servant of all." **Mark 9:35 NIV**

"Truly I tell you, anyone who gives you a cup of water in my name because you belong to the Messiah will certainly not lose their reward." **Mark 9:41 NIV**

Jesus called them together and said, "...whoever wants to become great among you must be your servant, and whoever wants to be first must be slave of all. For even the Son of Man did not come to be served, but to serve, and to give his life as a ransom for many." **Mark 10:42-45 NIV**

Christ did not die to make good works merely possible or to produce a half-hearted pursuit. He died to produce in us a passion for good deeds. Christian purity is not the mere avoidance of evil, but the pursuit of good. **John Piper**

Being happy with Him now means loving like He loves, helping like He helps, giving as He gives, serving as He serves, rescuing as He rescues, being with Him twenty-four hours a day—touching Him in his distressing disguise. **Mother Teresa**

If you do not find yourself among the needy and the poor, where the Gospel shows us Christ, then you may know that your faith is not right, and that you have not yet tasted of Christ's benevolence and work for you. **Martin Luther**

How could it be anything less than a joy to serve the One who has given us all things for life, and enrichment, and enjoyment? **Joni Eareckson Tada**

Trying to do the Lord's work in your own strength is the most confusing, exhausting, and tedious of all work. But when you are filled with the Holy Spirit, then the ministry of Jesus just flows out of you. **Corrie ten Boom**

> It is impossible at the same time to give the impression both that I am a great Christian and that Jesus Christ is a great Master. So the Christian will practice curling up small, as it were, so that in and through him or her the Savior may show himself great. **J.I. Packer**

Let us remember, there is One who daily records all we do for Him, and sees more beauty in His servants' work than His servants do themselves...And then shall His faithful witnesses discover, to their wonder and surprise, that there never was a word spoken on their Master's behalf, which does not receive a reward. **J.C. Ryle**

Our Gratitude to Jesus

> Sing and make music from your heart to the Lord, always giving thanks to God the Father for everything, in the name of our Lord Jesus Christ. **Ephesians 5:19-20 NIV**

Let the message of Christ dwell among you richly as you teach and admonish one another with all wisdom through psalms, hymns, and songs from the Spirit, singing to God with gratitude in your hearts. And whatever you do, whether in word or deed, do it all in the name of the Lord Jesus, giving thanks to God the Father through him. **Colossians 3:16-17 NIV**

Rejoice always, pray continually, give thanks in all circumstances; for this is God's will for you in Christ Jesus. **1 Thessalonians 5:16-18 NIV**

When we learn to read the story of Jesus and see it as the story of the love of God, doing for us what we could not do for ourselves—that insight produces, again and again, a sense of astonished gratitude which is very near the heart of authentic Christian experience. **N.T. Wright**

Our names are written in Heaven not because we were smart and strong and moral. Rather, "because of him you are in Christ Jesus, who became to us wisdom from God, righteousness and sanctification and redemption" (1 Corinthians 1:30). In other words, Jesus became for us, and remains for us, what we could never be for ourselves. And that should overwhelm us with unending gratitude. **Randy Alcorn**

God is calling us to receive with thankful joy our Savior. He is calling us to join in the heavenly celebration, that we might be happy as he is glorified. God has come to us in Christ to bring glory to himself in the highest as he grants us peace here in our lives. What can we do but rejoice? **Nancy Guthrie**

Scripture commands us, "Whatever is true, whatever is honorable, whatever is just, whatever is pure, whatever is lovely, whatever is commendable, if there is any excellence, if there is anything worthy of praise, think about these things" (Philippians 4:8). Who is more excellent and worthy of praise than Jesus Christ? We should trace all secondary joys and pleasures back to him as we'd trace a sunbeam back to the sun. We should thank him and worship him, so that when we ponder and delight in every good thing he gives us, we'll be thinking of and delighting in Jesus. **Randy Alcorn**

Jesus went without comfort so that you might have it. He postponed joy so that you might share in it. He willingly chose isolation so that you might never be alone in your hurt and sorrow. He had no real fellowship so that fellowship might be yours, this moment. This alone is enough cause for great gratitude! **Joni Eareckson Tada**

Just get to know Jesus...not who you want Him to be or who other people say He is. Get to know Him through the power of the Spirit as you study the Word. The more you get to know Him the more thankful you will be for Him. **Deb Wolf**

Help us not only to receive him but to walk in him,
depend upon him,
commune with him,
follow him as dear children,
imperfect, but still pressing forward,
not complaining of labour, but valuing rest,
not murmuring under trials, but thankful for our state.
The Valley of Vision: A Collection of Puritan Prayers and Devotions

I am continuously grateful to Jesus, the Creator and Master Builder, who has paid the price of redemption and will one day completely fix all that's broken and bring into full flower the New Heavens and New Earth, the home of relentless and unending happiness. **Randy Alcorn**

Our Love for Others in Jesus

"A despised Samaritan came along, and when he saw the man, he felt compassion for him. Going over to him, the Samaritan soothed his wounds...Then he put the man on his own donkey and took him to an inn, where he took care of him. The next day he handed the innkeeper two silver coins, telling him, 'Take care of this man. If his bill runs higher than this, I'll pay you the next time I'm here.'" **Luke 10:33-35 NLT**

"Your love for one another will prove to the world that you are my disciples." **John 13:35 NLT**

If you really fulfill the royal law according to the Scripture, "You shall love your neighbor as yourself," you are doing well. **James 2:8 ESV**

Whoever wishes to meet Jesus must meet him in places where brothers and sisters of Jesus are hungry, thirsty, naked, unwanted, sick or in prison. Whoever keeps himself distant from these places remains distant from Jesus. **Richard Wurmbrand**

I see Jesus in every human being...I serve because I love Jesus. **Mother Teresa**

Jesus will meet me today in the person of someone in need—I must not miss him. **E. Stanley Jones**

Christianity is not about building a...secure little niche in the world where you can live with your perfect little wife and your perfect little children in your beautiful little house where you have no gays or minority groups anywhere near you. Christianity is about learning to love like Jesus loved and Jesus loved the poor and Jesus loved the broken. **Rich Mullins**

I don't know how your theology works, but if Jesus has a choice between stained glass windows and feeding starving kids in Haiti, I have a feeling he'd choose the starving kids in Haiti. **Tony Campolo**

Agape is an overflowing love, a spontaneous love, which seeks nothing in return. And theologians would say that it is the love of God operating in the human heart. When you rise to love on this level you love all men, not because you like them, not because their ways appeal to you, not because they are worthful to you, but you love all men because God loves them. And you rise to the noble heights of loving the person who does the evil deed while hating the deed that the person does. And I think this is what Jesus means when he says, "Love your enemies." **Martin Luther King Jr.**

Jesus' decree to love and pray for our opponents is regarded as one of the most breathtaking and gut-wrenching challenges of his entire Sermon on the Mount, a speech renowned for its outrageous claims. There was no record of any other spiritual leader ever having articulated such a clear-cut, unambiguous command for people to express compassion to those who are actively working against their best interests. **Lee Strobel**

Jesus didn't wait until we got better to die for us. He died when we were in our most unlovely state. The person who doesn't deserve love actually needs love more, not less. If you know someone unworthy of love, that's great! You now have a chance to emulate Christ, because the essence of His love is unconditional. **Tony Evans**

Jesus gives the world the right to judge whether you and I are born-again Christians on the basis of our observable love toward all Christians. **Francis Schaeffer**

Learning how to love your neighbor requires a willingness to draw on the strength of Jesus Christ as you die to self and live for Him. **John C. Broger**

By depicting a Samaritan helping a Jew, Jesus could not have found a more forceful way to say that anyone at all in need—regardless of race, politics, class, and religion—is your neighbour. Not everyone is your brother or sister in faith, but everyone is your neighbour, and you must love your neighbour. **Timothy Keller**

The love of Christ always helps us see beyond the faults of others. **Victor Manuel Rivera**

The single most loving act we can do is share the good news of Jesus Christ, that God saves sinners. **Matt Chandler**

Our Living Out the Gospel of Jesus

He destroyed death, and through the Good News he showed us the way to have life that cannot be destroyed. **2 Timothy 1:10** NCV

"The time promised by God has come at last!" [Jesus] announced. "The Kingdom of God is near! Repent of your sins and believe the Good News!" **Mark 1:15** NLT

The Christian Gospel is that I am so flawed that Jesus had to die for me, yet I am so loved and valued that Jesus was glad to die for me. This leads to deep humility and deep confidence at the same time. It undermines both swaggering and sniveling. I cannot feel superior to anyone, and yet I have nothing to prove to anyone. I do not think more of myself nor less of myself. Instead, I think of myself less. **Timothy Keller**

Turn around and believe that the good news that we are loved is better than we ever dared hope, and that to believe in that good news, to live out of it and toward it, to be in love with that good news, is of all glad things in this world the gladdest thing of all. **Frederick Buechner**

If you read Scripture carefully, you will never get the idea that the work of Christ is for well-adjusted people who just need a little redemptive boost. It never presents any human condition or dilemma as outside the scope of the gospel. Redemption is nothing less than the rescue of helpless people facing an eternity of torment apart from God's love. **Paul David Tripp**

The good news as Jesus preached it is not just about the minimal entrance requirements for getting into heaven when you die. It is about the glorious redemption of human life—your life. **John Ortberg**

The gospel is the life of Jesus for sinners. His righteousness is our righteousness, and this gives us hope and confidence before God. Here the broken find encouragement, for in Christ we are righteous. **Joe Thorn**

Jesus is "mighty to save," the best proof of which lies in the fact that He has saved you. **Charles Spurgeon**

God can give you a whole new set of instincts, a new set of moral desires, a new moral bent so that you will do right because you *are* right...This is what the gospel promises. **A.W. Tozer**

The gospel isn't merely a "game changer"; it's an everything changer.
Scotty Smith

Our Public Acknowledgment of Jesus

"Peace be with you! As the Father has sent me, I am sending you."
John 20:21 NIV

"Everyone who acknowledges me before men, I also will acknowledge before my Father who is in heaven." **Matthew 10:32 ESV**

He commanded us to preach to the people and to testify that he is the one appointed by God to be judge of the living and the dead. **Acts 10:42 ESV**

We must show our Christian colors, if we are to be true to Jesus Christ. We cannot remain silent or concede everything away. **C.S. Lewis**

Even after all our frailties and failures, Christ Jesus can hardly wait to acknowledge us before the very angels of God. If He is that unashamed of us in all our imperfections, how can we be ashamed of Him, our Redeemer and Deliverer?
Beth Moore

Are you a champion of Christ on Twitter, but not in your neighborhood?
Michael Oh

Christ is the King. He calls the shots; we're just his ambassadors. So let's represent the real Jesus, the Jesus of Scripture, not the culturally accommodated "pop Jesus." If we seek our culture's approval, we may get it only at the expense of failing to represent Christ. **Randy Alcorn**

What other people think of me is becoming less and less important; what they think of Jesus because of me is critical. **Cliff Richard**

The greatest single cause of atheism in the world today is Christians who acknowledge Jesus with their lips, walk out the door, and deny Him by their lifestyle. **Kevin Max**

After 18 years of pastoral ministry, I have never met a person who fell in love with Jesus because a Christian scolded them about their ethics. Have you? **Scott Sauls**

The world takes its notions of God from the people who say that they belong to God's family. They read us a great deal more than they read the Bible. They see us; they only hear about Jesus Christ. **Alexander Maclaren**

The most effective way to win people to Jesus is to treat them the way Jesus would day in and day out. **Jacob Peterson**

The dying boy said: "Father, don't you weep for me; when I get to heaven I will go straight to Jesus and tell Him that ever since I can remember you have tried to lead me to Him." I would rather have my children say that of me...than to have a monument over me reaching to the skies. **Dwight L. Moody**

I love to tell the story;
'twill be my theme in glory
to tell the old, old story
of Jesus and his love. **Katherine Hankey**

Alexander Maclaren (1826–1910), looking out over his congregation one Sunday, was shocked to see a well-known skeptic in the audience...the man told Maclaren he had decided to become a Christian. The preacher asked which message had brought the man to that decision. The former skeptic replied: Your sermons, sir, were helpful, but they were not what finally persuaded me to become a Christian. A few weeks ago, as I was leaving church, I noticed an elderly lady with a radiant face. Because she was making her way with difficulty along the icy street,

I offered to help her. As we walked along together, she looked up at me and said, "I wonder if you know my Savior, Jesus Christ? He is everything in the world to me. I want you to love Him, too." Those few words touched my heart, and when I got home, I knelt down and received the Savior. **Calvin Miller**

I can't imagine more surprising places for God to appear than a manger or a cross. Yet all through his life and resurrection, Jesus demonstrates the power of showing and sharing God's love. Every time I write a script or a song or walk into the studio, I pray "Let some word that is heard be Thine." That's really all that matters. **Fred Rogers**

Don't wait for a feeling of love in order to share Christ with a stranger...take those first steps in evangelism because you love God. **John Piper**

God save us from living in comfort while sinners are sinking into hell! **Charles Spurgeon**

Would that God would make hell so real to us that we cannot rest; heaven so real that we must have men there; Christ so real that our supreme motive and aim shall be to make the Man of Sorrows the Man of Joy by the conversion to Him of many. **J. Hudson Taylor**

Unbelievers are not the enemy—they are people for whom Christ died. We need to remember we were each one of them once. **Greg Laurie**

When your heart is ablaze with the love of God, when you love other people—especially the ripsnorting sinners—so much that you dare to tell them about Jesus with no apologies, then never fear, there will be results. **Catherine Marshall**

Ministry is when you point out Jesus—nothing more and nothing less. **Priscilla Shirer**

This is what every follower of Jesus should be engaged in on a regular basis:

sharing our faith, leading others to Christ, discipling them, and helping them to get grounded in the church—and then going out and doing it all again. **Greg Laurie**

This is the grand purpose for which we were created: to enjoy the grace of Christ as we spread the gospel of Christ from wherever we live, to the ends of the earth. **David Platt**

Let my name die everywhere, let even my friends forget me, if by that means the cause of the blessed Jesus may be promoted. **George Whitefield**

Our Reign with Jesus

"His master replied, 'Well done, good and faithful servant! You have been faithful with a few things; I will put you in charge of many things. Come and share your master's happiness!'" **Matthew 25:21 NIV**

If we endure, we will also reign with him. **2 Timothy 2:12 NIV**

In the messianic kingdom the martyrs will reclaim the world as the possession which was denied to them by their persecutors. In the creation in which they endured servitude, they will eventually reign. **Irenaeus**

Jesus said, "I confer on you a kingdom, just as my Father conferred one on me, so that you may eat and drink at my table in my kingdom and sit on thrones, judging the twelve tribes of Israel" (Luke 22:29-30). This is an astounding statement. Christ has conferred to human beings a kingdom? a *kingdom*? The apostles will rule most prominently, but Scripture makes it clear that Christ will make rulers of everyone who serves him humbly and faithfully here and now. **Randy Alcorn**

Pascal, as no other, plotted humanity's story in these terms when he referred to man as a king who has lost his crown. "All the miseries of man prove his grandeur;

they are the miseries of a dethroned monarch." Redemption reverses this tragic abdication...The wretch will ascend the throne. The rebel will reign. The condemned will be crowned. **Bruce Milne**

The emphasis on the present heaven is clearly rest, cessation from earth's battles and comforts from earth's sufferings. The future heaven is centered more on activity and expansion, serving Christ and reigning with Him...In other words, the emphasis in the present heaven is on the absence of earth's negatives, while in the future heaven it is the presence of earth's positives, magnified many times through the power and glory of resurrected bodies on a resurrected Earth, free at last from sin and shame and all that would hinder both joy and achievement. **René Pache**

As Christians, we've been born into the family of an incredibly wealthy landowner and King—he owns every square inch of the universe. His government has no end. He will entrust management of his vast and limitless country to us, his heirs, and that's what we'll do for eternity: manage God's assets and rule his universe. We'll represent him as his children, his image-bearers, and his ambassadors. With such a destiny offered us, why would we settle for sin? Why would we waste our lives in self-preoccupation and self-pity? **Randy Alcorn**

Our Future with Jesus

"This is eternal life, that they know you, the only true God, and Jesus Christ whom you have sent." **John 17:3 ESV**

It will happen in a moment, in the blink of an eye, when the last trumpet is blown. For when the trumpet sounds, those who have died will be raised to live forever. And we who are living will also be transformed. **1 Corinthians 15:52 NLT**

All creation is waiting eagerly for that future day when God will reveal who his children really are. Against its will, all creation was subjected to God's curse. But with eager hope, the creation looks forward to the day when it will join God's children in glorious freedom from death and decay. **Romans 8:19-21 NLT**

After my skin has been destroyed, yet in my flesh I will see God; I myself will see him with my own eyes—I, and not another. How my heart yearns within me! **Job 19:26-27 NIV**

"Look! God's dwelling place is now among the people, and he will dwell with them. They will be his people, and God himself will be with them and be their God." **Revelation 21:3 NIV**

This is life eternal, that they might know Thee! That is where I cast my first anchor! **John Knox (his final words)**

Before you long for a life that is imperishable, you must accept that you are perishing along with everyone you care about. You must recognize that anything you might accomplish or acquire in this world is already fading away. Only then will you crave the unfading glory of what Jesus has accomplished and acquired for you. And you need to recognize you are going to lose everything you love in this world before you will hope in an inheritance kept in heaven for you. **Matthew McCullough**

When God writes our names in the "Lamb's Book of Life," He doesn't do it with an eraser handy. He does it for eternity. **R.C. Sproul**

Jesus, our head, is already in heaven; and if the head be above water, the body cannot drown. **John Flavel**

If we can learn to fix our eyes on Jesus, to see through the fog and picture our eternal home in our mind's eye, it will comfort and energize us, giving us a clear look at the finish line. **Randy Alcorn**

Until my work on this earth is done, I am immortal. But when my work for Christ is done...I go to be with Jesus. **John Wesley**

We but trade heartbeat for glory, and it will be most exciting. We shall go from the instant pain of our passing to the full presence of knowing the Lord face to face. **Calvin Miller**

Dying is worth it when Jesus is in it, because resurrection is far better than if you never died. **Greg Cahalan**

The most astonishing sight we can anticipate in Heaven is not streets of gold or pearly gates or loved ones who've died before us. It will be coming face-to-face with our Savior. Seeing God will be like seeing everything else for the first time. **Randy Alcorn**

I have often tried to imagine what the first five minutes with Jesus Christ in heaven will be. But I have in vain sought to picture the novelty and freshness of that wondrous time when the soul, filled with amazement, will exclaim, "The half has never been told me." **Charles Spurgeon**

Heaven isn't a place for people who are scared of hell; it's for people who love Jesus. **Jefferson Bethke**

The presence of Jesus will dissipate all gloom, disperse all slavish fears, chase away all darkness, free from all pain, deliver from all sorrow…raise us above all temptations, and fill us with unspeakably glorious joy…To be with Christ forever—this comprises all that we now desire, and all that we can wish. **James Smith**

What shall we do in heaven? Not lounge around but worship, work, think, and communicate, enjoying activity, beauty, people, and God. First and foremost, however, we shall see and love Jesus, our Savior, Master, and Friend. **J.I. Packer**

John was Christ's dearest friend on Earth. But seeing Jesus in Heaven, he "fell at his feet as though dead." One day we'll see Christ in his glory. The most exhilarating experiences on Earth won't begin to compare with the thrill of seeing Jesus. **Randy Alcorn**

When we are on the beach we only see a small part of the ocean... We only see a small part of God's great love, a few jewels of His great riches, but we know that there is much more beyond the horizon. The best is yet to come, when we see Jesus face to face. **Corrie ten Boom**

Heaven without Christ? Absurd. It is the sea without water, the earth without its fields, the heavens without their stars. There cannot be a heaven without Christ. **Charles Spurgeon**

To not only worship God, but to see God, run alongside God, eat with God, play catch with God...that is about as stunning a truth as there is. **Randy Alcorn**

Thy main plan, and the end of thy will is to make Christ glorious and beloved in heaven where he is now ascended, where one day all the elect will behold his glory and love and glorify him forever. Though here I love him but little, may this be my portion at last. In this world thou hast given me a beginning, one day it will be perfected in the realm above. ***The Valley of Vision: A Collection of Puritan Prayers and Devotions***

When the followers of Christ lose their interest in heaven they will no longer be happy Christians, and when they are no longer happy Christians they cannot be a powerful force in a sad and sinful world. **A.W. Tozer**

Heaven enters wherever Christ enters, even in this life. **C.S. Lewis**

The birth, death, and resurrection of Jesus means that one day everything sad will come untrue. **J.R.R. Tolkien**

One day Jesus is going to split the eastern sky and come for His own. It will not matter then how much money we have in a mutual fund or how many bedrooms we have in our homes...Only what we have done for the cause of Christ will matter. **James Forlines**

Jesus's resurrection is the beginning of God's new project not to snatch people away from earth to heaven but to colonize earth with the life of heaven. That, after all, is what the Lord's Prayer is about. **N.T. Wright**

The Nazareth carpenter had experience building entire worlds throughout the universe. Jesus is an expert at *repairing* what has been damaged—whether people or worlds. This damaged creation cries out to be repaired, and it's his plan to remodel the old Earth on a grand scale. How great will be the resurrected planet that he calls the New Earth—the one Jesus says will forever be our home…and *his*. **Randy Alcorn**

Peter was made to walk on water in his old body. Imagine what Christ will enable you to do in your new one. **Larry Dick**

Life on the New Earth will be a treasure hunt, with every day yielding new and delightful discoveries in Christ. **Randy Alcorn**

Our Treasure in Jesus

One thing have I asked of the Lord, that will I seek after: that I may dwell in the house of the Lord all the days of my life, to gaze upon the beauty of the Lord and to inquire in his temple. **Psalm 27:4 ESV**

I count all things to be loss in view of the surpassing value of knowing Christ Jesus my Lord, for whom I have suffered the loss of all things, and count them but rubbish so that I may gain Christ. **Philippians 3:8 NASB**

Treasuring Jesus is more than simply saying you like the guy. We give our time, our talents, our very selves to the things we treasure. Do you treasure him? **Jeremy Adelman**

It seems to me that we ought to be unconscious of ourselves, and that the nearer we get to Christ the more we shall be taken up with him. **Elizabeth Prentiss**

I believe there is no one deeper, lovelier, more sympathetic and more perfect than Jesus—not only is there no one else like him, there never could be anyone like him. **Fyodor Dostoevsky**

Is it any wonder that to this day this Galilean is too much for our small hearts? **H.G. Wells**

Jesus is the yes to every promise of God. **William Barclay**

Christ is worth all, or he is worth nothing. **George Whitefield**

They lose nothing who gain Christ. **Samuel Rutherford**

When you are deeply peaceful and confident that, because of Christ, God will bring you safely to his eternal kingdom and be the all-satisfying Treasure of your life forever, then you are free to see the truth, and love the truth, and speak the truth no matter what, and joyfully spread a passion for the truth whose name is Jesus. **John Piper**

I have one passion. It is He, only He. **Count Zinzendorf**

Sometimes when my heart has been hard, dead, slothful, blind, and senseless, which indeed are sad frames for a poor Christian to be in, yet at such a time...then has the blood of Christ...the admirable blood of the God of Heaven, that run out of His body when it did hang on the Cross, so softened, livened, quickened, and enlightened my soul, that truly, reader, I can say, O it makes me wonder! **John Bunyan**

Since He looked upon me my heart is not my own. He hath run away to heaven with it. **Samuel Rutherford**

O Jesus, grant the gift to see
The treasure that you are,
And as the night eclipses me,
O be my Morning Star. **John Piper**

Our Satisfaction in Jesus

"Blessed are you who are hungry now, for you shall be satisfied. Blessed are you who weep now, for you shall laugh." **Luke 6:21 ESV**

Our actions will show that we belong to the truth, so we will be confident when we stand before God. Even if we feel guilty, God is greater than our feelings, and he knows everything. Dear friends, if we don't feel guilty, we can come to God with bold confidence. And we will receive from him whatever we ask because we obey him and do the things that please him. **1 John 3:19-22 NLT**

Look to the living One for life. Look to Jesus for all you need between the gate of hell and the gate of heaven. **Charles Spurgeon**

The rattle without the breast will not satisfy the child; the house without the husband will not satisfy the wife...the world without Christ will not satisfy the soul. **Thomas Brooks**

If we only trust Christ to give us gifts and not himself as the all-satisfying gift, then we do not trust him in a way that honors him as our treasure. **John Piper**

God is the one who satisfies the passion for justice, the longing for spirituality, the hunger for relationship, the yearning for beauty. And God, the true God, is the God we see in Jesus of Nazareth. **N.T. Wright**

How completely satisfying to turn from our limitations to a God who has none. Eternal years lie in His heart. For Him time does not pass, it remains; and those who are in Christ share with Him all the riches of limitless time and endless years. God never hurries. There are no deadlines against which He must work. Only to know this is to quiet our spirits and relax our nerves. **A.W. Tozer**

The secret is Christ in me, not me in a different set of circumstances. **Elisabeth Elliot**

Christ with anything would have satisfied me; nothing without Christ would do it. **Thomas Boston**

How do I know that the resurrection and the whole Gospel is real? I know not only because of an acquaintance with the primary sources from the first century A.D., or even because of the words of the Bible. I know primarily, and I affirm this truth to you, on the basis of what I have witnessed in my own life...Jesus Christ provides a basis for hope and for the most profound personal satisfaction. **Glenn C. Louis**

Are you satisfied with Christ? If you are not, you have not really got him. If you have got him, he is everything to you. **Charles Spurgeon**

Other Great Reading by Randy Alcorn

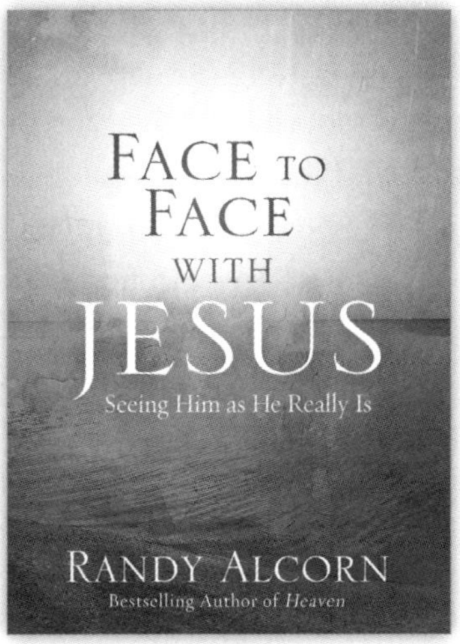

Face to Face with Jesus

Bestselling author Randy Alcorn shares brief meditations, Scripture readings, and inspirational quotes that help reveal the rich identity of God's Son. Are you ready to see Jesus face to face as you never have before?

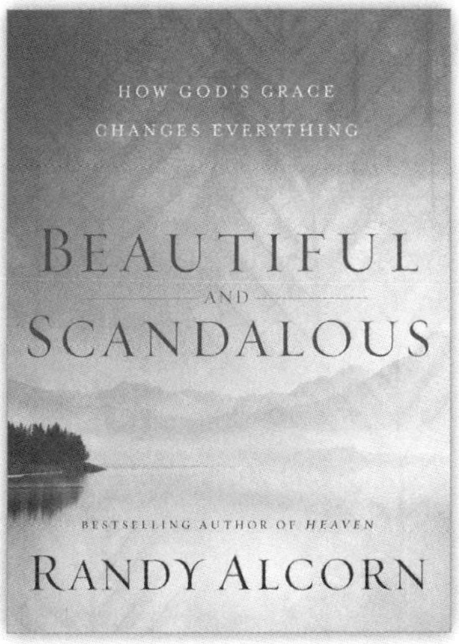

Beautiful and Scandalous

Beautiful and Scandalous offers daily meditations, Scripture readings, and inspirational quotes that will enable you to grasp more fully the grace God lavishes on you. Come explore the many facets of God's grace...and fall more in love than ever with the One whose faithful love for you is both beautiful and scandalous.

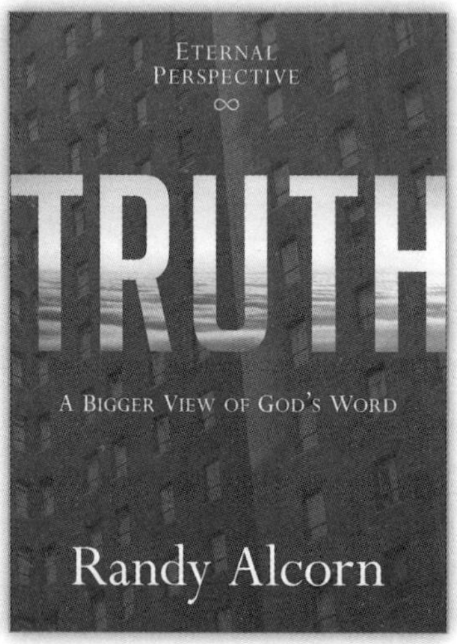

Truth

The world is a sea of clashing beliefs and thoughts. Your own feelings and circumstances change from one day to the next. Your heart longs for something to hold on to—and only God's truth can satisfy that longing. This is your invitation to refresh your heart and find lasting security.

About the Author

RANDY ALCORN is the founder and director of Eternal Perspective Ministries (EPM), a nonprofit organization dedicated to teaching the principles of God's Word and assisting the church in ministering to unreached, unfed, unborn, uneducated, unreconciled, and unsupported people around the world. His ministry focus is communicating the strategic importance of using our earthly time, money, possessions, and opportunities to invest in need-meeting ministries that count for eternity. He accomplishes this by analyzing, teaching, and applying biblical truth.

Before starting EPM in 1990, Randy served as a pastor for fourteen years. He has a bachelor of theology and a master of arts in biblical studies from Multnomah University and an honorary doctorate from Western Seminary in Portland, Oregon, and he has taught on the adjunct faculties of both institutions.

A *New York Times* bestselling author, Randy has written more than fifty books, including *Heaven, The Treasure Principle*, and the award-winning novel *Safely Home*. More than eleven million copies of his books have been sold, and his titles have been translated into more than seventy languages. All royalties from his books are given to the works of Christian ministries, including world missions and organizations that care for the poor.

Randy has written for many magazines, including EPM's *Eternal Perspectives*. He is active on Facebook and Twitter and has been a guest on more than 800 radio, television, and online programs, including *Focus on the Family, FamilyLife Today*, and *Revive Our Hearts*.

Randy resides in Gresham, Oregon, with his wife, Nanci. They have two married daughters and are the proud grandparents of five grandsons. Randy enjoys spending time with his family, biking, doing research, reading, and underwater photography.

Contact Eternal Perspective Ministries:

www.epm.org

39085 Pioneer Blvd., Suite 206, Sandy, OR 97055

503-668-5200

Follow Randy Alcorn:
Facebook: www.facebook.com/randyalcorn
Twitter: www.twitter.com/randyalcorn
Instagram: www.instagram.com/randyalcorn_epm
EPM website: www.epm.org
Blog: www.epm.org/blog